Memoirs of the Cardinal de Retz. Containing the particulars of his own life, with the most secret transactions at the French court during the administration of Cardinal Mazarin Volume 4 of 4

Jean François Paul de Gondi de Retz

Memoirs of the Cardinal de Retz. Containing the particulars of his own life, with the most secret transactions at the French court during the administration of Cardinal Mazarin, ... To which are added some other pieces written by the Cardinal de Retz, or explanatory to these memoirs. In four volumes. Translated from the French. With notes. ... Volume 4 of 4
Retz, Jean François Paul de Gondi de
ESTCID: T088963
Reproduction from British Library
Translated by P. Davall.
London : printed for Jacob Tonson, 1723.
4v.,plate : port. ; 12°

Gale ECCO Print Editions

Relive history with *Eighteenth Century Collections Online*, now available in print for the independent historian and collector. This series includes the most significant English-language and foreign-language works printed in Great Britain during the eighteenth century, and is organized in seven different subject areas including literature and language; medicine, science, and technology; and religion and philosophy. The collection also includes thousands of important works from the Americas.

The eighteenth century has been called "The Age of Enlightenment." It was a period of rapid advance in print culture and publishing, in world exploration, and in the rapid growth of science and technology – all of which had a profound impact on the political and cultural landscape. At the end of the century the American Revolution, French Revolution and Industrial Revolution, perhaps three of the most significant events in modern history, set in motion developments that eventually dominated world political, economic, and social life.

In a groundbreaking effort, Gale initiated a revolution of its own: digitization of epic proportions to preserve these invaluable works in the largest online archive of its kind. Contributions from major world libraries constitute over 175,000 original printed works. Scanned images of the actual pages, rather than transcriptions, recreate the works ***as they first appeared.***

Now for the first time, these high-quality digital scans of original works are available via print-on-demand, making them readily accessible to libraries, students, independent scholars, and readers of all ages.

For our initial release we have created seven robust collections to form one the world's most comprehensive catalogs of 18th century works.

Initial Gale ECCO Print Editions collections include:

> ***History and Geography***
> Rich in titles on English life and social history, this collection spans the world as it was known to eighteenth-century historians and explorers. Titles include a wealth of travel accounts and diaries, histories of nations from throughout the world, and maps and charts of a world that was still being discovered. Students of the War of American Independence will find fascinating accounts from the British side of conflict.

Social Science

Delve into what it was like to live during the eighteenth century by reading the first-hand accounts of everyday people, including city dwellers and farmers, businessmen and bankers, artisans and merchants, artists and their patrons, politicians and their constituents. Original texts make the American, French, and Industrial revolutions vividly contemporary.

Medicine, Science and Technology

Medical theory and practice of the 1700s developed rapidly, as is evidenced by the extensive collection, which includes descriptions of diseases, their conditions, and treatments. Books on science and technology, agriculture, military technology, natural philosophy, even cookbooks, are all contained here.

Literature and Language

Western literary study flows out of eighteenth-century works by Alexander Pope, Daniel Defoe, Henry Fielding, Frances Burney, Denis Diderot, Johann Gottfried Herder, Johann Wolfgang von Goethe, and others. Experience the birth of the modern novel, or compare the development of language using dictionaries and grammar discourses.

Religion and Philosophy

The Age of Enlightenment profoundly enriched religious and philosophical understanding and continues to influence present-day thinking. Works collected here include masterpieces by David Hume, Immanuel Kant, and Jean-Jacques Rousseau, as well as religious sermons and moral debates on the issues of the day, such as the slave trade. The Age of Reason saw conflict between Protestantism and Catholicism transformed into one between faith and logic -- a debate that continues in the twenty-first century.

Law and Reference

This collection reveals the history of English common law and Empire law in a vastly changing world of British expansion. Dominating the legal field is the *Commentaries of the Law of England* by Sir William Blackstone, which first appeared in 1765. Reference works such as almanacs and catalogues continue to educate us by revealing the day-to-day workings of society.

Fine Arts

The eighteenth-century fascination with Greek and Roman antiquity followed the systematic excavation of the ruins at Pompeii and Herculaneum in southern Italy; and after 1750 a neoclassical style dominated all artistic fields. The titles here trace developments in mostly English-language works on painting, sculpture, architecture, music, theater, and other disciplines. Instructional works on musical instruments, catalogs of art objects, comic operas, and more are also included.

MEMOIRS

OF THE

CARDINAL DE RETZ;

TRANSLATED FROM THE

FRENCH.

VOL. IV.

MEMOIRS

OF THE

CARDINAL DE RETZ;

TRANSLATED FROM THE

FRENCH,

WITH

NOTES.

VOL. IV.

LONDON,

Printed for T. BECKET, T CADELL, and T. EVANS, in the Strand.

MDCCLXXIV.

MEMOIRS

OF THE

CARDINAL DE RETZ;

WRITTEN BY HIMSELF;

To MADAM DE *****.

BOOK V.

A. D. 1654.

I STAID but four hours at Piombino, I left it as ſoon as I had dined, and took my way towards Florence I met at three or four leagues on this ſide of Volterre, one Signor Annibal (I do not remember his family name), he was a gentleman of the bed-chamber to the Great Duke, who, upon the advice which the Governor of Porto Ferraro had given him of my coming, had ſent him to compliment me, and to deſire me to conſent to make a ſlight quarantine before I came any further into his country.

The Great Duke was at ſome odds with the Genoeſe, which made him afraid that they might take this pretence of his communicating with perſons who came from the coaſt of Spain, which was ſuſpected of having the plague, to forbid all commerce with Tuſcany. Signor Annibal carried me to a houſe called L'Hoſpitalita, which is by Volterre, and which is built upon the field of battle where Catiline was killed. That houſe belonged formerly to the Great Lawrence of Medicis, and is fallen by alliances into the houſe of Corſini I ſtaid there nine days, during which time I was magnificently treated by the officers of the Great Duke. The Abbot Charrier, who upon the first notice of my arrival was gone to Porto Ferraro, came post from Florence to meet me at this house, where the Bailly de Gondi came likewise with the Great Duke's coaches, to fetch me away and to carry me to Camogliano, a fine and sumptuous seat belonging to the Marquis Nicolini, a near relation of his, where I lay that night. I left it the next morning pretty early, to go to Lambrosiano, which is a hunting house, where the Great Duke had been for some days. He did me the honour to come to meet me at Empoly, a pretty town enough, about a league from Lambrosiano. The first thing he said to me after the first compliment was, that I had not met in Spain with the Spaniards of Charles the Fifth's time. After he had carried me to the apartment prepared for me at Lambrosiano, and when I found myself in the chamber where I was to lie, sitting in a great chair above him, I asked him whether I acted the farce well. He did not understand my meaning at first, but when he knew that it was to let him see that I did not forget myself, and that if I took the upper hand of him, it was not at least without making due reflections upon it, he said to me, "You are the first Cardinal that ever spoke to me in this manner, but you are likewise the first for whom I have done what I now do without regret." I staid three days with him at Lambrosiano, and upon the second he came into my chamber pretty much moved, saying to me, "I am come to shew you a letter from the Duke d'Arcos Viceroy of Naples, which will let you see in what conditon that kingdom is." I found by the letter that Mr. de Guise was landed there, that there had been a great fight near the Grecian Tower; that the Viceroy hoped that the French would make no progress there, that it was at least what his soldiers insinuated; "For, added the Viceroy, as * Io non sor soldato, I am obliged to rely upon their judgment." The confession, as you see, was odd enough for a Viceroy.

* I am no soldier.

roy The Great Duke made me many offers, though Cardinal Mazarin threatened him in the King's name with a rupture, if he gave me passage through his dominions. Nothing could be more ridiculous, and the Great Duke for answer caused his Resident (as this last has since assured me) to desire the Cardinal to furnish him with some invention to bring the Pope and the Sacred College to consent to such refusal Of all the Great Duke's offers, I took only four thousand crowns, which sum I thought I should want, the Abbot Charrier having told me that there were as yet no remittances for me at Rome I gave the Great Duke a note under my hand for the repayment of that sum, which I owe him still, his highness having consented to be put the last in the list of my creditors, as being certainly the least in want of being repaid.

From Lambrosiano I went to Florence, where I staid two days with the Cardinal John Charles de Medicis, and with the Prince Leopold his brother, who has been since likewise a Cardinal. They gave me one of the Great Duke's litters to carry me to Sienna, where I met with Prince Mathias, who was Governor of it. Nothing could be added to the civilities that I received from that house, some of whom have borne, and all have certainly deserved the title of Magnificent I continued my journey in their litters, and accompanied by their officers, and the rains having been excessive in Italy, I had like to have been drowned near Ponte Cantine, in a torrent into which a thunder clap that frightened my mules, caused my litter to fall during the night I was certainly in a great deal of danger on that occasion.

At half a day's journey from Rome, the Abbot Rousseau, who held the rope at Nantes by means of which I escaped, and who having found means afterwards to make his own escape out of the Castle, as he did in a very resolute and in a very fortunate manner, was come to Rome to wait there for me, the Abbot Rousseau, I say, came to inform me that the French faction had declared very much against me at Rome, and that they even threatened to hinder me from coming thither. I continued my journey however, and having met with no obstacle, I arrived there, and I went to St. Peter's church to prayers, from whence I alighted at the Abbot Charrier's house. I found there Monsignor Febey, master of the ceremonies, who waited for me, and who was ordered by the Pope to direct me at my first coming Monsignor Franzoni, Treasurer of the Chamber, and who is now a Cardinal, came thither afterwards with a purse in which there were four thousand crowns in gold, which his holiness sent me with all possible marks of civility. I went incognito that evening in a chair, to wait on the Signora Olympia, and on the Princess of Rossane, and I came back to the Abbot Charrier's, accompanied only by two gentlemen.

The next morning as I was in bed, the Abbot de la Rocheposai, who was altogether unknown to me, came into my chamber, and after having first complimented me upon some relation that was between us, he told me, that he thought himself obliged to give me notice that the Cardinal d'Est, Protector of France, had terrible orders from the king against me, that at the time he was speaking, the Cardinals of the French faction were holding a congregation at the Cardinal d'Est's house, where they were to resolve upon the particular measures which they were to take against me, for they were before come to a general resolution, conformably to his Majesty's orders, not to suffer me to stay at Rome, but to drive me away from thence at any rate. My answer to the Abbot de la Rocheposai was, that I had such violent scruples, as to the conduct which I had formerly followed at Paris, that I was resolved rather to die a thousand times, than to think upon defending myself, but that I thought on the other side that it was contrary to the duty of a Cardinal to come so near the Pope, and afterwards to leave Rome without having kissed his feet, so that all that I could do in the extremity I found myself in, was to commit myself to the Divine Providence, and to go alone with him in a quarter of an hour's time, if he pleased, to Mass, at a little church which was in sight

of

of my houſe. The Abbot perceived that I bantered him, and he left me pretty much diſpleaſed with his negotiation, which had in my opinion been put upon him by poor Cardinal Anthonio, a good man, but weak beyond imagination I thought fit however to let the Pope know of theſe threatenings, upon which his Holineſs ſent immediately the Abbot Charrier to Count Vidman, a noble Venetian, and Colonel of his Guards, to tell him that he ſhould be anſwerable for my perſon, in caſe that, if he ſaw the leaſt appearance of ſtirring in the French faction, he did not diſpoſe as he thought fit of his Switzers, his Corſes, his Lanciers, and his Light-horſe I was ſo civil as to ſend notice of this order to the Cardinal d'Eſt, though I did it in an indirect manner by the means of Monſignor Scotti; and the Cardinal d'Eſt was likewiſe ſo civil as to leave me at quiet.

The Pope gave me the next day an audience that laſted four hours, wherein he expreſſed a more than ordinary good-will to me, and wherein he ſhewed a very uncommon genius. He even deſcended ſo low as to make me ſome excuſes for not having acted more vigorouſly for my liberty. He wept, and even abundantly, and he ſaid to me, "God forgive thoſe who have been negligent in giving me the firſt advice of your impriſonment. That raſcal Valancey impoſed on me, and told me that you were convicted of having attempted on the king's perſon. I received no expreſs, either from your friends or relations. The Ambaſſador had all manner of time allowed him to put upon us what he pleaſed, and to cool the firſt fire of the Sacred College, half of whom thought that you were forſaken by the whole kingdom, when they ſaw nobody ſent from you hither" The Abbot Charrier, who for want of money was kept ten or twelve days at Paris after my detention, had informed me of theſe particulars at l'Hoſpitalita, and he had even told me further that he ſhould have been kept at Paris longer, if the Abbot Amelot had not lent him two thouſand crowns. That delay coſt me dear, for it is certain that if the Pope had received firſt an expreſs ſent by my friends, he had not given the Ambaſſador audience, or had ſtaid to give it him till he had fixed upon ſome reſolution. That fault was a capital one, and the more ſo, becauſe it might eaſily have been prevented. My Steward had 14000 livres of my money in his hands when I was arreſted. My friends did not want money even for my ſervice, as it appeared by their manner of aſſiſting me afterwards. This is not the only conjuncture in which I have obſerved, that the averſeneſs which moſt men have to part with their money, is the cauſe that they never do it time enough, even in conjunctures when they are moſt reſolved to do it. I have never diſcovered theſe particulars to any body, becauſe they nearly concern ſome of my friends. But as I am entirely yours, I owe you the full and entire truth.

The Pope held a conſiſtory the day that followed my audience, on purpoſe to give me the hat, and ſaid to me, "Conſidering that * voſtro protetore di quanto baiocchi [he never called the Cardinal d'Eſt otherwiſe] is altogether likely to commit ſome impertinence in this conjuncture, he muſt be amuſed, and made to believe that you will not aſſiſt at the conſiſtory." It was an eaſy matter for me to make him think ſo, becauſe I really was extremely ill of my ſhoulder, and ſo ill, that Nicolo, the moſt famous ſurgeon at Rome, had ſaid that if it was not quickly looked after I was like to fall into worſe ſymptoms ſtill. I went to bed upon that pretence at my return from the Pope, who cauſed ſome reports to be ſpread in relation to that conſiſtory, which ſerved to deceive the French Cardinals. They all went thither thinking no harm, and they were much ſurpriſed when they ſaw me come in with the Maſter of the Ceremonies, and in a condition to receive the hat. The Cardinals d'Eſt and Urſini went out, but Cardinal Bichi ſtaid. It is impoſſible to imagine the effect which theſe ſorts of tricks produce, in favour of thoſe who act them well, in a country

* Your two-penny Protector.

where

where the discredit of passing for a dupe is greater than any where else

The Pope's good disposition towards me, which he carried so far as to have some thoughts of adopting me for his nephew, and his evil disposition towards Cardinal Mazarin, had in all likelihood quickly produced some other scenes, if his holiness had not fallen ill within three days of the distemper of which he died five weeks after. All that I could do before the conclave began was to have my shoulder looked after. Nicolo put it out of joint a second time, in order to set it right He put me to intolerable pain, and did not succeed in his operation. The Pope died, and as I had been most of that while confined to my bed, I had had but very little time to prepare myself for the Conclave, which was likely however in all appearance to give me a great deal of trouble The Cardinal d'Est was saying publicly that he had the King's order to forbear, not only communicating with me, but even saluting me. The Duke de Terra-Nova, the Spanish Ambassador, had made me all the offers imaginable, in his Catholic Majesty's name, as had likewise the Cardinal Harrach, in the name of the Emperor The old Cardinal de Medicis, Dean of the Sacred College, and Protector of Spain, took at first an inclination to me, but it is easy for you to judge, by what passed at St Sebastian's and at Vivaros, that I had no design to enter into the faction of the house of Austria I was not ignorant that a foreign Cardinal persecuted by his King, could make but a very mean figure, at a place where the regard which both public and private persons have for the Catholic Crowns, is still greater than any where else, by reason that it is the more pressing and more immediate interest of every one not to displease them. It was however, not only important, but even necessary for me to consider of some measures in a Court where foresight is not less reputable than it is useful To tell you the truth, I found myself very much perplexed in this conjuncture, and this is the method which I thought fit to follow. Pope Innocent, who was a great man, had particu-

 larly

larly applied himself to make a right choice of persons, at the promotions he had made of Cardinals, and it is certain that he mistook but in a very few. The Signora Olympia forced him in some manner, by the ascendant which she had over him, to honour with this dignity Maldachini his nephew, who was yet a child: but it may be said, that excepting this, all the others were either good, or supported by considerations that justified them. It is even true, that in most of them their merit, joined to their birth, concurred to render them illustrious. Those of that number who did not find themselves attached to the Catholic crowns by their nomination, or by their faction, found themselves altogether at liberty at the death of the Pope, because Cardinal Pamphilio, his nephew, having resigned his hat to marry the Princess of Rossane, and the Cardinal Astali whom his Holiness had adopted, having since lost that adoption even shamefully, there was no body that could set up himself at the head of that faction during the Conclave. Those that found themselves in that state, which might be called a free one, were the Cardinals Chigi, Lomelini, Ottoboni, Imperiali, Aquaviva, Pio, Borromeo, Albrizi, Gualtieri, Azolini, Omodei, Cibo, Odescalchi, Vidman, and Aldobrandini. Ten of them, which were Lomelini, Ottoboni, Imperiali, Borromeo, Aquaviva, Pio, Gualtieri, Albrizi, Omodei, and Azolini, took it into their heads to make use of their liberty, to deliver the Sacred College from the custom which subjects the Cardinals in the giving their vote, to the faction of their benefactors, when they ought only to hearken to what the Holy Ghost inspires them with. They resolved to stick close only to their duty, and to profess publicly at the entering into the Conclave a perfect independency on any faction or crown. The faction of Spain being at that time the strongest at Rome, both by reason of their own number, and by the conjunction of those attached to the House of Medicis, it was that faction that made the greatest noise at the independence of the flying squadron, for so they called the ten Cardinals whom I have named

I took

I took my time when the Cardinal John Charles de Medicis was exclaiming, in the name of the Spanish faction, against the flying squadron, to unite with it, after having however observed the necessary decorum in respect to France; for I desired Monsignor Scotti, who had been Nuncio in Extraordinary there, and who was agreeable to the court, to go to all the Cardinals of the French faction, and to intreat them in my name that they would let me know what I was to do for the King's service; that I did not desire to be let into the secret, but only to be acquainted day by day with what steps I was to take to perform my duty

The Cardinal Grimaldi sent me a very civil and obliging answer by Monsignor Scotti; but the Cardinals de Est, Bichi, and Ursini, treated me with a great deal of haughtiness, and even with contempt I declared the very next day in public, that since they would afford me no manner of means to be serviceable to France, I thought, that the best thing I could do, was to join at least with those who were the least dependant on the Spanish faction I was received amongst the flying squadron with all the civility possible, and the event shewed that I was in the right to do as I did.

I cannot say the like of my conduct at that same time with Mr de Lionne. That Gentleman was reconciled to Cardinal Mazarin, who sent him to Rome to solicit against me, and who gave him the quality of Ambassador Extraordinary to the Princes of Italy, that he might appear at Rome with more dignity. Lionne being a pretty great friend of Montresor's, had seen him before he left Paris, and had desired him to write me word that he would do his best to soften matters, and that I should perceive it by the effects. He spoke sincerely, having tolerable good intentions for me. But I answered it in another manner than I ought, which was not one of the least faults that I have committed in my life-time. I will give you the particulars of it, with the reasons of my conduct, which was not good, after I have given you an account of the Conclave.

The first step that the flying squadron took during the nine days that are spent in the Pope's obsequies, was to unite with Cardinal Barberini, who had it in his head to bring to the chair Cardinal Sachetti, a man much resembling the late President le Bailleul, of whom Menage used to say, that he was good for nothing but to have his picture drawn. It is certain, that Cardinal Sachetti was a man but of mean parts, but being a creature of Pope Urban's, to whose house he had always been truly attached, Barberini had set his thoughts on him, and the more strongly, because his exaltation appeared, and was really difficult to the last degree. Cardinal Barberini, whose life is angelical, has an oddness of humour which renders him, as they say in Italy, "Inamorato de l'impossibile." The exaltation of Sachetti was little less than impossible. His intimate friendship with Mazarin, who had been, if not a domestic, a table companion at least of his brother's, was not a good recommendation for him with Spain: but what kept him still further from the chair, was the public declaration which the house of Medicis, which was besides at the head of the Spanish faction, had made against him, at the Conclave preceding this.

Those of the squadron who had in view the making Cardinal Chigi Pope, thought that the only way to engage Cardinal Barberini to serve him, was to oblige him to do it out of a principle of gratitude, by using truly and sincerely their utmost efforts to bring Sachetti to the chair, because they foresaw, that all their endeavours would come to nothing, or would serve at least only to unite them to Cardinal Barberini in so intimate a manner that nothing could hinder him afterwards from concurring with what they desired. This was the whole mystery of a Conclave that hath furnished all those who have been pleased to give us the history of it, with a thousand impertinencies. And I am ready to maintain, that the way of reasoning of the squadron was very just. It was this. "We are persuaded that Chigi is the candidate of the greatest merit that is in the college, and we are no less per-

persuaded that we cannot make him Pope but by doing our utmost in favour of Sachetti The worst that can happen, is, our succeeding in bringing Sachetti to the chair, which indeed, would not be a very good choice, but not the worst that we could make In all appearance we shall not succeed in it, in which case we shall bring Barberini to give his vote and interest to Chigi, as well out of gratitude as to keep us all attached to him We shall bring over to Chigi the factions of Spain and of Medicis, for fear that we should at last carry it in favour of Sachetti, and the faction of France likewise when they find it impossible for them to hinder it " These measures, which were solid and profound, and of which it must be confessed, that Cardinal Azolini was the chief contriver, were approved of unanimously at the Transpontine, where the flying squadron assembled from the first days that the obsequies of the Pope began, and they were approved of even after having examined maturely the difficulties of such an undertaking, which would have appeared unsurmountable to persons of a mean understanding Great names are always of a mighty weight with such sort of persons. France, Spain, the Empire, Tuscany, were names very fit to frighten them. There was no appearance that Cardinal Mazarin could be for Chigi, who was Nuncio at Munster at the time that the peace was negotiating there, and who had declared himself openly more than once against Servien, who was there Plenipotentiary of France Neither was there any likelihood that Spain would approve of him Cardinal Trivulce, the ablest Cardinal of that faction, and perhaps of the whole College, exclaimed publicly against him as a bigot, and he was at the bottom much afraid of his exaltation, by reason of the severity of Chigi, a candidate very unfit to bear with his debaucheries, which were indeed very scandalous It was not to be supposed that Cardinal John Charles of Medicis could be well inclined towards Chigi, both for the same reasons as Trivulce, and by reason of his birth, for he was of Sienna, and known to be a passionate lover of his country, which is likewise known not to be much inamoured with the dominion of Florence

Every one of these considerations were weighed and examined All that was probable, or doubtful, or possible, was entered into, and the squadron fixed at last upon the resolution which I have mentioned, and which was so much the wiser, because it carried with it the appearance of boldness. It must be confessed, that perhaps there never was any thing concerted, of which the harmony kept so true as it did in this, and it seemed as if all those that concurred in it, were formed on purpose to act in concert together. The vivacity of Imperiali was corrected by the phlegm of Lomelini, Ottoboni's profound sense made a right use of Aquaviva's haughtiness, the candour of Omodei, and the reservedness of Gualtieri, served to cover, when occasion required, the impetuosity of Pio, and the duplicity of Albrizzi: Azolini, whose genius is one of the finest and supplest in the world, was continually upon the watch to observe all these different motions; and the inclinations which the Cardinals de Medicis, and Barberini, heads of the two most opposite factions, had taken at first for me, supplied in me upon occasion the want of those qualities which were necessary to maintain my character with them. All the actors did their parts well; the action went on without any interruption; there was no great variety of scenes, but the play was the finer for not being overcharged with plot. Whatever was writ about it, there was no other mystery that what I have explained to you before, but it must be owned, that the episodes of it were curious I now come to the particulars.

The Conclave, if I am not mistaken, lasted eighty days We gave every morning and every afternoon, two or three and thirty votes to Sachetti; which votes were made up of the faction of France, of the creatures of Pope Urban, uncle to Cardinal Barberini, and of the flying squadron. The votes of the Spaniards, of the Germans, and of the Medicis, were dispersed among several candidates in every scrutiny, and they affected to act in this manner to give their conduct an

air

air more ecclesiastical, and more free from any cabal or intrigue than ours had. But their projects did not succeed, because the disorderly way of living of Cardinal John Charles of Medicis, and of Cardinal Trivulce, who were properly the souls of their factions, gave more lustre to the exemplary piety of Cardinal Barberini, than they were able by their artifices to remove Cardinal Cesy, a pensionary of Spain, and the greatest ape in every respect that I ever knew, was telling me one day very wittily on that occasion: "You will beat us at last, by reason of the discredit we bring upon ourselves, by assuming the appearance of godly persons: hypocrisy may sometimes deceive, but it cannot do it long, when able persons undertake to unmask it." Their faction lost in a little time the concetto, as they call it there, of being well-meaning men, and we soon gained that reputation, because the truth was that Sachetti, who was beloved for his mildness, passed for a man of right and good intentions; and because the regard which those of the house of Medicis were obliged to shew for Cardinal Rasponi, though at the bottom they would not have been willing to have had him for Pope, gave us room to make the public believe that they would instal in St. Peter's chair the Volpe, (for so Cardinal Rasponi was called, because he passed for a cheat.) These dispositions, to which might be added many others of too long a discussion, made those of the Spanish faction perceive that they were losing ground, and though that discovery went not so far as to make them believe that we had it in our thoughts to make a Pope without their participation, it was however great enough to make them apprehend that their faction being made up of many old men, and ours of many young ones, we might easily have the benefit of time on our side. We intercepted a letter of the Spanish Ambassador's to Cardinal Sforce, which shewed that fear in express terms, and we even perceived by the air of that letter, more than by the words, that the Ambassador was not very well pleased with the conduct of those of the faction of Medicis. It was Monsignor Febey, if I am not mistaken, that intercepted that letter. This

feed

ſeed was cultivated with a great deal of care as ſoon as it was perceived to ſpring up, and the ſquadron, who by means of Borromeo, a Milaneſe, and of Aquaviva, a Neapolitan, preſerved a great regard for the Ambaſſador of Spain, did not omit to inſinuate to him, that the ſervice of the King his maſter, as well as his own private intereſt, required of him that he ſhould not truſt the Florentines ſo much as to ſubject to their maxims and to their caprices, the conduct of a Crown which all the world reſpected

This worked inſenſibly, and produced its effect at laſt. I have already told you that the faction of France joined heartily with us in favour of Sachetti. The difference was, that they gave into it blindly, thinking that they might ſucceed, and that what we did was almoſt with a certain aſſurance that it would not do, ſo that thoſe of the French faction took no hypothetical meaſures, if I may uſe that expreſſion; that is, they did not form any other ſcheme in caſe that of Sachetti ſhould fail. Ours being founded upon the ſuppoſition of which I have ſpoken, which we counted almoſt as certain, we applied ourſelves beforehand to weaken the French faction, againſt the time that we judged that it might turn againſt us I opened a way by chance to the Cardinal John Charles of bringing over to him Cardinal Urſini, the doing of which coſt him but little In this manner, at the time that the Spaniſh faction was wholly bent againſt Sachetti, and the French for him, we were at work upon a project of which either of them little thought, which was to divide that of Spain, and to weaken that of France. The advantage of finding one's ſelf in a condition to act in this manner, is great, but is ſeldom to be met with It required juſt ſuch a concurrence of circumſtances as that that happened in this conjuncture, and which perhaps would not happen again in ten thouſand years We had Chigi in our view, and we could not come at him but by uſing our utmoſt endeavours in favour of Sachetti, though without any probable hopes of ſucceſs in reſpect to this laſt, ſo that we were obliged to do out of good conduct what our promiſes to Barberini required

quired of us This advantage was not the only one, the steps we took, covered our march, and our enemies shooting at random, and always where they could do us no harm, lost every one of their shots You shall see what success that conduct had, after I have explained to you that of Chigi, and our reasons for having him in our view

He was a creature of Pope Innocent's, and the third in rank of the promotion of which I was first He had been inquisitor at Malta, and Nuncio at Munster, and he had gained every where the reputation of an integrity without blemish, and of a conduct free, from his infancy, from any manner of reproach He had enough of liberal learning to make a shew of his not being quite ignorant in other sciences His severity had an allay of mildness in it, and his maxims appeared honest. He was not very communicative, but in the little conversation he had, he shewed himself more reserved and wise (savio col silentio) than any man I ever knew. All the outward shew of a true and solid piety, set off admirably well all these good qualities, or rather all these appearances. What gave them a body, at least a fantastic one, was what had passed at Munster between Servien and him. Servien, who was known and acknowledged to have been the destroying dæmon of the peace, had fallen out there cruelly with Contarini, Ambassador of Venice, a wise and good man. Chigi signalised himself for Contarini, being conscious that it was a good way of making his court to Pope Innocent. His opposing Servien, who was the execration of the people, gained him the love of the public, and raised him into credit The steps he took whilst he was either at Aix-la Chapelle, or at Brussels, at his coming back from Munster; I say the steps he took with Cardinal Mazarin pleased his Holiness. Innocent called him back to Rome, and made him secretary of state and a Cardinal He was known there only by the character under which I have represented him The Pope being a sharp-sighted man, discovered quickly that Chigi was not the man he had taken him for, but this penetration of the Pope's was no obstacle to Chigi's for-

tune,

tune, but on the contrary was a help to it, because Innocent finding himself a dying would not condemn his own choice, and because Chigi, who, for that same reason, was not much afraid of a dying Pope, was glad to set up in the eyes of the world for a man of an unshaken virtue, and of an inflexible rigidness. He made not his court to the Signora Olympia, who was abhorred in Rome, and he even blamed pretty openly all that the public disapproved in her conduct, so that all the world, which is, and will be for ever deceived in things which flatter their passions, admired his courage and his virtue, when they ought at most to have praised only his good sense, which made him sow the seeds of a future papacy, in a field where there was nothing now for him to reap.

Cardinal Azolini, who had been secretary of the briefs at the time that the other was secretary of state, had observed in his memorials about state affairs, some sort of finesses that did not agree with the candor of which he made profession. He had acquainted me with it before the Conclave began, but he had told me at the same time that he knew of no better choice, and that besides, Chigi's reputation was upon such a foot, even with those that composed the flying squadron, that whatever he could say against him would pass with them but as a sequel only of some little fallings out, which the competition of their posts had occasioned betwixt them. I made the less reflection upon what Azolini said, because I was myself prepossessed in favour of Chigi. He had shewn a special regard for the Abbot Charrier during my imprisonment. He had made this last believe, that he did in my behalf with the Pope, beyond what ever could be imagined He exclaimed with Charrier against the Pope, and even with a greater shew of passion than Charrier himself, because he did not push Cardinal Mazarin vigorously enough upon my account. The Abbot Charrier had as free an access to him as any one of his domestics, and he was persuaded that Chigi was better affected to me, and more passionate for my interest, than I was myself. I had no reason to suspect any thing to the contrary during

ing

ing the whole Conclave. I was ſeated immediately above him at the ſcrutiny, and I had an opportunity of conferring with him ſo long as the ſcrutiny laſted. I believe, that that was the reaſon which made him affect to have an ear for nobody but for me, as to what related to his promotion to the chair. His anſwer to ſome of the ſquadron, who were diſcovering their deſigns to him, was ſo full of diſintereſtedneſs, that they were much edified at it He was ſeen neither at the windows where the Cardinals uſed to take the air, nor in the * corridors where they walk together. He kept all along ſhut up in his cell, where he would even receive no viſits He could not forbear hearkening to the advices I ſometimes gave him during the ſcrutiny, but he did it always in a manner ſo remote from any deſire of the triple Crown, that he always filled me with admiration; or, at leaſt, he hearkened to me with ſuch an eccleſiaſtical ſpirit, that it had been impoſſible for malice itſelf to imagine in him any other deſire, than that of which St. Paul ſpeaks, when he ſays, that "qui epiſcopatum deſiderat, bonum opus deſiderat." All his diſcourſes to me were full of nothing elſe but of his zeal for the church, and of his regret, that they did not ſtudy enough at Rome the ſcripture, the councils, and tradition. He never grew weary of hearing me ſpeak of the maxims of our Sorbonne. Indeed, as it is impoſſible to keep one's ſelf ſo much upon the reſerve, as never to diſcover any thing of one's natural temper, he could not hide himſelf ſo well, but that I found out, that he was a man addicted to trifles, which is always a ſign, not only of a ſmall genius, but even of a low mind. He was one day mentioning to me ſomething of his ſtudies in his younger years, and he was ſaying, that he uſed the ſame pen for two years together. This is inſignificant in itſelf, but having often obſerved, that the leaſt things are ſometimes more diſtinguiſhing marks than the greateſt, I own that I diſliked what he was mentioning to me. I expreſſed my diſlike to the Abbot Charrier, who was one of my conclaviſts I remember that he chid me for it, and that he called me a repro-

* Galleries that lead from one apartment to another.

bate

bate for not knowing how to value christian simplicity.

In short, Chigi acted the part of a counterfeit so extremely well, that notwithstanding his meanness, which he could not hide in respect of many little things, his physiognomy, which was low, having much the air of a physician, though he was a man of good birth, he acted, I say, his part so extremely well, that we thought that by setting him upon St. Peter's chair, we should renew in him the glory and the virtue of St Gregory, and of St Leo. We were frustrated in our hopes as to this last point, though we succeeded in respect to his exaltation, because the Spaniards were afraid, for the reasons I have already mentioned, that the obstinacy of the young cardinals would hold out longer than that of the old, and because Barberini despaired at last of making Sachetti Pope, considering the engagements and public declarations of the Spanish faction, and of that of Medicis. We resolved to take hold of the opportunity, when it should offer, to insinuate to both these factions of what advantage it would be to them to think on Chigi Borromeo was to persuade the Spaniards that they could do nothing better, considering the averseness that the French faction had for him, and I was to represent to Cardinal Barberini, that there being no candidate amongst his creatures whom he could possibly bring to the chair, the whole church would repute it as the greatest piece of merit in him, if without any interested view, he caused the choice to fall upon the most worthy candidate We expected to find some help to our design in the disposition of some private members of the several factions, the ground of which expectation was this: Cardinal Montalte, who was of the Spanish faction, a man of small talents, but a good man, who lived high, and had the air of a great Lord, was mightily afraid that Cardinal Fiorenzola, a Dominican, and a man of a vigorous spirit, should be proposed by Cardinal Grimaldi his intimate friend, who had something odd in him, pretty much resembling Fiorenzola We resolved to make a right use of that fear of Montalte's, to bring him by degrees to a liking a liking of Chigi The old Cardinal de Medicis, who was the mildest tempered man in the world, found himself very much fatigued, both with the length of the Conclave, and with the impetuosity of the Cardinal John Charles, his nephew, who would not, sometimes, spare his own uncle. I was upon very good terms with the old man, and so much as sometimes to occasion jealousy in the Cardinal John Charles What had chiefly procured me the old Cardinal's friendship, was his natural candour, that had caused him to be pleased with my manner of proceeding with him I made it my business besides to honour him publicly, and I even paid him my respects very carefully. This attachment had not prevented me however from explaining myself clearly with him about my engagements with Cardinal Barberini, and with the flying squadron He had been pleased with my sincerity, which proved, by the event, more useful to me than artifice I managed the old man with a great deal of care, and judged that I should quickly be in a condition to dispose him by degrees to a reconciliation with Cardinal Barberini, who was at odds with all his house, and to look upon Cardinal Chigi as on a man not so dangerous as he had been represented to him. You see by this, that we were not idle in respect to the factions of Spain and of Tuscany, though neither of these factions suspected any thing of our doings, because it was not yet time to discover ourselves The attention of the squadron was not less, in respect to France, whose opposition to Chigi was still more public and more declared than that of the others. Mr de Lionne, nephew to Servien, spoke of Chigi to any body that would but hear him, as of a pedant, whom he did not so much as suppose any way likely to stand as a candidate Cardinal Grimaldi, who in the time of their prelacy, had had some kind of misunderstanding with him, said publicly that his merit was but imaginary It was impossible but that the Cardinal d' Est should be afraid, as brother of the Duke of Modena, of the exaltation of a Cardinal who was disinterested and firm, which are the two qualities that the princes of Italy are altogether afraid

of

of in a pope. I have already told you that ſomething perſonal had happened in Germany, between Chigi and Cardinal Mazarin, and all theſe conſiderations joined together, made us judge that it was neceſſary to reconcile matters, as much as poſſible, with the French faction, who, though weak, might poſſibly be an obſtacle to us I ſay, though weak, becauſe it is certain that the French faction made not a figure conſiderable enough in that Conclave to hinder us from pretending, as we did in effect pretend, that we had it in our power to make a Pope in ſpite of them. Not that that faction wanted men, and even men of capacity. Eſt, who was Protector of France, ſupplied by his quality, by his high living, and by his courage, what his natural darkneſs and the ambiguity of his expreſſions took off from the regard that was otherwiſe due to him. Grimaldi joined to the reputation he had all along preſerved, of being a man of vigour, a ſuperiority of air, oppoſed to the ſervile manners of the other cardinals of his faction, which gave him a reputation above the others. Bichi, an able man, and extremely well practiſed in buſineſs, ought naturally to hold a great poſt among thoſe of that faction. Cardinal Anthonio ſhone by his liberality, and Cardinal Urſini by his name. One would think that that was enough to preſerve that faction from being contemptible, and yet it was very near being contemned, becauſe the advantages which I have mentioned, were unhappily mixed with defects that ſpoiled the reſt. Grimaldi, who hated Mazarin as much as he was hated by him, acted hardly at all, and was prevented the more from acting, becauſe he believed, and that truly enough, that Mr. de Lionne, who had the ſecret of the French court, would not entruſt him with it Eſt, who, notwithſtanding his courage, trembled becauſe the Marquis de Caracena entered juſt at that time into the territory of Modena with the whole forces of the Milaneſe, was prevented, for that reaſon, from doing all that he might have done againſt Spain. I have already told you, that Cardinal John Charles of Medicis had, in ſome meaſure, brought Urſini over to him.

him. Cardinal Anthonio had neither activity nor parts, and besides it was hardly doubted, but that Cardinal Barberini, his brother, who was upon a very ill foot at the Court of France, would win him at last. Mr de Lionne could not, for that reason, confide intirely in Cardinal Anthonio, because he was not sure that Cardinal Barberini, who had hitherto been for Sachetti who was agreeable to France, would not change for some other that might be disagreeable to that Court, and that same reason lessened likewise in a great measure Mr de Lionne's confidence for the Cardinal de Est, because Lionne knew that Est preserved a great regard for Cardinal Barberini, both by reason of the long friendship they had had together, and by reason of the Duchess of Modena, who was Barberini's niece. Bichi was not a man after Mazarin's heart, because Mazarin thought him too cunning, and besides, very ill affected to him, as it was true. This detail will, I suppose, prevent your being surprised that the faction of a Crown that was both powerful and in happy circumstances, was not so much regarded as it ought to have been in that conjuncture. You will still be the less surprised at it, when you are pleased to consider the man to whom the secret of the French affairs was intrusted, and who had the government of a machine so very much out of order. Lionne was known in Rome only as an under secretary to Cardinal Mazarin. He had been seen at that place during the ministry of Cardinal Richlieu, as a private man, and in a mean state enough, and besides as a gamester, and as one that publicly kept a concubine. He had indeed had some sort post in Italy relating to the affairs of Parma, but not considerable enough to expect that he should jump at once from that, to the post he had now at Rome, neither was he a man well enough practised in affairs to intrust into his hands the direction of a Conclave, which of all affairs is certainly the most arduous. I know that it is common enough to states that are in a prosperous condition to commit such faults, because the incapacity of those they employ, is often supplied by the respect that

that is shewn to the master that sends them. Never state relied more on that respect than France did in the time of Cardinal Mazarin That minister however experienced on this occasion, that the doing so is not always a sure Game. Mr de Lionne had neither respect enough paid him, nor the capacity required to keep in a due equilibrium the several springs of a machine so ill set together. It was not long before we discovered it, and we made an advantageous use of it in respect to our design.

I ought to have acquainted you before, that having been informed that Lionne had disobliged Cardinal Ursini about an arrear of pension, which amounted only to one thousand crowns, I gave notice of it timely enough to Cardinal John Charles de Medicis, to give him an opportunity of winning Ursini, which he did at so cheap a rate, that for the honour of the purple I believe that I shall do better not to mention the particulars The sequel will shew you that we made still a better use of the evil disposition of Cardinal Bichi against Lionne, to divide the French faction, and to break its measures still more than before But as that faction was not that of which we were the most afraid, though it was that which opposed us most, we advanced our work in respect to it, in proportion only to the progress we made in respect to the two others, from whence we expected, and with good reason, to meet with more difficulties. I have already told you the reasons we had to believe that the two factions, of Spain and of Medicis, would be brought to approve of Chigi but with great difficulty, and you have likewise already seen the management we used to cure, by degrees, and even imperceptibly, their evil dispositions Our hardest task was to act in this imperceptible manner, which was a thing however altogether necessary, for if Barberini had perceived in the least, that we had Chigi in view, we had infallibly lost him, because, with all the virtue imaginable, he is capricious to the last degree, and that nothing could ever have prevented his fancying, that we had a design to deceive him in respect to Sachetti. It was properly on on this occasion that I admired the sincerity, the foresight, the activity, and the penetration of those that composed the flying squadron, and of Azolini chiefly, who was the man that stirred the most in this affair. There was not one step taken, in relation to Barberini and Sachetti, which might not have been approved of by the most rigid men in their morals As it was clearly perceived that all that could be done for Sachetti, would, by the event, prove ineffectual, the Squadron omitted not one step that was thought necessary to remove the evil dispositions which they foresaw that they should find on the part of France, of Spain, and of Florence, and even on the part of Barberini, about the exaltation of Chigi, when that matter was in a disposition fit to be proposed. As there was not the least room to doubt, that if Barberini perceived any thing of our design, he would immediately distrust us, we covered our march with so great an attention, and with so much good fortune, that he discovered it only by our means, when we thought it necessary for us that he should know it The greatest impediment we had to surmount, was, that being to rely on him as our chief support, we were obliged as a thing previous to all, to go about removing the obstacles which we foresaw would be very great from the whole faction of his late uncle Pope Urban. We knew that the only and daily application of the old Cardinals of that faction, who saw, as well as we, the impossibility of making Sachetti Pope, was to insinuate to Barberini, that it would be extremely shameful to him, that a Pope should be chosen that was not one of his creatures The whole faction conspired to persuade him of the same thing, every one of them conceiving some hopes of being the chosen man Genetti made no doubt but that his constant attachment from the beginning to the family of the Barberini, ought to give him the right of preference, Cecchini was persuaded that it was due to his merit, Rappacioli, who was but one and forty years old, or but little more, for I do not remember it precisely, fancied however, that his piety, his capacity, and his want of health, might raise him

up

up to the Papacy, even with ease; Fiorenzola suffered himself to be flattered by the imaginations of Grimaldi, in being natural to give an easy belief to what one desires. It is impossible for those who have never seen a Conclave, to imagine the illusions of men, in relation to the Papacy, which is rightly called Rabia Papale. That illusion however was a thing very likely to make us fail in our attempt, because the clamours of the whole faction of Pope Urban were very likely to make Barberini afraid of losing all his creatures in a moment, if he chose a Pope that was not one of that faction. That inconveniency, as you see, was very great, but we found a remedy in the very place from whence we expected the evil should come, for the jealousy that reigned among them, obliged them to take betimes such measures one against another, as incensed Barberini, because they wanted the discretion which we had used in keeping our sentiments hid in respect to the impossibility of Sachetti's exaltation Barberini thought that they were willing to believe that exaltation impossible, that they might advance their own interest. From that time he looked upon them as upon a pack of ambitious and ungrateful men, and that disposition of mind was the cause that when he came himself to be persuaded that it was impossible to make Sachetti Pope, he resolved the more easily upon setting his faction aside, being willing to persuade himself that he should run a less risk of losing his creatures, by giving them to understand that he was carried into another faction by his allies, than by incensing his whole faction against him, for the preference he must give to one of them over all the rest. For as to their yielding unanimously to Sachetti, they did it in favour of his old age and of his manners, which indeed were very amiable. Not but that in my opinion, it would have been with him as with Galba, who would have been thought worthy of the empire, if he had not been made Emperor. But however matters stood not on that foot. Barberini's creatures were indeed induced to favour Sachetti for that reason; but, not thinking his exaltation possible, their deference for him

him ſerved only to increaſe the cruel jealouſy they had conceived before-hand one againſt another

Old Cardinal Spada, a man well verſed in affairs, but whom affairs had corrupted, declared againſt Rappacioli ſo far as to write a libel againſt him, wherein he accuſed him of having believed that the devil might be received to mercy Montalte ſaid publicly, that he had ſufficient cauſes to oppoſe in form Fiorenzola's exaltation Fiorenzola, on his ſide, made a pleaſant deſcription enough of the fine diverſions, which la Signora Baſti, a neice of Cecchini's, handſome and a coquet, would give the public at the time of the carnival, if her uncle was choſen Pope All theſe piques and fooleries, which, to ſay the truth, were unworthy of a conclave, diſpleaſed Baberini to the laſt degree, he being a pious and grave man; and were no obſtacles to our deſigns, as you will preſently ſee

I think I have told you, that this Conclave laſted about eighty days, two thirds of which were ſpent in the manner I have already told you, becauſe Cardinal Barberini could not get it out of his head, but that our obſtinacy would at laſt carry it in favour of Sachetti We were leſs able to undeceive him than any body, for the reaſons which I have mentioned, and I do not know, whether the thing had not been carried ſtill much farther, if Sachetti, who grew weary to ſee himſelf amuſed by their balloting four times a day, without any proſpect of ſucceſs for him, had not himſelf opened Barberini's eyes. It was not, however, without a great deal of pain; but he ſucceeded at laſt; and after we had obſerved all manner of precautions, to prevent his ſuſpecting in the leaſt that we had any ſhare in that ſtep of Sachetti's, as it was true that we had not, we entered into a diſcuſſion with him of the Cardinals of his faction, and of the poſſibility of raiſing one to the chair. We perceived at firſt, that he was himſelf very much embaraſſed at it, and not without good reaſon We were not ſorry to find him embaraſſed, becauſe that gave us room to mention Cardinals of other factions, and to fall inſenſibly upon Cardinal Chigi. Cardinal Barberini, who, from his youth, has been a passionate lover of piety, and who admired much that which he thought that Chigi had, yielded to him pretty easily, with this only scruple, that Chigi, who was a great friend to the Jesuits, might probably strike at the doctrine of St Augustine, which Cardinal Barberini had a greater respect for, than knowledge of I was charged to inquire exactly about that matter with Chigi himself, and I acquitted myself of my commission in a manner which hurt neither my duty, nor the tenderness of conscience of Chigi That Cardinal, in the long conversations I had with him, during the time of the scrutinies, having penetrated me easily enough, because I had no reserve for him, he had discovered that I did not approve of people's infatuation in respect to persons, and that, in my opinion, truth only deserved to be examined and approved of He seemed to espouse the same sentiments, and he gave me room to believe, that his maxims made him altogether a fit man for restoring peace to the church. He explained himself upon that subject, publicly and reasonably enough, for Cardinal Albizi, a pensionary of the Jesuits, having exclaimed, even indecently, against St Augustine, whom he accused of carrying things to extremes, Chigi took him up vigorously, and spoke according to the respect due to that great supporter of grace This adventure served much more than all that I had said, to remove intirely Barberini's scruple As soon as we saw him determined, we began to make use of the materials which we had only hitherto been preparing Every one of us performed the task that was set him We began to explain what we had hitherto either kept carefully hid, or had at least only insinuated. Borromeo and Aquaviva disclosed themselves more fully to the Spanish Ambassador. Azolini had a greater liberty allowed him of shewing his parts with the several factions I spoke fully, and with all the vigour I could, to the Dean of the Sacred College, who intrusted me with his desire of appeasing the Great Duke in favour of the Barberinis; and Cardinal Barberini kept not hid from me the joy that that gave him. Azolini, or Lomelini, I do do not precisely remember which, discovered, that Bichi, who was allied to Chigi, was at the bottom extremely well disposed for him Bichi acted in his favour with a great deal of address, as well as prudence; for believing that Mazarin would not confide enough in him, to concur, upon what he should write, to Chigi's exaltation, he made use of Sachetti, to persuade him, who being tired, as I have said, of having been so long amused, dispatched an express to Mazarin, to give him notice, that Chigi would be Pope in spight of France, if that Crown offered to give him the exclusion, as the report went. It is certain, that as soon as Chigi was put up for candidate, all the Frenchmen in Rome said publicly, according to the style used by those of that nation, that their King would never suffer it. Mazarin was of another mind, for by the same express he sent an order to Lionne, not to exclude him. He was in the right, for I am persuaded, that if the exclusion had come, Chigi had been Pope three days sooner than he was. It is never prudent for Crowns to venture too easily on these exclusions. There are some Conclaves where the thing may succeed, but there are others where the success is impossible The Conclave I am speaking of was of this number; the Sacred College was not only strong, but the members were conscious of their own strength.

Things being in the condition which I have mentioned, the Cardinals de Medicis and Barberini sent me about nine at night to carry the news to Cardinal Chigi. I found him in bed, and I approached to kiss his hands. He understood what my errand was, and embracing me, he said, "Ecco l'efetto de la buona vicinanza*." I have already told you that I sat near him during the time of the scrutiny All the Cardinals came running to him afterwards. He sent for me again that same night about eleven, after he was left alone, and I cannot express to you how kindly he treated me. We went in a body the next day to take him out of his cell, and we carried him to the chapel

* This is an effect of your good neighbourhood.

where the ſcrutiny is made, where he had, if I am not miſtaken, all the votes for him, except one, or at moſt two. The ſuſpicion fell upon old Spada, Grimaldi, and Roſetti, becauſe they were the only ones that diſapproved, at leaſt publicly, of his exaltation. Grimaldi himſelf told me, that I had made a choice which I ſhould repent of as to my particular, and the event juſtified what he had told me. I attributed theſe words to the oddneſs of his temper, as I did Spada's diſlike to his envious temper, and that of Roſetti to the fear he had of Chigi's ſeverity. I am ſtill perſuaded that I was not miſtaken in my judgment, though I muſt confeſs that at the bottom they were likewiſe in the right. What is moſt certain is, that there never was any election of a Pope more univerſally applauded. The new Pope acted his part extremely well in theſe firſt moments, in which, by an odd kind of defect enough, to which moſt men are ſubject, thoſe that are expecting that dignity with the greateſt impatience, appear the moſt ſurpriſed when it comes. What followed after his election ſhewed, that his probity was not great enough to ſtifle his ardent deſire for the papal chair. He was ſo far, however, from giving any demonſtrations of his having been impatient, that we had room to believe that he was rather ſorry for it. He wept bitterly, whilſt the ſcrutiny, by which he was elected Pope, was reading over again; and finding, that I was obſerving of it, he embraced me with one arm, and Lomelini, who was ſeated below him, with the other, and he ſaid to us, "Forgive this weakneſs to a man who has always loved his relations tenderly, and who finds himſelf parted for ever from them." After the uſual ceremony, we went down to St. Peter's church, where he affected to ſit only upon a corner of the altar, though the Maſters of the Ceremonies told him that the cuſtom for Popes was to ſit juſt in the middle of it. He received there the adoration of the Sacred College with much more modeſty than grandeur, and more dejection than joy. When my turn came to kiſs his feet, he embraced me, and ſaid to me, with ſo loud a voice, that the Ambaſſadors of Spain and Venice,

nice, as well as the Conneſtable Colonna heard him; "Signor Cardinal de Retz, Ecce opus manuum tuarum." You may judge of the effects which theſe words produced. The Ambaſſadors told it to thoſe that were near them, and in an inſtant it was ſpread all over the church. Morangis, brother to Barillon, meeting me an hour after, regaled me with it; and I went back to my houſe, accompanied by above ſixſcore coaches, full of perſons, altogether perſuaded that I was going to govern St. Peter's bark. I remember, that Barillon whiſpered theſe words into my ears, "I am reſolved to count the number of coaches, that I may this evening give an account of it to Mr. de Lionne; we muſt not deprive the cuckold of this regale."

I have promiſed you ſome epiſodes, in which I will be as good as my word. You have already ſeen, that the French faction had received orders from the King, not only to forbear having any commuuication with me, but even to forbear ſaluting me. The Cardinal d'Eſt carefully avoided the meeting me; and, when it was not in his power to do ſo, he either turned his head another way, or he feigned to take up his handkerchief, or he affected to ſpeak to ſome of thoſe he had with him. In ſhort, as he always affected to appear an eccleſiaſtic, he affected likewiſe, in my opinion, to ſhew that, upon ſuch an occaſion, a conduct that went even againſt the appearances of chriſtian charity was unpleaſant to him. Cardinal Anthonio ſaluted me always very civilly when no body obſerved him, but being very cringing to the court, and a timorous man beſides, he acted in public according to his direction. Urſini, who was the man in the world of the vileſt ſoul, braved me every where equally. Bichi always ſaluted me civilly, and Grimaldi obſerved the King's orders no otherwiſe than in not viſiting me, for he even ſpoke to me, and always very civilly, when we met by chance. Theſe particulars will, I doubt, appear trifling to you; but my reaſon for not omitting them is, becauſe they are, in my opinion, a true and very natural image of the baſe politics of courtiers, each of them having his particular rule whereby he winds them up, or lowers them to his own pitch, in which rule they shew a greater regard by much to their own inclination than to their true interest

Conformably to that maxim, all the Cardinals of the French faction used me differently during the Conclave, though they all spoke of me alike in their letters to the Court of France. I have since made an application of that example to a thousand others As to my behaviour in respect to them, it was as civil as if they had used me in a civil manner. From as far as they could perceive me when we met, I held always my cap in my hand, and my civility to them was even carried to humility. I told every body, that I paid them this respect, not only as being my brothers, but as being likewise attached to the King my master. My language in this was like that of a Frenchman, of a christian, and of an ecclesiastic Ursini having one day braved me in so public a manner that it shocked every body, I redoubled my civilities to him to a point that pleased every body. What happened to me the next day helped to set off that modesty, or rather that affectation of modesty Cardinal John Charles de Medicis, who was naturally impetuous, stood up against me, for being, as he said, too much united with the squadron. I answered him with all the regard I owed to his person and his house This did not prevent his growing warm, and his telling me, that I ought to remember the obligations which my family had to his house, to which I answered, that I should never forget them, and that the Cardinal de Medicis, Dean of the Sacred College, was altogether persuaded of it, as was likewise the Great Duke. " But I am not persuaded of it, said he in a heat: have you forgot, that if it had not been for Queen Catherine of Medicis, you would be now but a private gentleman of Florence?" " Sir, replied I, in the presence of twelve Cardinals, I must beg your pardon; and, to convince you, that I am not at all ignorant of the rank which I should hold at Florence, if I was there upon the foot of my birth, I should be there as much above you, as my predecessors were above yours 400 years ago." Having said this, I turned to the company, and said,

ſaid, "You ſee, my Lords, how eaſy it is for French blood to ferment againſt the Spaniſh faction." The Great Duke, and the Cardinal Dean, were both ſo kind as not to reſent theſe words, and the Marquis Riccardi, Ambaſſador to the firſt, told me, after the Conclave was ended, that for his part he was pleaſed at them, and that he had blamed the Cardinal John Charles.

There happened another ſcene ſome days after, which was lucky enough for me. The Duke de Terra Nova, the Spaniſh Ambaſſador, preſented a memorial to the Sacred College, about ſomething which I have forgot, in which he ſtyled the King his maſter eldeſt ſon of the church. As the Secretary of the College was reading of it, I took notice of that expreſſion, which I believe was not obſerved by the Cardinals of the French faction, or at leaſt was not complained of by them. I allowed them time enough to have done it, being unwilling to ſhew either any precipitation, or affectation. But finding, that not one of them offered to ſay any thing, I roſe from my ſeat, and advancing towards the Cardinal Dean, I oppoſed in form the article of the memorial, in which his Catholic Majeſty was ſtyled eldeſt ſon of the church. I aſked for an act of my oppoſition, which was granted me in due form, being ſigned by four Maſters of Ceremonies. Cardinal Mazarin was ſo kind as to tell the King, and the Queen Mother, at the Queen's circle, that this was an invention of mine, concerted with the Spaniſh Ambaſſador, to give me the credit of it in France. It never becomes a miniſter to be an impoſtor, but it is even impolitic in him to carry his impoſtures beyond all probability.

Now I am upon Conclaves, I cannot leave this ſubject, without giving you a deſcription that may give you a knowledge of them, and correct the idea, which, without doubt, you muſt have formed upon common report, or perhaps upon reading ſome fabulous relations which have been written about them. And even what I have been writing to you of this Conclave of Alexander the VIIth, may have proved a further help for keeping you in your error, because I have spoke of murmurs, of complaints, and of little passions, which, as I think, ought to be set in their true light. It is certain, that there were more of these murmurings, of these complaints, and of these passions, in this conclave, than in any other at which I have been present. But it is not less certain, that excepting what passed between Cardinal John Charles and me, of which I have given you an account, a much slighter reproof, which that Cardinal drew upon him from Cardinal Imperiali, for pressing him over much; and the libel of Spada against Rappacioli; there was not in these murmurs, in these complaints, and in these little seeming passions, not only the least particle of hatred, but even of evil disposition. We lived all the while with one another, upon the same terms of respect and civility that is observed in the cabinets of princes, with the same politeness that rendered the court of Henry the Third remarkable, with the same familiarity that is used among the members of the same College; with the same modesty observed by novices during their probation time, and with the same love, at least in outward appearance, that ought to reign amongst well united brothers. I do not at all magnify the matter, and I say even less about it, than what I have seen in other Conclaves in which I have been. I cannot better express my thoughts upon this subject than by saying, that even in this Conclave of Alexander the VIIth, which the impetuosity of Cardinal John Charles de Medicis heated, or rather disordered a little, the answer which I made him was excused for no other reason but because he was not a man beloved; that that of Imperiali was disapproved of, and that Spada's libel was looked upon with detestation, and was disowned by him the very next day, because every body cried shame upon him. I may truly say, that in all the Conclaves at which I have assisted, I never saw one Cardinal, nor one Conclavist, fall into a passion, and that I have even seen very few of them warmed. It is very rare to hear there any loud voice, or to see any body's countenance altered. I have often tried, whether I could observe any such alteration

teration in the countenance of thoſe that had been juſt excluded, and I may ſay with ſincerity, that excepting one time, I could never diſcover any They are even there ſo far from ſuſpecting any thing like thoſe ſort of revenges, which common error charges the Italians with, that it is pretty common for the Cardinal elected to drink, at his dinner, wine ſent him in the morning by the excluded Cardinal. In ſhort, I dare maintain, that there is nothing wiſer or greater than the outward appearance commonly obſerved in a Conclave. I am not ignorant, that the form practiſed there ſince Pope Gregory's bull, contributes much to regulate it; but it muſt be confeſſed, that none but the Italians are capable of obſerving that rule with the decency they do. I return to my narration

You will eaſily believe, that I did not fail, during the time that the Conclave laſted, of adviſing with Cardinal Chigi and my friends of the ſquadron, in reſpect to the conduct which I was to follow after the Conclave was ended. I foreſaw that I ſhould meet with many difficulties, both on the ſide of Rome, and on that of France, and my firſt converſations with my friends convinced me that I was not miſtaken. I will begin with thoſe which I met on the ſide of Rome, and which I will mention at once, that I may not interrupt the thread of my diſcourſe, intending to explain my conduct in reſpect to Italy, before I mention the ſteps I took in reſpect to France My friends there, who underſtood little of the manners of Italy, and who (according to the genius of our nation, which is to think, that all others are to conform to our own manners) thought that a Cardinal, that was perſecuted, might, and even ought, to live at Rome in ſome meaſure like a private man, were telling me in all their letters, that decency required, that I ſhould keep in the houſe of the Fathers of the Miſſion, where I had indeed took an apartment ſeven or eight days after my coming to Rome They were adding, how neceſſary it was that I ſhould live frugally, both upon account of my revenues, which being ſeized upon in France in a very extraordinary and rigorous manner, deprived me of the means of making even a middling figure; and because that that modest way of living would work admirably upon the minds of the clergy of Paris, whom I should stand in great need of afterwards I mentioned this to Cardinal Chigi, who passed for the greatest ecclesiastic on that side the Alps, and I was very much surprised when he said to me. "No, Sir, no, when you are settled in your Archbishoprick, you may live after what manner you please, because people there will know what you are, or what you are not able to do. You are now at Rome, where your enemies are every day saying, that your credit is lost in France, the falsity of which it is necessary for you to shew You are not an hermit, but a Cardinal, and one of a rank which is called here Dei Cardinaloni Modesty is perhaps more valued here than any where else, but, in a man of your age, of your birth, and of your rank, modesty ought to be tempered. It ought besides to appear so much an act of your choice, that the least suspicion of its being forced, would spoil it quite There are a great many in Rome who love to trample upon those whom they see creeping. Do not fall so low as that, dear Sir, and consider, I beseech you, what figure you will make in the streets with the six footmen you speak of, when you meet with a sorry citizen of Paris, who, instead of paying you the least respect, will brave you, to make his court to the Cardinal d'Est. You ought not to have come to Rome, except you had found yourself resolved and enabled to support your dignity Christian humility does not consist in disgracing it, and all I can say is, that poor Cardinal Chigi, who is now speaking to you, who has but five thousand crowns a-year revenue, and who is reckoned one of the poorest Cardinals, even of those that are monks, cannot assist at any congregation, without four coaches with liveries for his equipage, though he is sure that he will meet with no body in the streets of Rome that will be wanting to the respect due to his rank"

This is but part of what Cardinal Chigi was telling me every day; and what my other friends, who were not, or at least who appeared not such zealous Ecclesi-

astics

aſtics as he, enlarged upon ſtill much more. Cardinal Barberini exclaimed ſtill more than the reſt againſt this project of retrenching my expences He offered me his purſe, but being unwilling to make uſe of it, and even to be a charge to my relations and my friends in France, I found myſelf in a great trouble, and ſo much the greater becauſe I ſaw theſe laſt very much diſpoſed to believe that a great expence was in no manner neceſſary to me at Rome. I have hardly found myſelf during my whole life in any circumſtance more vexatious to me than that was, and I may truly ſay that I remember but one, where I needed more to make a terrible effort on myſelf, to prevent my acting in the manner I ſhould have wiſhed If I had followed my own inclination I had reduced myſelf to two footmen. But I gave way to neceſſity, when I became convinced that I ſhould infallibly fall into contempt if I did not appear with ſome dignity I looked out for a palace to live in. I gathered together all my attendants, which were in great number, I got liveries made that were modeſt, but for no leſs than eighty perſons, and I kept withal a great table. The Abbots of Courtenai and of Sevigné came to me at Rome, as did likewiſe Campi, who had commanded the Italian regiment of Cardinal Mazarin, but who had ſince attached himſelf to me, in ſhort, I ſaw all my former domeſtics come flocking thither to rejoin me My expence was great during the Conclave, and greater after the Conclave was done But it was neceſſary, and the event ſhewed that the advice of my friends in Italy was better grounded than that of my friends in France. For the Cardinal d'Eſt having enjoined in the King's name, the very next day after the Pope's election, all the French that were at Rome to forbear ſtopping before me in the ſtreets, and even having forbid the Superiors of the French churches to receive me, I had fallen into a great ridicule, if I had not been in a condition to make my dignity reſpected You will be fully convinced of the truth of what I ſay, by the anſwer the Pope made me, when I entreated him to preſcribe to me in what manner he deſired that I ſhould behave

 myſelf

myfelf in refpect to the orders given out by the Cardinal d'Eft. I will mention that anfwer, after I have given you an account of the firft fteps the Pope took after his creation.

He caufed the next day his coffin to be laid under his bed, the day after he gave particular habits to the Train-bearers of the Cardinals; the third day he forbad the Cardinals to wear any perfonal mourning, even for their fathers. This was enough to convince me (and I told it even to Azolini, who owned it) that we had been bubbled, and that the Pope would never be but a poor fort of a man. The Cavalier Bernini, who is a man of good fenfe, obferved two or three days after, that the Pope had taken notice, in a ftatue which he was fhewing him, only of a little fringe that was at the bottom of the gown. Thefe obfervations feem flight; but they are certain. Great men may have great weakneffes, and are not even exempt from all fmall ones, but there are fome fort of weakneffes, of which they are not capable; and I have never feen a great man, for example, begin his entrance into a great employment with trifling matters. Azolini, who made the fame obfervations as I, advifed me not to lofe one moment in engaging Rome to protect me, by granting me the * Pallium of the Archbifhoprick of Paris.

* The Pallium is a Pontifical ornament peculiar to Popes, Patriarchs, Primates, and Metropolitans, which they wear over their Pontifical habits as a mark of their jurifdiction. It is made of white wool, fhorn from two lambs, which fome Nuns of the order of St Agnes offer every year, the day of the feftival of that Saint, whilft the Agnus Dei is finging at Mafs. Thefe lambs are received by two Canons of the church of St John of Lateran, who put them into the hands of the Apoftolick Sub-Deacons. Thefe take care to feed them, and to fheer them in the proper feafon, and to them only belongs the making of thefe Palliums, which they afterwards lay on the bodies of St Peter and St Paul, at the great altar of their church, upon which they fay prayers all night, as it is expreffed in the Roman Ceremonial. The Pope only has now the right of granting the Pallium, and a metropolitan, before his receiving it, cannot confecrate Bifhops, dedicate Churches, be called Archbifhop, &c. See Furetiere's Dictionary at the word PALLIUM, where you have more about it. And fee what Pafquier fays of the hurt which

is

Paris. I asked it in the first consistory, before any body had even the least thought that I intended the asking of it. The Pope gave it me naturally, and without reflecting upon what he did. The thing was regular, and he could not have refused it, without violating the rules of the church, but you will see by what followed, that he was not governed by these rules This step made me believe that he would make no difficulty to suffer that I should at least be treated at Rome as a Cardinal. I made therefore my complaint to him about the order given by the Cardinal d'Est to all the Frenchmen in that city, representing that that Cardinal was not satisfied with acting in Rome like a Sovereign, by degrading me from all temporal honours, but that he likewise acted like the Pope himself, by interdicting me the French churches. I had matter enough to enlarge upon, which you may be sure I did. The Pope, to whom Mr de Lionne had made his complaints about his granting me the Pallium, and to whom he had spoke with an air and in a tone which expressed his insolence; the Pope, I say, appeared to me very much embarrassed. He spoke a great deal against the Cardinal d'Est; he deplored the sad custom (that was the expression he used) that had subjected rather than attached Cardinals to Crowns, so far as to have formed amongst themselves a scandalous schism. He enlarged much upon that point; but I had but a bad opinion of my affair, when I saw him dwell so long upon generals without entering into particulars, and I soon perceived that my fear was well grounded, when I heard him, after many circumlocutions, explain himself in this manner: " The politics of my predecessors have not left me so much elbow-room as my good intentions deserve I confess that it is a shame to the Sacred College, and even to the Holy See, to suffer the licentiousness, which the Cardinal d'Est, or rather Cardinal Mazarin, take on this occasion. But

it was like to have done to the liberty of the Gallican church, at its first being sent into France, in the seventh chapter of the third book of his Recherches de la France.

the

the Spaniards had a quarrel almost like this concerning Cardinal Barberini in the last Pope's time And even in the time of Pope Paul the Vth, the Mareschal d'Estrées did not use Cardinal Borghese much better. These examples should not at another time authorize the evil, which I should then be fully able to redress. But you must consider, Charo mio Signor Cardinale, that Christendom is all in a fire, which none but Pope Alexander is able to extinguish, and that he is obliged for that reason on many occasions to shut his eyes, for fear of disabling himself from serving the public in so necessary a work as that of a general peace. What will you say when I tell you what Lionne has declared insolently to me, three days since, upon my giving you the Pallium, that France would give me no share in the treaty which is talked of, and which is not so remote as people think? What I am saying does not mean that I intend to abandon you; but it is only to convince you that I ought to behave myself with a great deal of circumspection, and that it is proper that you should help me. in short, that we ought both of us to give way to time"

If my design had been to make my court to his Holiness, I should have retired after this discourse, which was, as you see, only a prelude for refusing to answer me in a direct manner But as I wanted, and even quickly, that direct answer, because I might find myself at every instant in the trouble which I would avoid, I thought that it was best for me to bring the Pope to explain himself, and I took the liberty to represent to him with a profound respect, that perhaps at my parting from his Holiness, I should meet in the street the Cardinal d'Est, who being but a Cardinal Deacon ought to stop before me, and that I should infallibly meet with Frenchmen, Rome being filled with them, that I entreated him therefore to give me his orders, which would prevent my committing any fault, and for want of which I should be put to a non-plus; that if I should suffer that what the ceremonial orders to be paid to Cardinals, should be refused me, I was afraid that the Sacred College would not approve

prove of my conduct; that if I put myself in a condition to have it paid me, I was afraid to be wanting to the respect which I owed his Holiness, to whom alone it belonged to determine of what concerned Cardinals, that I therefore most humbly entreated him to prescribe to me exactly what I was to do, assuring him, that I would without the least difficulty execute whatever he would please to order, because I should think it as glorious to me to submit to his commands, as I should think it shameful to give way to those of the Cardinal d'Est.

It was on this occasion that I discovered for the first time the true genius of Pope Alexander, which was to make use of finesses in every thing. That defect is great, and is so much the more so, when it is to be met with in men possessed with great dignities, because they are never reclaimed from it, the respect which is borne them, and which affords no room to any complaints, being the cause that they remain almost always persuaded that they blind the eyes of every body, even when there is not one soul but what perceives their finesses. The Pope, who with a view of justifying what he did, or rather of ceasing to have any thing more to do with my conduct, either in respect to France or to the Sacred College, would have been pleased that I should have contested with him upon what he had been saying, took me up sharply when I spoke of submitting to his commands, saying "No, but to those of the Cardinal d'Est, when they derive from the King of France." The tone with which this was said, and what the Marquis Riccardi, Ambassador of Florence, had said to me the day before, of much such a turn which the Pope gave to a conversation he had lately had with him, made me judge that the Pope expected that I should take the change, and that I should go about distinguishing, what were the King's orders, and what those of the Cardinal d'Est; by which means he would have room given him, for telling Mr de Lionne that he had exhorted me to submit, and for telling my brethren the Cardinals, that he had only advised me to keep within the terms of respect which

which I owed the King But I afforded him no room either for one or for the other, for I anſwered him without any heſitation, that what he propoſed was juſt the cauſe of my trouble, and the thing upon which I entreated him to determine, becauſe the name of the King appeared on one ſide, to which I ought to ſhew all manner of ſubmiſſion; and that I ſaw on the other ſide the authority of his Holineſs ſo much wounded, that I did not think that I ought, in my own particular, to give way to a ſtroke of ſuch a nature, except at leaſt I had an expreſs order for it. The Pope talked much and went a great way about, in order to draw me off from my demand, or rather to draw himſelf off from the determination I was aſking for, but I remained fixed and firm to my point He roved up and down, and diverted himſelf, which is always eaſy to thoſe that are our ſuperiors. He repeated ſeveral times that the King of France was a great King At other times he told me that God was ſtill a greater. Sometimes he enlarged upon the obligations which Eccleſiaſtics were in to preſerve the liberties and immunities of the church; and ſometimes upon the neceſſity there was of managing the minds of Kings in the preſent conjuncture He recommended to me chriſtian patience, he recommended to me epiſcopal vigour. He blamed the ceremonial, to which the Court of Rome was too much tied up; he praiſed the obſervation of it, as a thing neceſſary for the ſupport of its dignity. The literal ſenſe of all his diſcourſe was, that let me act in what manner I pleaſed, I could do nothing but what he might ſay he had forbidden me I preſſed him to explain himſelf, as much as it is poſſible to preſs a man that is ſitting in St Peter's chair, but I could draw nothing out of him. I gave an account of my audience to Cardinal Barberini, and to my friends of the ſquadron, and I will acquaint you with the conduct they put me upon, after I have given you the particulars of a converſation which Mr de Lionne had had ſome days before with the Pope, and of what paſſed at that time between Mr. de Lionne and me.

Mr.

Mr. de Lionne, who was but lately re eſtabliſhed at the French Court, was touched to the quick that the Pope had granted me the Pallium, becauſe he was afraid that Cardinal Mazarin would have charged him with that action, as an effect of his negligence The thing was done before he knew that it was to be propoſed, which might prove a great crime with a man that had told Lionne, at parting, that there was not one body at Rome but would willingly ſerve him as a ſpy The fear he had of being reprimanded, obliged him to make the Pope a terrible reprimand, for the manner in which he ſpoke to his Holineſs cannot be called otherwiſe. He declared to his face, that notwithſtanding my Bulls, my Act of Poſſeſſion, and my Pallium, the King did not, nor would ever look upon me, as Archbiſhop of Paris. This was one of the ſofteſt expreſſions of his whole diſcourſe, the rhetorical figures of which were filled up with menaces of arreſts of Parliament, of decrees of the Sorbonne, and of reſolutions of the French Clergy. Lionne mentioned ſomething, but in dark words, about a ſchiſm, but he explained himſelf clearly and frankly about excluding the Pope entirely and abſolutely from the congreſs for a general peace, which would, as it was ſuppoſed, be very ſoon treated of This laſt article frightened Pope Alexander to ſuch a degree, that he aſked Lionne a million of excuſes, ſo low, and even ſo ridiculous, that they will not be believed by poſterity. He told him, with tears in his eyes, that I had over-reached him ; but that he would inſtantly name a congregation of Cardinals that ſhould be agreeable to the King, in order to examine what could be done towards his ſatisfaction, he deſired for that effect, that Mr de Lionne would, with all manner of expedition, get a memorial drawn of all that had paſſed in the civil war ; aſſuring him, that the King might depend upon it, that he would make ſuch a quick and good example of me, as would ſatisfy his Majeſty. In ſhort, Mr de Lionne was ſo well pleaſed, and ſo fully ſatisfied with what the Pope told him, that he immediately ſent an expreſs about it to Cardinal Mazarin, to whom he he wrote a letter, in which were the following words: "I hope, in a few days, to send your eminence a piece of news still more acceptable, which will be that of the Cardinal de Retz's imprisonment in the Castle of St Angelo. The Pope looks upon the amnesties granted to the rebels at Paris, as insignificant, and as a thing, as he has told me, of which the Cardinal de Retz can make no use, because as none but the Pope can condemn Cardinals, so none but his Holiness can absolve them. I have not however taken this for granted, and my answer to him has been, that the Parliament of Paris pretends, that they may condemn Cardinals, and that they would already have proceeded to the trial of the Cardinal de Retz, if your eminence had not opposed it vigorously, moved to it purely from the respect you bear to the Holy See, and to his Holiness in particular The Pope, my Lord, has expressed a great obligation to your eminence for it, and has charged me to assure you, that he would do the King more justice than the Parliament of Paris would have done." This was one of the articles of Lionne's letter.

I desire that you would observe, that the conversation I had with the Pope, the particulars of which I have given you, happened but two or three days after that which he had with Lionne, and which served for a ground to the letter I just now mentioned. But supposing I had had no knowledge of that letter, I might however have easily perceived the evil disposition of the Pope, of which I had not only probable, but sure evidences Monsignor Febey, first master of the ceremonies, a wise and an honest man, and who, in concert with me, had served the Pope very worthily about his exaltation, gave me notice that he found him very much changed in respect to me "And so much, added he, that I am scandalized at it * almaggior segno" The Pope had even told the Abbot Charrier, that he understood nothing in the pleasure he took to spread a report in Rome, as if I governed the

* To the greatest degree possible.

Pope-

Popedom. Father Hilarion, a Bernardine, and Abbot of the Holy Crofs at Jerufalem, who was one of the honefteft men in the world, and with whom I had contracted a ftrict friendfhip, advifed me, upon what the Pope had faid to the Abbot Charrier, to take a turn into the country, under pretence of taking the air, but in effect, to let his Holinefs fee, that I was very far from being a bufy-body at Court. I followed his advice, and I went for a month or five weeks to Grotta Frefcati, which is at four leagues diftance from Rome. It was in ancient times the Tufculum of Cicero, and it is now an Abbey of the order of St. Bazil, and belongs to Cardinal Barberini. The place is extremely agreeable, and by what it appears to me, I do not think it even flattered in what its ancient lord has faid of it in his Epiftles. I was diverting myfelf there in what is ftill to be feen of fome things mentioned by that great man. The columns of white marble which he caufed to be brought from Greece, for his porch, fupport the church of the Monks there, who are Italians, but who perform the offices in Greek, and who have a particular way of finging which is very fine. It was at that place that Mr. de Lionne's letter, of which I fpoke, came to my knowledge. Croiffi brought me a copy of it taken from the original It is neceffary I fhould explain to you who Croiffi was, and that I fhould mention the particulars of the intrigue which opened me a way to fee that letter

Croiffi was a Counfellor of the Parliament of Paris, who had been deeply engaged, as you have feen, in the intrigues of that time. He had been at Munfter with Mr. de Avaux, who fent him at that time to Ragotfki, Prince of Tranfilvania. He had fince fallen out with Mr Servier about fomething that related to Mr de Avaux's concerns, and that quarrel, and his temper, which was naturally unquiet, carried him to fignalize himfelf againft Mazarin, as foon as the movements of his company had opened him a way to do it The accefs which Mr. de St. Romain, his particular friend, had to the Prince of Conti, and that

which

which * Mr. Courtin, who has the honour to be known to you, had to madam de Longueville, attached him, during the siege of Paris, to their interests. He followed those of the Prince of Condé, as soon as that Prince had fallen out with the Court, he was of great service to him during his imprisonment, he was in the secret of the negotiation, and of the treaty which the Fronde made with that Prince, he remained attached to him when the Fronde fell out for the second time with his Highness, after his coming out of prison, but he preserved all along all manner of regard for us. A few days after my being taken up, he was arrested at Paris, whither he was returned against the King's orders, and where he kept himself hid. He was brought to the Castle of Vincennes, where I was kept prisoner, and was lodged in a chamber just over my head. We found means to have a correspondence together. He tied his letters to a thread, which he let down to one of my windows in the night-time. As my custom was to study till two in the morning, I took the opportunity of my guards falling asleep, to take up his letters, and to tie mine to the same thread. The advices I gave him during his trial, which was going upon with a great deal of eagerness, were not unuseful to him. The Chancellor came twice to Vincennes to interrogate him. He was charged with holding intelligence with the Prince of Conde, even since the condemnation of that Prince, and his retreat among the Spaniards. It was Croissi who had first proposed the setting a price upon Cardinal Mazarin's head, which was a circumstance not very favourable to his justification. Though he was guilty, he came off, however, tolerably well, by the assistance of the President de Bellievre who was one of his judges, and who told me, when he came to take me out of Vincennes, that he had given Croissi a certain sign which had set him right, and saved him, in

* He was the first that attempted a French translation of Grotius de jure belli belli & pacis.

the

the anſwer he was making to one of the Chancellor's interrogatories. In ſhort, he was proſecuted no further, and he came out of priſon upon giving his word to part with his employment, and to quit either Paris or the kingdom, I do not remember which. He came to Rome, where he found me, and he took up his lodging, if I am not miſtaken, with Châtillon who was his friend They came together to ſee me, almoſt every evening, not daring to come in the day-time, becauſe of the orders given to all the French to the contrary. Theſe two gentlemen had a particular acquaintance with little Fouquet the preſent Biſhop of Agde, who was at Rome at that time, and who diſapproved the liberty which Mr. de Lionne took of lying with his own wife, with whom little Fouquet was much in favour That gentleman having in view to get for himſelf the poſt which Lionne had in Rome, was very glad beſides, to put him upon acting his part ill, that he might thereby have an opportunity of diſſerving him at court. He thought that the beſt way to bring his project to paſs, was to embroil and imbarraſs the chief, or rather the only negotiation that Lionne had there, which was that concerning me. To that effect he ſpoke to Croiſſi, whom he charged to aſſure me, that he would inform me punctually of every ſtep which Lionne ſhould take, that I ſhould have a copy of all the cuckold's diſpatches (he never called Mr. de Lionne otherwiſe) before they were ſent away; that I ſhould have likewiſe a copy of Mazarin's Letters a quarter of an hour after the cuckold had received them; and that it was in his power to do what he promiſed, becauſe he could intirely diſpoſe of Madam de Lionne, from whom the huſband kept nothing ſecret, that Lady beſides being at that time extremely incenſed againſt him, for being paſſionately in love with one of her women named Agathe, who was very pretty. This conſiderable advantage which I had over Lionne, was the chief cauſe of my not valuing, as I ought to have done, the advances which he had made me, by the means of Montreſor It ought not to have produced that effect, and

and I was certainly in the wrong Two other motives contributed to the making me commit that error. The first was the pleasure we had every evening, Crossi, Châtillon, and I, to turn the cuckold into ridicule, and I observed on this occasion, though too late, what I have since observed in others, that one ought to be extremely intent, in great affairs still more than in others, upon guarding one's self against the pleasure one is inclined to take in raillery. It is a thing which amuses, tickles, and flatters, and this pleasure has in many occasions cost the Prince of Condé dear The other motive, which incensed me at first against Lionne was, that immediately after the Conclave, he sent, by an express order from the Court, as he has told me since, at St. Germains, one La Borne, who was an officer in Rome who took care Cardinal Mazarin's dispatches, to the palace of our Lady of Loretto, where I lodged, with a notification in form to all my domestic servants that were Frenchmen, to abandon me, upon pain of being declared guilty of high treason, as abettors to a rebel to his King, and a traitor to his country I was incensed at those expressions. The name of the King saved the man that pronounced them from receiving some insult; but the Chevalier de Bois David, who belonged to me, and who was young and wanton, shewed him, as he was going, a pair of horns, which was a thing very well adapted to the subject You see by this, that words spoken, often engage more than actions, and this reflection has obliged me to say to myself more than once, that in great affairs the least words cannot be too nicely weighed.

I return to the letter which Croissi brought me at Grotto Frescati. I was surprised at it, but with that kind of surprize which causes no emotion Things incredible have always worked that effect on me. Not but that I know that what is incredible proves often true; but as it ought not to be so, according to the best rules of foresight, I could never be moved at it, because I have always looked upon those sorts of events, as upon thunderbolts, that are uncommon, but not impossible.

We

We made however a great many reflections, Croissi, the Abbot Charrier, and I, upon that letter I sent the Abbot to Rome to communicate the contents of it to Cardinal Azolini, who made no great account of the Pope's words, on which Lionne seemed to reckon so much. The Cardinal told the Abbot Charrier, with a great deal of good sense and penetration, that he was persuaded that Lionne, whose interest it was to hide, or rather to disguise and retrieve at the Court of France, his want of care about my receiving the Pallium, magnified the words and promises of his Holiness, "who is besides, added Azolini, the best man in the world at finding out expressions, the most promising, and the least significant." He advised me to return to Rome, and to set a good face upon the matter; to continue to express an entire confidence in the Pope's justice and in his good-will, and to go on in the same manner I used to do, as if I knew nothing of what he had told Lionne. I believed him, and I followed his advice I declared at my return to Rome, as my friends had advised me before my going thence, that I bore such a respect for the King's name, that I was ready to suffer every thing without exception from those who could shew the least character from his most Christian Majesty, that not only Mr. de Lionne, but even Mr. Gueffier, who was only an Agent for France, might live with me in the manner they thought fit; but that I should, on all occasions, shew them all the civility that was in my power; that I would observe the same rule in regard to my brother Cardinals, being persuaded that there was no reason whatever that could exempt Ecclesiastics even from all the outward duties of union and of charity that ought to be professed among them; that this rule, which was evangelical, and consequently far superior to that of the ceremonials, taught me that I ought not to examine whether they were elder or younger in rank than me; that I would stop equally before them all, without considering whether they would do the like by me, or whether they would salute me or not, that as to private men, who had no manner of character from the King,

King, and who should refuse to pay me the respect due to my dignity, I could not follow the same conduct with them, because it would prove a detriment to that dignity, considering the consequences which laymen would not fail to draw from it to their advantage, against the prerogatives of the church; that knowing myself however to be, both by my inclination and by my maxims, very remote from any thing that carries with it the least appearance of violence, I would order my servants to offer none to the first that should be wanting to the respect he owed to my character, but only to cut the ham-strings of his coach-horses. You will easily believe that no body would expose themselves to receive such an affront. Most of the French stopped before me, those who chose to obey the orders of the Cardinal d' Est, carefully avoided the meeting me in the streets The Pope, to whom Cardinal Bichi had much magnified the public declaration which I had made in relation to my conduct, mentioned it to me with a reprimand, saying that I ought not to threaten those that should obey the King's orders As I began to be acquainted with the manners of the Pope, which consisted all in cunning, I thought that my best way was to give him only such an answer as would oblige him to explain himself, which is an infallible rule of acting with men of that character. I answered, that I took it for a great obligation that he would be so kind as to honour me with his orders; that I would for the future bear with any thing from any Frenchman of the lowest kind, and that it was enough for my justification with the Sacred College, to say that what I did was his Holiness's command. The Pope stopped me hastily at that word, and said, "You do not take me right, my meaning is not that the respect due to a Cardinal should be denied him, you go from one extreme to another. I charge you to take care not to speak after this manner in Rome." I took hold of these words of the Pope with no less eagerness than he had taken up what I was saying to him. I begged that he would forgive me if I had mistaken his meaning. I told him that I presumed

presumed that he approved in general of the conduct which I had declared that I would follow, and that he would have me only keep the right medium between the two extremes. The Pope thought not fit to contradict me, finding, in some manner, his account in what had passed by reason of his ambiguous expressions. I found mine likewise in it, because I was not obliged to change my conduct. My audience ended in this manner, and at my coming out from it, I spoke mightily in commendation of his Holiness to Monsignor il Maestro di Camera, who accompanied me, and who failed not to report it in the evening to the Pope, to which his Holiness answered with a sour look, '* Questi maledetti Francesi sono piu furbi di noi altri' This Master of the Chamber, who was Monsignor Bandinelli, and who became a Cardinal afterwards, told this two days after to Father Hilarion, from whom I had it. I continued to live upon that foot, till I took a journey to the waters of St. Cassien that are in Tuscany, to try to find some relief for a new accident that had happened to my shoulder by my own fault.

I have already told you that the most famous surgeon in Rome had tried in vain to set it right, though in order to it, he had put it out of joint a second time. I suffered myself to be wheedled by a country fellow who lived in Prince Borghese's territories, upon the recommendation of a gentleman of Florence of the house of Mazzinghi, who was allied to me, and who assured me that he had seen prodigious cures performed by this quack. He put my shoulder out of joint for the third time, and he put me to intolerable pain, without bringing it to itself The weakness which this operation left me in, obliged me to have recourse to the waters of St. Cassien, which afforded me but little relief I came from thence to spend the rest of the summer at Caprarola, which is a very fine house at forty miles distance from Rome, belonging to the

* These cursed Frenchmen are greater cheats than we are.

Duke of Parma I staid there for the Rinfrescata *, after which I returned to Rome, where I found the Pope as much altered in respect to every thing without exception, as I had already found him altered in respect to me † He had nothing left of the piety he had before affected, but only his gravity, which he still preserved whilst he was at church I call it gravity, and not modesty, because a great deal of pride appeared to be joined with it He did not only continue the abuse of Nepotism, by causing all his relations, to come to Rome, but he consecrated it by causing the Cardinals to approve of it, having asked their advice in private, for fear of being obliged to follow one contrary to his inclination, in case any Cardinal had publicly opposed it He grew vain to a ridiculous degree, valuing himself upon his gentility, as a country 'Squire would if his coat of arms was questioned at the herald's office. He envied every body without exception Cardinal Cesy used to say, that he would make him burst with anger by the continual praises he gave St Leo. It is certain that he almost fell out with Monsignor Magalotti, because he thought that he pretended to be better versed than he in the Dictionary of the Academy of La Crusca He never spoke one word of truth, and the Marquis Riccardi, Ambassador from Florence, expressed himself in these words in the latter end of a letter to the Great Duke, which he shewed me, "In fine, serenissimo Signore, habbiamo un Papa, chi non dice una parola di verita" He was continually applying himself to trifles, and was so foolish as to promise a public reward to the man who should find out a Latin word for a calash He once spent seven or eight days in finding out whether

* The time when the heats begin to abate

† The luxury of this Pope, and the tyranny of his nephews during his Popedom, are described in a book called, Sindicato di Alexandro VII Amongst other Pasquinades against him that are there to be met with, there is one in which Marforio having asked Pasquin, what the Pope said to the Cardinals as he lay a dying, Pasquin answers, 'Maxima de seipso, plurima de Parentibus pauca de Principibus, turpia de Cardinalibus, pauca de Ecclesia, de Deo nihil.'

wosco

mosco came from *musca*, or *musca* from *mosco*. Cardinal Imperiali having told me the particulars of what had passed at two or three sittings of the Academy, that had been held upon that subject, I thought that he magnified the thing to divert himself, but I was undeceived the very next day, for the Pope having sent for Cardinal Rappacioli and for me, and having taken us with him in his coach, he held us for three hours long that were spent in taking the air, upon as poor trifles as the low criticism of a little school-master could have produced, and Rappacioli, who was a man of refined wit, told me, after we had waited on him to his apartment, that as soon as he was at home he would distil the whole discourse of the Pope, to try how much good sense he could extract out of a conversation that had lasted three hours, in which the Pope had had all the talk to himself He shewed an affectation some days after, which appeared to be extremely childish. he carried all the Cardinals to the seven churches; but the way being too long to go in the forenoon with so great a train, he gave them a dinner in the refectory of St Paul's, each of them having their separate allowance served before them, as pilgrims have in the time of the Jubilee. All the silver plate, which was used with profusion on this occasion, was made on purpose in a form like to the utensils common to pilgrims. I remember among others, that the vessels which our wine was served in, were altogether like the gourd-bottles used by pilgrims. But nothing in my opinion shewed more the Pope's want of judgment than the pride he took in being thought the author of the Queen of Sweden's conversion She had abjured her heresy eighteen months before she had any thought of coming to Rome And yet as soon as Pope Alexander heard of it, he acquainted the Sacred College with it in a full consistory in a speech very much studied. He omitted nothing to give us to understand that he had been the only instrument which God had made use of for that conversion. There was no body but was very well informed of the contrary, so I leave you to judge of the effect which a piece of vanity so ill contrived could produce. It will be an easy thing for you to imagine that the way which the Pope took was no encouragement for me to expect any great matters from his protection, and besides I quickly perceived that the more he grew attached to small matters, the weaker he grew in respect to great

There is every year an anniversary performed for the soul of Henry the Great, in the church of St. John of Lateran, where the Ambassadors of France and the Cardinals of the French faction never fail to be present. The Cardinal d' Est was pleased to declare that he would not suffer me to be there. I was told of it, and I asked an audience of the Pope to acquaint him with it He refused it me, upon pretence of an indisposition I got Monsignor Febei to know of him what he would have me do on this occasion, but he could draw from him nothing but equivocal answers. As I foresaw that if any thing happened between the Cardinal d' Est and me, wherein any blood should be shed, the Pope would not fail to run me down, I did whatever I could decently do to oblige him to put out an order that should forbid my being present at the ceremony But finding that I could not succeed in it, and being unwilling on the other side to degrade myself from the title of a French Cardinal, by excluding myself from the functions which were peculiar to that nation, I resolved to venture on, happen what would. I went to St John of Lateran very well accompanied; I took up my seat there, I assisted at the service, I saluted very civilly at my coming in and at my going out the Cardinals of the faction, who contented themselves with refusing to do the like to me, and I came back to my house very well pleased with my having come off so cheap. I had a like adventure at the church of St. Lewis, whither the Sacred College went upon that Saint's holy-day. Having heard that La Bussiere, who is now Master of the Chamber to the Ambassadors at Rome, and who was at that time Master of the Horse to Mr de Lionne, had said publicly that I should not be suffered to be there, I did what in me lay, to oblige the Pope to prevent the harm that might ensue. I

spoke

ſpoke of it to him with vigour, but he would never explain himſelf It is true that at my firſt mentioning the thing to him, he told me, that he did not ſee what could oblige me to aſſiſt at theſe ceremonies, when I had ſo good an excuſe for forbearing the doing of it, as the French King's command was, for not admitting me there But after I had anſwered him, that if I once acknowledged theſe orders to be the King's, I could not ſee how I could excuſe myſelf from obeying his other orders by which I was diveſted of the Archbiſhoprick of Paris, he was put to a nonplus. He told me that I ought to be my own adviſer; that as for him he would never forbid a Cardinal from aſſiſting at the functions of the Sacred College, and ſo I parted from him juſt as wiſe as I was before I went to St Lewis's church in a condition to diſpute the ground. La Buſſiere ſnatched away from the Curate's hands the * Aſperges, as he was going to preſent me with holy water, which one of my Gentlemen had fetched. Cardinal Anthonio forbore making me the uſual compliment made to other Cardinals on this occaſion This however did not hinder me from taking my ſeat there, nor from ſtaying all the time the ceremony laſted, which ſerved to maintain me at Rome upon the foot of a French Cardinal The expence which was neceſſary to ſupport me in that poſt, was not one of the leaſt difficulties I met with. I was no longer at the head of a great faction, which I have always compared to a great cloud, wherein every body fancies that he ſees what is moſt pleaſing to him. Moſt people looked upon me during the commotions of Paris, as on a man that was in a condition to take advantage of every revolution. The tree was thought to be well rooted, and every body expected to gather ſome fruit from it This ſtate I was in, occaſioned immenſe offers to be made me, and ſuch that if my averſion for borrowing had not been ſtill greater than my inclination was to ſpend, I might have counted my debts to amount to more millions of piſtoles than they

* A ſprinkler for holy water.

amounted to millions of livres I was not at Rome upon the same foot. I was a Refugee there, and persecuted by my King, and I was besides ill used by the Pope. The revenues of my Archbishoprick and of my Benefices were seized upon, and all the French bankers were expresly forbidden to help me. The animosity against me had been carried so far as to require all those who were thought to have both the will and the power to do it, not to assist me The Court, in order to deprive me of all manner of succour, had even affected to declare to all my creditors that the King would never suffer them to touch a penny of all the revenues he had in his hands. They had besides affected there, to cause these revenues to be dissipated in so profuse and prophane a mannner, that two bastards of the Abbot Fouquet's were publicly maintained at the Archbishop's palace, a fund being set aside for it out of these revenues. No manner of precautions had been omitted to prevent my farmers from succouring me, or to put my creditors upon troubling me, by proceedings which had signified nothing to them for the present, but of which all tne charge must have fallen upon me

The industry which the Abbot Fouquet used upon this last article, had no success but with a butcher, every one of my other creditors having refused to trouble me in the least. Cardinal Mazarin's application upon other heads, succeeded better. The receivers of the Archbishoprick assisted me but poorly, and even some of my friends took hold of the King's orders against it, to excuse themselves from assisting me. Mr and Madam de Liancour sent two thousand crowns for me to the Bishop of Châlons, after they had offered twenty thousand to my father, whose most particular and intimate friends they were, alledging for their excuse the promise they had made to the Queen The Abbot Amelot, who took it into his head to be made a Bishop by Cardinal Mazarin's interest, made answer to those who would have persuaded him to assist me, that I had given such marks of distinction to Mr. de Caumartin in a visit which both of of them had made me at Nantes, that he did not think that he ought to fall out for my sake with the Cardinal, at the time that he was giving him particular marks of his esteem. Mr de Luines, with whom I had contracted a pretty intimate friendship since the siege of Paris, thought that he should acquit himself of what he owed me upon that account, in sending me six thousand livres In short, Messieurs de Châlons, de Caumartin, de Bagnols, and de la Houssaye, who were so kind as to take upon them at that time the care of my subsistence, found themselves sufficiently embarrassed with it, and it may be said that they met with no hearty assistance, but in Mr. de Manevillette, who gave them twenty-four thousand livres for my use, in Mr Pirion de Mastrac, who sent eighteen thousand, in Madam d' Asserac, who furnished as much, in Mr. de Hacqueville, who out of his little spared me five thousand, Madam de Lesdiguieres lent me fifty thousand, and Mr. de Brissac thirty-six thousand, Messieurs de Châlons and de la Houssaye furnished forty thousand between them two, and Mr de Caumartin helped me with fifty-five thousand. The Duke de Retz, my brother, kindly supplied the rest, which he had even done with a better grace, if his wife had had as much generosity and good nature as he had. You will perhaps tell me that it is surprising that a man who seemed to be so much sunk under the weight of disgrace, could be supplied with such sums. But I will answer, that it is beyond comparison more surprising that I had not more considerable supplies offered me, considering the engagements which an infinite number of persons had entered into with me.

I insert in these Memoirs out of gratitude, the names of those who assisted me, whilst I spare out of good-nature the names of most of those who abandoned me, and I had even suppressed with pleasure the others I name, if the desire which you have expressed, that I should leave such Memoirs as might prove instructive to the young gentlemen your sons, had not obliged me not entirely to bury in silence, particulars which may be of use to them Their birth may naturally enough raiſe them to the higheſt poſts, and nothing in my opinion is more neceſſary to ſuch perſons than to be informed betimes, that nothing but a continuation of good fortune is able to fix moſt men's friendſhips I was good-natured enough not to believe it, though all the books I had read had given me that caution. The number of faults which I have fallen into by believing otherwiſe, is inconceivable; and I have been, during my diſgrace, twenty times upon the point of wanting what is moſt neceſſary, becauſe during my good fortune I had never dreamt that it was poſſible for me to want what is moſt ſuperfluous. It is likewiſe from my regard for the young gentlemen your ſons, that I will mention ſome other particulars which otherwiſe would not be worthy your attention. It is impoſſible for you to imagine how great domeſtic troubles are during a diſgrace. There is no body but thinks that he does honour to a diſgraced man in ſerving him, or if there are ſome men of honour who think otherwiſe, they are very few in number, becauſe that evil diſpoſition inſinuates itſelf ſo imperceptibly into the minds of thoſe that ſtand not extremely upon their guard, that they feel nothing of this diſtemper, which pretty much reſembles ingratitude I have often conſidered of both theſe defects, and I have found that a ſymptom common to them both is, that moſt of thoſe that are tainted with them, do not ſo much as ſuſpect it in the leaſt. Thoſe that are guilty of ingratitude, ſeldom perceive it, becauſe the ſame inclination that leads them to it, leads them firſt to leſſen in their own thoughts the obligations they have received from their benefactors. Thoſe that are tainted with the firſt defect, perceive it as little, becauſe the complacency they find in their conſtant attachment to the ill fortune of a friend, hinders them from perceiving that they have ſometimes been troubled at it ten times in a day

Madam de Pomereu was ſaying one day in one of her letters to me, upon occaſion of a miſunderſtanding that had happened between Meſſieurs de Caumartin and de la Houſſaye, that the friends of unfortu-

nate

nate persons were a little hard to please; she ought to have said the like of their domestics Familiarity, which a person of quality who is well bred can defend himself from less than another, lessens insensibly (when he falls into trouble) the respect which is constantly paid him during the time of his good fortune. This familiarity produces at first the liberty of speaking, which is soon followed by the liberty of complaining. The true food of these complaints is the fancy which a domestic is full of, that he would be much better with some other than with the disgraced person. He will not own to himself however that he is possessed with such a fancy, because he cannot but see that it would not agree, either with the engagements of honour into which he has entered, or with the affection which he at the bottom often preserves, in the midst of these evil dispositions This obliges him to disguise to himself, even without thinking that he is doing of it, the true spring from which what he feels in the most secret part of his heart proceeds, attributing to other causes, what is occasioned by the pain he suffers for a disgrace which he is forced to share in. The choice of a domestic preferably to another, which is often necessary and even inevitable on a thousand occasions, is always looked upon by the rest as an injury. The most difficult thing that a disgraced master does for them, is no more than duty in him: what he does not do, let it be never so much impossible, is no better than ingratitude or hardness of heart. What is still worse than all that I have mentioned, is, that the remedy which a truly good natured man is willing to apply on these occasions, by favouring the distemper, increases it instead of healing it It is necessary that I should explain all this. Having always lived with my domestics as if they had been my brothers; it was far from my thoughts to imagine it possible that I could meet among them any thing but complacency and good humour I began to perceive upon the galley that familiarity is attended with many inconveniencies; but I thought that it might be in my power to remedy them by my good usage, and my first step when I arrived at Florence was to divide as well amongst those of my domestics who had accompanied me during my voyage, as amongst those that had joined me upon the road, the money which the Great Duke had lent me I gave to each of them sixscore pistoles to buy themselves cloaths and other necessaries, and I was very much surprised at my arrival at Rome, to find them, at least for the most part, upon an ill foot, and having pretensions, greater beyond comparison in many respects, than if they had lived with a prime Minister. They took it ill that they had not the chambers marked out for them in my palace, hung with the finest tapestry This circumstance is but a sample of a hundred and a hundred such, and it is enough for me to tell you that matters came to that point, both by their murmurings, and their divisions which commonly follow murmurings, that I was obliged for my own satisfaction to take an exact memorandum, during the great leisure I had at the Masters of St. Cassien, of what I had given to my gentlemen since my arrival at Rome, and I found that they would not have cost me near so much if I had had them with me at the Louvre, supposing I had lived there in Mazarin's post Bois-guerin alone, who had indeed a great fit of sickness at St Cassien, where I left him with my litter and my physician, cost me in less than fifteen months that he staid with me, five thousand eight hundred livres in money paid him and laid out for him, which is perhaps more than he had received, had he been a domestic to Cardinal Mazarin His health obliged him to return into France for change of air, where it did not appear to me afterwards that he remembered much the manner in which I had treated him I am obliged to except from the number of murmurers which I had in my family, Malclerc, who has the honour to be known to you, and who received from me much less than the others, because as chance would have it, he was not present at the time of the distributions. He was continually upon travelling, as you will see by the sequel of this narration, and I am obliged

liged to ſay for truth's ſake, that I never obſerved in him upon any occaſion, any marks either of diſſatiſfaction or of private intereſt. The Abbot de Lamet, my Maſter of the Chamber, who would never touch a penny of me, during the whole time of my diſgrace, was leſs capable of this laſt vice than any man I know. But being naturally of an uneaſy temper, he was pretty much ſubject to the firſt, being excited to it by Joly, who with an honeſt heart, and upright intentions, has a ſort of oddneſs in him altogether oppoſite to the temper which is required for the keeping the balance even in governing a great family. It was not without pain that I could behave myſelf right with theſe two, and with the Abbot Charrier, they being all three pretty apt to be jealous one of another The Abbot Charrier inclined altogether in favour of the Abbot Bouvier, who was my agent, and my officer for diſpatches at the Pope's Court, to whom all my bills of exchange were directed Joly declared himſelf for the Abbot Rouſſeau, who being brother to my ſteward, pretended that he ought to perform the functions of that office, of which he was in truth not at all capable I muſt again beg your excuſe for troubling you with theſe trifles, and I do not doubt but that you believe that I would willingly have kept theſe little defects in my domeſtics altogether hid, when you come to reflect that it has not prevented me from doing for all of them without exception, ſince my return into France, whatever lay in my power. What I have ſaid upon this ſubject, is only as I have told you in relation to your children, who perhaps will meet no where elſe with ſo particular an account, having, as to myſelf, found nothing like it in any book. You will perhaps aſk me of what advantage this will be to them? For anſwer to that queſtion, I would have them to conſider once a week, that a prudent man ought always to keep his natural goodneſs under ſome reſtraint, and that a perſon of great quality, whoſe ſoul can never be too much inclined to goodneſs, ought by his good conduct to keep it carefully hid, and not to disclose it but with precaution, that he may preserve the dignity of it, chiefly, during his disgraces It is incredible to believe how much vexation and trouble my natural easiness, so opposite to that maxim, has cost me

I believe that I have said enough to convince you how hard a part I had to act. You will still conceive it the better when I have given you an account of the conduct which I was obliged to follow at the same time, in respect to France As soon as I had made my escape out of the castle of Nantes, Cardinal Mazarin caused an arrest of the King's Council to be issued out, whereby my Vicars general were forbidden to put out any mandates before they had communicated about it with the Kihg's Privy-council. Though this arrest tended towards destroying the liberty which is essential to the government of the church, it might have been alledged that those who had given it had affected to preserve some appearance of order and discipline, because they acknowledged at least my jurisdiction But they soon broke through all this pretended order, by declaring my see vacant by an arrest given at Peronne. This happened a month or two before the Holy See declared that it was filled up, by granting me the Pallium of the Archbishoprick of Paris in a full consistory At the time that this last arrest was given, Messieurs Chevalier and l'Avocat, Canons of the church of Notredame, my vicars-general, were sent for to Court, and their absence was made use of for a pretence to force the Chapter to take upon them the administration of my Diocese. This proceeding, so uncanonical, gave no less offence to the church of Rome than to that of France, and they agreed intirely both of them in their sentiments upon that subject I observed it, and took care to confirm them in these sentiments, and after I had staid as long as I thought it necessary, considering the temper of those I lived with, to clear my conduct of any air of precipitancy, I wrote, conformably to these

these sentiments, a letter to my Chapter, which I insert here, because it will present you at one view with what passed upon that account, since my getting out of prison.

GENTLEMEN,

"ONE of my greatest satisfactions after God had restored me to my liberty, having been the assurances of your affection and esteem, which you expressed in a manner so advantageous to me, both in private by your obliging and speedy answer to my letter, and in public, by your public thanksgiving, offered to God for my deliverance; I can in like manner assure you, that among so many traverses and dangers which I have since run, I have felt no greater affliction than that of receiving the sorrowful news of the manner in which your company has been treated, in order to divide you from my interest, which is no other than that of the church, and to oblige you to abandon, by forced and involuntary resolutions, the man whose right and authority you had maintained with so much vigour and constancy. The end which it has pleased God to put to my travels and to my labours, by leading me to the capital city of the kingdom of Jesus Christ, and to the most ancient and most sacred sanctuary for his Ministers, persecuted by the great men of this world, has not been able to make me forget what has been done in Paris for the subjecting of you Neither has the reception which the head of all the Bishops and the Father of all the Faithful, vouchsafed to give me in so favourable a manner, before God took him from this world, the marks of kindness and of affection with which he was pleased to honour my exile and my innocence, in so public and in so glorious a manner, and the Apostolical protection which he did me the honour to promise me with so much tenderness and generosity; neither I say has all this been able to allay entirely the grief, which the deplorable state your company has been reduced to for these last six months, has brought upon me. For as the extraordinary marks of your true

true friendship for me, have drawn upon you the aversion of my enemies, and as you have been persecuted for no other reason but because you have always opposed the persecution which I laboured under; I have been wounded to the very heart with the same wounds which your company has received, and the same generosity which will oblige me so long as I live to preserve a particular sense of gratitude for your good offices, obliges me still more for the present to feel inwardly an uncommon sense of compassion and tenderness for your afflictions and sufferings.

"I have heard with sorrow, gentlemen, that those who, since my liberty, have imputed to me as a crime the zeal which you have expressed for me, have reproached me in a public and defamatory libel, with having caused actions scandalous and injurious to his Majesty to be committed in his capital city, for no other reason but your expressing by one of the Canticles of the church, your joy to God for my deliverance, after having asked it of him by so many prayers. I have learnt that that act of piety of yours, which has rejoiced all those who were afflicted at the violation of the ecclesiastical, liberty in imprisoning a Cardinal and an Archbishop, has provoked my enemies to a degree that they have taken occasion from thence of treating you like seditions men and disturbers of the public peace, that they have made use of that pretence to oblige my two Vicars-general and other persons of your company to go to Court, under colour of making them give an account of their actions, but in reality to expose them to contempt, to insult them with railleries and affronts, and to daunt them if possible by menaces. But what has touched me the most was my hearing that that first persecution of my Vicars general and of some others of your brethren, has served only as a step to come up afterwards to a greater against your whole body. They have been driven away on purpose only to weaken your company, and to take an opportunity from their exile to signify an arrest to you of the twenty-second of August last, whereby secular persons, usurping the authority of the church, have declared my my ſee vacant, and have commanded you, in conſequence of that pretended vacancy, to name within eight days other Vicars to govern my Dioceſe in the room of thoſe I had named, accompanying that command with threats that other meaſures ſhould be taken, in caſe you refuſed to obey it I make no doubt but that you have all looked upon the bare propoſal of an enterprize ſo injurious to the epiſcopal dignity, as a ſignal affront given to the church of Paris, in expreſſing by this arreſt the thoughts which the authors of it have, that you can be capable of giving your conſent to the ſhameful ſubjection of the Spouſe of Jeſus Chriſt, to the violence and uſurpation of the eccleſiaſtical authority, by a lay power (which is always venerable whilſt it keeps in its due bounds) and to ſo ſcandalous a degrading of your Archbiſhop

" But my enemies at the ſame time, being conſcious of your averſeneſs to do of your own accord any thing like this, I have learnt that beſides the taking away ſome of your brethren from you, they had made uſe of all manner of means to win ſome. to intimidate others, and even to ſlacken the zeal of thoſe who are the leaſt mindful of their private intereſt, by making them afraid of loſing your rights and your privileges. And that all might be conformable to that ſame ſpirit, I have found by reading the act of notification of that arreſt which has been ſent me, that two of the under-officers of the Council that are the bearers of the orders that are iſſued from that board, being entered into your aſſembly, declared there that they ſignified that arreſt to you by an expreſs command, that you might not pretend ignorance, but that you might obey it and becauſe it is a known thing that the firſt impreſſions of fear are always the moſt powerful, theſe two officers being unwilling to give you any time to come to vourſelves, commanded you to deliberate immediately about that arreſt, declaring to you that they would not leave the place till you had done it.

" There is room however to praiſe God that ſuch an extraordinary proceeding has rendered ſtill more viſible to all the world the inſult which my enemies have

have offered to the church in my person. Whatever violence has been used to hinder you from acting according to the true impulse of your heart, and whatever fear has been infused into the minds of people, it has not been possible to make you consent to that sacrilegious degrading of an Archbishop by a tribunal composed of lay men; and your refusing to do it, notwithstanding all the instances of my enemies, will be a more than sufficient proof to posterity, of their attempting against the church, things so wicked and insupportable, that even those whom they have oppressed and whom they have reduced to act no longer like free men, could not but conceive an horror at it. Instead therefore of declaring my See vacant according to the tenor of that arrest, you have declared that my Vicars-general were the true and lawful administrators of the spiritual jurisdiction of my Diocese, and that nothing but a violence that came from abroad, hindered them from exercising it. You have resolved upon making remonstrances to the King for their return as well as for mine, whereby you have shewn how much concerned you were at the wounds that were endeavoured to be given to my character. This is your true disposition of mind: all that has been done since can be imputed only to the unjust breakers of the inviolable rights of the church.

" I have learned, gentlemen, that many of you have remained firm and unmoveable during this tempest, and have preserved in part the honour of your body, by a courageous resistance against all the enterprizes of my enemies. But I have learned besides that those who have not been so firm, and who have not had the courage to oppose openly the injury that was attempted against their Archbishop, have given way to that weakness only because they were not suffered to follow the laws of the church, and because they thought themselves obliged to submit to necessity, which they were told had no law. They have acted not like free persons, but like persons reduced to the greatest extremity. They have felt on this occasion, the struggle which St. Paul describes, of the flesh against the spirit,

spirit, and they may say upon this occasion, We have not done the good which we would, but we have done the evil which we would not.

"All the world knows that when you were forced to take into your hands the spiritual administration of my Diocese, my Vicars-general had been absent but a few days, and that there was room to believe that they would soon return Now I would ask whether any body has ever heard that a Diocese ought to pass for deserted and forsaken, and that there is an obligation to force a Chapter to usurp the authority of its Archbishop, four days after his Vicars-general have been sent for to Court? Does not even the passage out of the Decretals, which, as I am informed, has been the only ground for what has been done, destroy clearly what it is pretended that it establishes? If a Bishop says, that Decretal of Pope Boniface VIII is taken either by Pagans or Schismatics, it is not the Metropolitan but the Chapter that is to administer the Diocese, in relation to spiritual or temporal matters, as if the See was vacant by death, till the time that the Bishop gets out of the hands of those Pagans or Schismatics, and is restored to his liberty, or till the time that the Pope, to whom it belongs to provide for the necessities of the church, and whom the Chapter ought to advise with without loss of time, has ordered it otherwise.

"This is the passage out of the Decretal, which is in question; and it is a formal condemnation of all that has been attempted against the authority which I have received from God. For if there had been any room to make use of this Decretal to take away from me the exercise of my episcopal functions, it must have been whilst I was a prisoner, because it relates only to a Bishop who is deprived of his liberty But my enemies have been so far from pretending any thing like it, that during the whole time of my imprisonment, and to the day of my deliverance, my Vicars-general governed my Diocese peaceably in my name, and by my authority. And in effect how could my enemies have made use of this Decretal, except they had

had been willing to take upon them, in respect to me, the dishonourable name of Pagans or Schismatics, who having either no fear of God or no respect for the church, make no conscience of persecuting the Ministers of God, and the Prelates of his church, by reducing them to subjection and to the misery of a prison. But if my enemies could make no use against me of this Decrecretal whilst I was kept in captivity, because I was not detained by Pagans or Schismatics, which is the only thing meant by it, what right could they have to make use of it after it had pleased God to break my fetters? since Pope Boniface orders expresly that that administration of the Chapter ought to last only till the Bishop be restored to liberty By this it is plain that if you had taken into your hands the administration of my Diocese whilst I was kept in captivity (which you would never do) you ought necessarily to have quitted it, according to the express meaning of that Decretal, as soon as God was pleased to restore me to my liberty. And supposing that it should be pretended that the absence of an Archbishop who is free, and the obstacles which a lay power may create against the functions of his Vicars-general, gave the Chapter the same right to take into their hands the administration of his Diocese, as if the Bishop was kept prisoner by Schismatics or Infidels, such a pretence would confound things which are entirely different, that is, a Bishop who is a captive, with a Bishop who is free, a Bishop who can act neither by himself or others, with a Bishop that can and ought to do it, a Chapter, a clergy, and a people, who can receive no manner of orders or letters from their Bishop, with a Chapter and a Diocese who can receive both, and who ought even to receive them with respect, according to all the Canons of the church

" When a Bishop is kept prisoner in the hands of Infidels, it is a foreign force which suspends the episcopal functions, which puts him under an absolute impossibility of governing his Diocese, and over which the church has no power But in the present case, the Bishop being free as I am, thanks be to God, he may

may send his orders and establish persons to govern it in his absence, and the obstacles which passion or animosity would oppose to it, ought to be considered only as wicked attempts against episcopal authority, to which ecclesiastics cannot yield without betraying the honour and interest of the church. And as when the person of a Bishop is captive among Infidels, there is nothing but what his church ought to do to redeem him, even to the selling of their holy vessels, if no other means can be found for his ransom; in the same manner when endeavours are used to keep, not his person, because it is out of his enemies reach, but his authority captive; his church ought to use all the power it has, not against him, but for him, not to usurp his authority, but to defend it against those that would destroy it.

" For you know, gentlemen, that it is in time of persecution and troubles, that the clergy ought to keep more than ever inseparably united to their Bishop; and that as the hands are naturally carried to the head, in order to preserve it when it is threatened with any danger, so the prime ecclesiastics of a Diocese, who are the hands of the Prelates whereby they act and govern the people, ought never to act with more zeal and more vigour for maintaining the authority of their chiefs and of their pastors, than when it is violently attacked, and when a lay power will assume the right of interdicting his Vicars-general from their ecclesiastical functions, and of putting into other hands, in an arbitrary manner, the administration of his Diocese

" But if it could be supposed that a Bishop should leave his See vacant and abdicated in a manner that others may take in hand the conduct of it whether he will or no, because he is persecuted, and that his enemies will hinder him from governing it, either by himself or by his officers, so many great Prelates whom several persecutions have formerly obliged to fly away and to hide themselves, either upon account of their faith, or for some pretended interest and quarrels of state, relating to the liberty of the church, and who continued

continued notwithstanding to govern their Dioceses by their letters, and by the orders which they sent to their clergy and to their people, so many Prelates, I say, ought to have remained during the whole time, without authority, as deserters of their Sees; and their Priests would have had a right to assume their power, and to deprive them, by a detestable schism, of the functions of their characters.

"The great St. Cyprian, Bishop of Carthage (to mention only that example out of antiquity) perceiving the persecution that was kindling against him, and that the Pagans required that he should be exposed in the Amphitheatre to the lions, thought himself obliged to retire, for fear of exciting by his presence the rage of the Infidels against his people This occasioned some Priests of his church who did not love him, to take hold of his absence to usurp his authority, and to assume the power which God had given him over the church of Carthage. But he soon convinced them that his See was not deserted, though he was absent and hidden, and though persecution prevented him from performing the functions of a Bishop He never governed his church with more firmness and vigour. He established Vicars to govern it in his name and by his authority; he excommunicated those Priests who were endeavouring to take away his power from him, and he likewise excommunicated all their abettors; in short, he did by his letters all that he had done if he had been present. The account in writing which he sends himself to the clergy of Rome, shews clearly that he never had the government of his church more at heart than after the proscription of his person and of his goods had obliged him to remove from it From the place of his retreat he sent mandates about the conduct which was to be observed towards those who were fallen under persecution He named the Readers, the Sub-deacons, and the Priests which he sent to his clergy. He comforted some, he exhorted others, and above all, he was labouring to prevent his enemies from taking hold of his absence to make a schism in

his

his church, and to ſeparate from him part of the flock which was committed to his conduct.

" But if that holy Biſhop of Carthage had loſt none of his right of governing his own church, is there not a much greater reaſon that an Archbiſhop of Paris ſhould preſerve the right of governing his, when he is neither hid nor inviſible, but is expoſed to the greateſt light in the world, by his being with the chief of all Biſhops, and the common father to all Catholic Kings, when he is acknowledged by his Holineſs for the lawful Prelate of his See, and when he performs publicly in the chiefeſt of all churches the ſacred functions of his dignity of cardinal.

" And it ſignifies nothing to ſay, that the cauſe of St Cyprian's proſcription being the war which the Pagans were making againſt our faith, his example ought not to be extended to the proſcription of an Archbiſhop who is only perſecuted for pretended reaſons of ſtate for let the ſubject for proſcribing a Prelate be what it will, ſo long as he remains veſted with the epiſcopal dignity, and that the church has given no judgment againſt him; as no proſcription or interdiction, made by any lay power, can hinder him from being a Biſhop nor from filling up his See, neither can it hinder him from having the right and the power of performing a Biſhop's functions, having received that right from Jeſus Chriſt and not from the King, for which reaſon nothing can prevent his clergy from being obliged in conſcience to ſubmit to his orders in reſpect to the ſpiritual adminiſtration of his Dioceſe

" It is therefore in vain that my enemies pretend to cover the violence of a proceeding unheard of and without example, with the cauſes which they make uſe of for a pretext, that is with chimerical and imaginary crimes of ſtate which they have begun to impute publicly to me, in order to deprive me of the exerciſe of my employment, which I enjoyed by means of my Vicars-general during my impriſonment, only from the day that it was pleaſed God to reſtore me to my liberty. But if I have been a Biſhop during my impriſon-

imprisonment, am I no longer one for being at Rome? Am I the first Prelate who has fallen into disgrace with the Court, and who has been forced to leave the kingdom? But if all those to whom such an accident has happened have notwithstanding governed their Dioceses by their Vicars general according to the inviolable discipline of the church, what means this new abuse of the lay power, that tramples under foot all ecclesiastical laws? What means this new yoke and this new thraldom which is endeavoured to be imposed upon the church of Jesus Christ, by subjecting the spiritual exercise of the episcopal power, to all the caprices and to all the jealousies of a favourite?

"The late Cardinal Richelieu, when he was yet only Bishop of Luçon, was exiled to Avignon after the death of the Mareschal d'Ancre. but notwithstanding his being out of the kingdom, it never came into any body's head to persuade his Chapter to take into their hands the government of his Bishoprick, as if his See had been deserted; but his Vicars-general still continued to govern it in his name and by his authority. And have we not seen besides, that the late Archbishop of Bourdeaux having been oblige to leave France, and to retire likewise into Avignon, he did not cease notwithstanding to govern his Diocese, not only by his Vicars-general, but likewise by his orders and regulations which he sent from the place of his retreat, some of which I have myself seen printed and published.

"Must a Bishop for being at Rome, which place may be called the common country of all Bishops, lose a right which he would preserve by being at Avignon? But why should not the church enjoy, during the reign of the most christian and the most pious Prince in the world, one of the most sacred and inviolable rights that belongs to her, and which she peaceably enjoyed during the reign of the late King his father? But what I have been sadly concerned at, is to have heard that there have been two Prelates so little sensible to the honour of their character, and so far devoted to the

the passions of my enemies, as to undertake to admit into holy orders in my church, or rather to prophane that holy Sacrament by so wicked an attempt, there being nothing more firmly established in all the ecclesiastical discipline than the right which every Bishop has to communicate the sacerdotal power of Jesus Christ to those who are submitted to him, no other Bishop having the power to do it against his will, except by a violence that makes him deserve to be deprived of the episcopal functions, the sacred unity of which he violates, according to the ordinances of all the ancient councils, which that of Trent has renewed

" But if even when a See is vacant by the death of a Bishop, councils have forbid the Chapter to cause holy orders to be administered without an urgent necessity, such a one as a vacancy that should last above a year would be, and if what the council of Trent has established upon that subject is only a renewing of what we find to have been established by the councils of France, which forbid all Bishops to ordain Clerks, and to consecrate altars, in a church deprived by death of its own Pastor. is it not visible that that which would not have been lawful, supposing my See to be vacant by my death, must be less so, by the violence which has been committed against me who am living and at liberty? Is it not visible that the precipitancy which has been used in this attempt renders it altogether inexcusable, so as to deserve the most severe punishments inflicted by our holy Canons?

" But it is time, gentlemen, that the church of Paris should be delivered from the oppression under which it groans, and that it should be reinstated in the order which a foreign force has deprived it of I make no doubt but that even those who have shewn the least courage in opposing the impetuosity of that torrent, will bless God when they shall see all the pretences which have occasioned this scandalous inter-regnum of the episcopal power to cease. It can no longer be said that the place of my residence is unknown, neither can I any longer be looked upon as shut up in a Conclave. Besides, I can no longer find out myself any pretences

or

or colours for the long patience which I have used, and which is so opposite to all the ancient practices of the church, and which would leave strange scruples upon me, if God, who is the searcher of all hearts, did not read in mine that the cause of my silence has proceeded only from the profound respect which I have always preserved, and still continue to preserve for ever, for all that bears the title of King, and from the hopes that the great and holy inclinations which shine in his Majesty, would bring him to see the injury which has been done to the church under his name. I cannot believe, gentlemen, but that the Holy Ghost, who has lately shewn by the election of that great and worthy successor of St. Peter so particular a protection to the universal church, has already inspired the heart of our great Monarch with sentiments altogether favourable to the re-establishing the church of Paris I make no doubt but that the ardent zeal which I have shewn for his service on all occasions has taken off from his royal soul those false impressions which are not capable of darkening innocence, and I am persuaded that at a time when the church is issuing out with abundance the treasure of her indulgences, the piety of the successors of St. Lewis will not suffer that they should pass through channels uncommon and unnatural I have all manner of room to believe that my Vicars-general are at present at Paris, that the King's goodness has recalled them, there to peform their functions under my authority, and that his Majesty has at last done you the justice which you have been continually asking him in all your acts, since you have always protested, even in the title of those acts, that what you do is only occasioned by their absence. I therefore, gentlemen, direct to them the Bull of our holy father the Pope, in order to have it published according to the usual forms, and in case they should not be at Paris, which I can however hardly believe, I direct it to the Arch-priests of the Magdalen of St. Severin, to do with it according to my orders and the common practice of the Diocese. By the same mandate I give them the administration of my Diocese in the absence of my

Vicars-

Vicars-general, and I am perſuaded that theſe reſolutions will give you great joy, ſince they will begin to give you a ſight of thoſe things which you have ſo long wiſhed for, and that they will free you from thoſe difficulties which you were put to by the apprehenſion of ſeeing the government of my archbiſhoprick deſerted and abandoned. I had given theſe orders immediately after the Conclave, if I had not rather choſen that you ſhould receive them at the ſame time that I am receiving from his Holineſs's hands the fullneſs of the archiepiſcopal power, by the Pallium, which is the mark and the conſummation of it. I pray to God to give me the neceſſary gifts, that I may uſe it as I am bound to do, for his ſervice and for his glory; and I beg that in your prayers you would implore for me the bleſſings of heaven. I hope that your charity will make you grant my requeſt; and I am, Gentlemen, your very affectionate ſervant and brother,

From Rome,
the 22d of May, 1655.

The Cardinal de Retz,
Archbiſhop of Paris."

This letter had all the effect that I could have wiſhed. The chapter, which was very well diſpoſed in my favour, quitted with joy the adminiſtration of my dioceſe, notwithſtanding the efforts which they made at Court to prevent it. But they met in that body but with three or four perſons that ſided with them, and who were no great ornament to their company.

Mr d'Aubigni *, who bore the name of Stuart, ſignalized himſelf on this occaſion as much by his firmneſs, as old Vantadour made himſelf remarkable by his weakneſs. In ſhort, my Vicars general took

* Lewis Stuart d'Aubigni, uncle to the late Duke of Richmond and Lenox, was ſent into France very young and educated at Port-Royal. Having taken orders betimes, he was made a Canon of Notre Dame at Paris. He came into England at the Reſtoration of King Charles the Second, and was made Almoner to Katherine his Queen. He was nominated to the Cardinalſhip, but he died at Paris ſome hours before the arrival of the courier who brought him the hat.

again courageoufly into their hands the government of my diocefe, and Cardinal Mazarin was obliged to fend a Lettre de Cachet to them, in order to remove them from Paris, and to force them upon going to Court for the fecond time. I will acquaint you with the fequel of this violence, after I have given you an account of fome particulars which you will find pretty curious, becaufe they will give you the true idea of the moft grievous misfortune that in my opinion attends difgrace.

A letter which I received from Paris fome time after my being entered into the Conclave, obliged me to difpatch Malclerc thither. That letter, which came from Mr. de Caumartin, acquainted me that Mr. de Noirmoutier was treating with the Court by the means of Madam de Chevreufe and of Laigues; that that Lady had affured the Cardinal, that Noirmoutier would give me only the appearance of friendfhip, but would in reality do nothing againft the intereft of his eminence; that the Cardinal had declared to that Lady, that Laigues would never be fuffered to enter into the exercife of his place of Captain of the guards to the Duke of Anjou, which was given him at the imprifonment of the Princes, till the King was mafter of Mezieres and Charleville; that Noirmoutier had difpatched to Court, Longrue, the King's Lieutenant in this laft place, to affure his Majefty, not only in his own, but likewife in the Vifcount de Lamet's name, that he might reckon at leaft upon an abfolute inaction in refpect to thofe two places, whilft they fhould treat about the chief matter; that this advice came from Madam de Lefdiguieres, who had it in all likelihood of the Marefchal de Villeroi, fo that I might rely upon it. This affair, as you fee, deferved to be confidered, and the reflection I made upon it, befides the neceffity of providing for my fubfiftence, obliged me, as I have faid, to fend Malclerc into France, with an order to reprefent to my friends the neceffity which put me upon expences, which they thought I might well fpare; and with an order likewife to do his beft with Meffieurs de Noirmoutier

moutier and de Lamet, to oblige them not to come to an accommodation with the Court, till the Pope was chosen I had by this time great hopes of Chigi's exaltation; and I had so good an opinion of his zeal for the interest of the Church, and of his gratitude for me, that I began to reckon upon those places as upon means only to shew, by my suffering their Governors to come to an accommodation, that I put my whole reliance of being restored upon his Holiness's protection. Malclerc found at his coming to Paris that the advice which had been given me was but too well grounded, and Mr. de Caumartin would even have prevented his going to Charleville, thinking that that journey would only give Mr de Noirmoutier an opportunity of making his court the better The Bishop of Châlons, whom Malclerc saw upon the road, tried likewise for the same reason to hinder him from going. But Malclerc was resolved to follow his directions As he passed through Montmirel he was known by some of Madam de Noirmoutier's people, which obliged him to see that Lady. He had sense enough to make her believe, that he yielded to the multitude of reasons which she alledged to prevent his going to her husband, which if he had not done, might probably, considering that Lady's humour, have occasioned his being sent to the Bastille However he saw Messieurs de Noirmoutier and de Lamet at a league's distance from Mezieres, at a Gentleman's house named d'Haudrey, Noirmoutier spoke of nothing but of the obligations which he had to Madam de Chevreuse, of the perfect union there was between Laigues and him, and of the reasons he had to complain of me, which is the ordinary language of all ungrateful persons. Lamet expressed all manner of good intentions for me, but he gave Malclerc to understand at the same time that it would be extremely difficult for him to separate himself from the interest, or rather from the conduct of Noirmoutier, considering the situation of their two places, it being certain that the one signifies but little without the other. In short, Malclerc, who reduced all the favours which he asked of them in my behalf to their staying before they made their accommodation, till there was a new Pope chosen, drew upon him the railleries of Noirmoutier, for being so simple as to suffer himself to be dazzled at the false lights, with which, as he said, I was affecting to amuse all the world, in respect to the exaltation of Chigi, the truth of which he heard however from the Bishop of Châlons at his arrival at Paris.

My friends, whom I had acquainted by Malclerc with the likelihood of the thing, began, when they heard it confirmed, to be filled with all the hopes which you may easily imagine. You will as easily imagine how troubled Noirmoutier was at his precipitancy. He had concluded his accommodation with the Cardinal, soon after his having spoken with Malclerc, and he was come to Paris to put the last hand to it. He expressed a desire of seeing Malclerc, as soon as he was informed that Chigi was really elected Pope. He discovered that he was still at Paris, though my friends, who mistrusted him much for his want both of secrecy and fidelity, had told him that he was gone, and he bestirred himself so much that he saw him in the suburb of St Anthony. He did whatever he could to excuse or rather disguise his precipitancy in making his accommodation, and he did not hide how sorely vexed he was for having refused to grant the small delay that was asked him. He betrayed his shame both by his discourse and his countenance. I ceased to be with him that discourteous and tyrannical man that would have sacrificed all my friends to my ambition and to my caprice. The whole conversation was spent in expressions of his tenderness for me, of the means which he was seeking after, jointly with Madam de Chevreuse and with Laigue, to reconcile me upon a solid foot with the Court, and of the ease which they hoped to find in it. The conclusion was a very earnest instance he made to Malclerc to accept of ten thousand crowns, whereby he hoped, considering the pressing necessity I was in for money, that he might lessen in respect to me, and

cover

cover in respect to the public, the cruel wrong which he had done me. Malclerc refused the ten thousand crowns, though all my friends pressed him very much to accept of them. They wrote to me about it, even in very strong terms, but without persuading me, for which I am pleased with myself even at this time. "Nothing is greater than to bestow favours upon those who have been wanting to us: nothing in my opinion is weaker than to receive any from their hands. The christian religion which commands the first, would infallibly have enjoined us the second, if it were a duty which we ought to observe." Though my friends had been of opinion that Mr de Noirmoutier's offers ought not to have been refused, because they came from himself, they thought that it would not be well to sollicit new recruits of money from others, at a time when prudence obliged them to affect rather to appear triumphant for the exaltation of Chigi. They supplied out of their own fund what was most pressing and most necessary, and so Malclerc came back to Rome, where I can assure you he was not chid for having refused Noirmoutier's money.

What you have seen of the behaviour of that gentleman, is a true image of what all those that are wanting to their friends during their disgraces, constantly practise. Their first care is, to whisper abroad the causes of discontent, which they pretend to have against those whom they design to forsake, and their second care is to lessen as much as they can the weight of the obligation which they have to them. Nothing can be of greater service to them for that purpose, than their appearing grateful to others, whose friendship can be in no manner troublesome. They impose by this means upon half mankind, who give but a slight attention to ingratitudes in which they are not concerned, and they set up a false gratitude in the room of the true one. Not but that there are always some persons more clear sighted, upon whom it is not easy to put the change, and this puts me in mind of a saying of the Prince de Guimené's, which may be applied to this subject. Montresor, to whom

I had procured an abbey of twelve thouſand livres a-year, at the time that the Princes were arreſted, ſaying one day at the Count de Bethune's that he was obliged for it to Mr de Joyeuſe, the Prince de Guimené made this repartee to him. "I had forgot that Mr de Joyeuſe had the diſpoſal of the benefices for that year." Mr. Noirmoutier did, in order to juſtify his ingratitude, what Montreſor had done to ſatisfy only his fondneſs for Madam de Guiſe. This made me excuſe the laſt, when I could not help being touched to the quick with the other's behaviour. The only or at leaſt the beſt remedy againſt theſe kind of vexations, which are more ſenſible to perſons in diſgrace, than the diſgrace itſelf, is never to do good but for the ſake of good itſelf. An ill-natured man is incapable of following that rule, which is the reſult of the moſt refined virtue. Neither is it much eaſier to a good-natured man to follow it, becauſe it is natural to him to join to the motives of doing good which he finds in the ſatisfaction of his own conſcience, the regard he has to his friendſhip. I return to what paſſed at that time in reſpect to the adminiſtration of my dioceſe.

As ſoon as the Court had learnt that the chapter had quitted it, they ſent there for my two Vicars-general, as well as for Mr. Loiſel, Curate of St. John's, and for Mr Briet, two Canons of my cathedral, who had both ſignalized themſelves for my intereſt.

F I N I S.

THE

HISTORY

OF THE

CONSPIRACY

OF THE

COUNT JOHN LEWIS DE FIESQUE.

Against the

REPUBLIC OF GENOA.

Written by the CARDINAL DE RETZ.

THE HISTORY OF THE CONSPIRACY OF THE COUNT DE FIESQUE.

IN the beginning of the year 1547, the republic of Genoa was in a condition which might have been called happy, had it been better secured. To all appearance, it enjoyed a glorious tranquility, acquired by its own arms, and preserved by those of the great * Charles the fifth, whom that State had chosen for the protector of its liberty. The weakness of its enemies sheltered it from their ambition, and the charms of peace restored plenty there, which the disorders of war had so long banished thence trade began to revive in the city, to the visible advantage of the public, and of private persons; and if the minds of the citizens had been as free from jealousy, as their fortunes were from necessity, that common-wealth had soon recovered from its past miseries, by a state of ease, wealth, and happiness But the want of union amongst them, and the seeds of hatred which the late divisions had left in peoples heart's, were dangerous remains, which plainly indicated, that that great body was not yet cured of its distempers, and that its seeming health was like that of those persons, whose bloated faces

* The Emperor.

carry with them a good appearance, but hide many ill humours. The nobility, who had the government in their hands, could not forget the injuries which they had received from the people, during the time that they had no ſhare in the management of affairs; and the people on their part could not ſuffer the dominion of the nobility, but as a new tyranny, which was contrary to the ordinances of the ſtate: ſome, even amongſt the noblemen who aſpired to a higher fortune, ſecretly envied the grandeur of the reſt. Thus the one commanded with haughtineſs, and the others obeyed with indignation, and many thought themſelves ſervants, becauſe they did not act enough like maſters. When Providence permitted an accident to happen, which made theſe different ſentiments break out on a ſudden, and which finally confirmed, the one in their command, and the others in their ſlavery.

This was the conſpiracy of John Lewis de Fieſque, Count de Lavagne, which we muſt take up a little higher, the better to underſtand the circumſtances of the events that followed.

At the time of thoſe famous wars, in which the Emperor Charles the fifth, and Francis the firſt, King of France, laid Italy waſte, Andrew Doria, born of one of the beſt families in Genoa, and the greateſt ſeaman at that day in Europe, followed the French party with a great deal of zeal, and maintained the grandeur and reputation of that crown at ſea, with ſuch courage and good fortune, as tended no leſs to the advantage of thoſe he ſided with, than to his own glory. But it is a misfortune common to great Princes not to regard ſufficiently thoſe who can do them ſervice, when once they think themſelves aſſured of their loyalty; from this cauſe proceeded the loſs which France ſuffered of ſo good a ſervant, and that loſs produced ſuch fatal effects, that the remembrance of them will ever be grievous and deplorable to that kingdom. Whilſt this great man was engaged, upon advantageous terms, in the King's ſervice abroad, as general of his gallies, thoſe who were firſt in favour and power at home began to envy both his glory and his

his post, and formed the design of undoing the man whom they saw too great ever to submit to be dependant on any one but his master. As they judged it at first neither safe nor useful to their design, to do him ill offices with the King, who had lately expressed too good an opinion of him, so soon to conceive an ill one; they took a more subtle method, and joining their praises to the public applause, which was given to Doria's first taking up arms for France, they resolved by degrees to give him such occasions of discontent, as might seem rather to proceed from the general necessity of affairs, than from their private malice, and which nevertheless would work the desired effect They sought the means of giving his proud and haughty mind room to display itself, that they might the better ruin him in the King's good opinion; and the business which his employment obliged him to have before the council, furnished those who were in full authority there, but with too many occasions of disobliging him. One time the Exchequer was too low to pay his large salary, another time it was assigned him upon insufficient funds; sometimes his demands were reckoned unjust and exorbitant; at length his remonstrances on the wrongs done him, were so criminally represented to the King by the artifices of his enemies, that he began to be importunate and troublesome, and by little and little came to be accounted by his Majesty, one of an interested, insolent, and turbulent spirit He was at last openly disobliged, by being refused the ransom of the Prince of Orange, whom his nephew Philippin Doria had taken prisoner before Naples, and whom the King had caused to be put into other hands. They demanded from him, even with threats, the Marquis de Gast, and Ascanio Colonna, taken prisoners at the same battle. They talked no longer of keeping the promise which they had made him, to restore Savona to the republic of Genoa; and as his enemies observed him to take fire, instead of concealing the reasons he had to complain, under an appearance of moderation they left nothing undone to encrease them. Monsieur de Barbezieux was ordered to take possession of his gallies, and even to secure his person if it were possible This fault was no less contrary to prudence than to good faith, and the Ministers of France cannot be sufficiently blamed, *for having preferred their private interest to their master's* service, and taken away from him the only man who could have maintained his party in Italy. and since they were resolved to ruin him, we may venture to say, that they were bad politicians not to have done it thoroughly, but to have left him in a condition wherein he was capably of doing a great deal of hurt, not only to France in general, but to themselves in particular, by the vexation and disgust which the King might take at their counsels, and by the ill consequences which they had brought upon his kingdom

Doria finding himself thus criminally treated, publishes a manifesto of his complaints, protesting that they do not so much proceed from his private interests, as from the injustice with which Savona was refused to be restored to his dear country, though so often promised them by the King. He treats with the Marquis de Gast his prisoner, declares for the Emperor, and accepts of the command of his fleet The conduct of this old politician was, in this, at least as malicious as that of the French Ministers, but much more cunning and judicious He cannot be excused from an extreme ingratitude, in suffering himself to be hurried away by his passion to so dangerous a piece of revenge, against a Prince to whom he may be said to have been obliged for all his honour, since he had gained the most glorious marks of it in the command of his armies, and it is hard to justify him from a base piece of treachery, unworthy his former actions, in ordering his Lieutenant, Philippin Doria to suffer provisions to come into Naples, which was then extremely distressed by Mr de Lautrec, at the time that he still protested that he would continue in the King's service. But it must also be owned that, for this way of acting, he ought to pass for a very able man in relation to political interest, in that he so artfully threw the appearances on his side, that his friends could say, that

that the breach of promise which he complained of for his country, was the true cause of his change, and that his enemies could not deny, but that he was drove to it by such usage, as was too severe, and too hard to bear. Besides, he was not ignorant that the means of being greatly considered in a party, is, to let the first coming into it be accompanied with great advantages. And indeed, he timed his revolt so well, and managed it with so much conduct, that he preserved Naples to the Emperor, which, in a few days, would have been taken from him by the French, if Philippin Doria had continued to serve them faithfully. *This change was the occasion that France lost one* * of the greatest generals that ever that kingdom produced, and at last put the commonwealth of Genoa under the protection of the Crown of Spain, to whom it is so necessary by reason of its neighbourhood to the Spanish dominions in Italy. And this was the first action of Andrew Doria's for the Emperor's service, after he had openly declared himself against the French King.

This skilful and ambitious man, acquainted as he was with the intrigues of Genoa, and the inclinations of the Genoese, did not fail to manage the minds of that people, who have always been accused of a natural love for novelty. As he had in the city many friends and secret favourers, who took care to give him intelligence *of all that passed there*, he took care, on his side, to confirm the one in the discontent which they expressed against the present government, and to use his endeavours to raise a like discontent in the others, to persuade the people that the French left them only the name of Sovereigns, whilst they themselves kept all the power, to set before the nobility the image of the ancient government which had always been *in their hands*; *and lastly, to inspire every one* with the hopes of a general re-establishment of affairs, by a revolution.

* Odet de Foix, Sieur de Lautres, and Mareschal of France, who died before Naples in the year 1528.

Having

Having formed his party, he came near to Genoa with his gallies, landed his troops, and ranged them in order of battle, without meeting with any resistance. He entered the city, followed by those of his friends, who had taken up arms at the appointed signal He possessed himself of the principal posts, of which he made himself master, almost without drawing his sword. Theodore Trivulcius, who commanded there for the King of France, lost with Genoa all the reputation which he had gained in the Italian wars, by neglecting to break the measures which were concerted there, though he had notice given him of them, and because, to save his life and his money, he preferred the making a shameful composition in the castle, to the burying himself honourably in the ruins of that place, which was of such importance to his master's service.

No sooner were the French driven out of Genoa, than the name of Doria was heard to echo through the streets; one side, in these acclamations, following their true sentiments, the other, by their dissembled shouts, endeavouring to conceal the opinion which they had expressed on divers occasions, that their thoughts were not agreeable to the public joy. And the greatest part rejoiced at these things (as it is common for the vulgar to do) for no other reason than because they were new.

Doria did not suffer this heat to cool; he assembled the nobility, he put the government into their hands, and protesting that he claimed no share in it, but what should be common to him and the rest of the noblemen, he gave a form to the common-wealth, and having received all imaginable testimonies of the obligations which his fellow citizens had to him, he retired to his palace to enjoy at ease the fruit of his past labours, and the Common-wealth erected a statue for him with the title of "Father of his country, and restorer of liberty."

Many people are of opinion, that Doria had fully satisfied his ambition, in the restoring liberty to his country, and that the general applause which he met

with

with from his countrymen, rather inspired him with the thought of enjoying that glory in quiet, than that of making use of it for higher purposes. Others cannot imagine, that the great employment which he had newly accepted of in the Emperor's service, and the continual care he had taken to keep the nobility of Genoa attached to his house, could proceed from a quiet and intirely disinterested mind. They think that he was too able a man, not to see that a Sovereign in Genoa could not be grateful to the Spanish council, and that he intended only to amuse them by an appearance of moderation, and to defer, to a more favourable opportunity, his more exalted enterprizes

His old age might, however, have justly diminished the fear they had of his authority, if they had not perceived a power almost equal to his lodged in a second self Jannetin Doria, his cousin and adopted son, aged about twenty-eight, was extremely vain, haughty, and insolent, he had the survivorship of all his father's posts, and by that means kept the Genoese nobility in his interests He lived with too much splendor for a citizen, who desired to avoid drawing envy on himself, and giving umbrage to the Common-wealth; and he even shewed pretty openly that he disdained that character. The extraordinary height which that House had attained to, produced the great agitation of which we are now going to speak, and may serve as a memorable example to all states, never to suffer within themselves, any person so eminent, that his authority may give rise to the design of bringing him down, and to the pretence of undertaking it

John Lewis de Fiesque, Count de Lavagne, issued from the most ancient and most illustrious family in Genoa; worth above two hundred thousand crowns a-year, not above two and twenty, endued with one of the finest and most elevated minds in the world, ambitious, bold and enterprising, led at that time in Genoa a life very contrary to his inclinations As he was passionately fond of glory, which he wanted opportunities of acquiring, he thought of nothing so much as the means of finding them out. but though the present time af-

forded

forded him none, he might neverthelefs have affured himfelf, that his merit would have opened him a way to the glory he afpired to, by ferving his country, if the extraordinary power of Janetin Doria, whom we have juft now mentioned, had left him any room to hope for an employment in it. But as he was too great by his birth, and too much efteemed for his good qualities, not to create an apprehenfion in the man who would have had all the reputation and ftrength of the Common-wealth center in himfelf; he forefaw that he could have no pretenfions likely to fucceed, in a place where his rival was almoft intirely mafter; becaufe it is certain, that all perfons in the higheft pofts who take umbrage at others, never think of thofe who are the occafion of it, but with a defign of ruining them Seeing therefore that he had every thing to fear from Doria's grandeur, and nothing to hope for his own advantage, he thought himfelf obliged to prevent, by his wit and his courage, the ill confequences of that greatnefs which was fo oppofite to that of his Houfe, not being ignorant that there is never any thing to be expected, from thofe who make themfelves feared, but an extreme diftruft, and a continual endeavour to keep down thofe who have any merit, and who are capable of raifing themfelves

All thefe confiderations made John Lewis de Fiefque defpair of growing great in his country's fervice, and put into his head the defign of bringing down the power of the family of the Dorias, before they had acquired a greater ftrength, and as the government of Genoa was annexed to that family, he refolved, with their ruin, to effect a change in that government

Great rivers never do any harm whilft nothing withftands their courfe but the leaft obftacle makes them rufh forward with violence, and a fmall dam is often the occafion of their drowning thofe plains, which they would elfe have watered with advantage

Thus we may judge, that if the Count de Fiefque had not found his way to glory blocked up by the authority of the Dorias, he had certainly kept within the bounds of a more moderate conduct, and had ufefully employed,

employed, for the ſervice of his country, thoſe talents which brought it to the brink of ruin.

Theſe ambitious thoughts were kept up in the Count's mind, by many perſons who hoped to find their private advantage in the public confuſion; and amongſt theſe none were more eager in their ſolicitations than the French, who made him great promiſes and conſiderable offers; firſt by Cæſar Fregoza and Cagnino Gonzague, and afterwards by Monſieur du Bellai, who had private conferences with him by means of Peter Luke de Fieſque

It was the common opinion of that time, that Pope Paul the third, hoping, by the ſame blow, to beat down Andrew Doria, whom he hated for ſome private reaſons, and to take away from the Emperor, who was already too powerful, a conſiderable ſupport of his party in Italy, had left nothing undone to feed the Count de Fieſque's ambition, and had raiſed in him the ſtrongeſt deſire of forming a deſign upon Genoa.

There is nothing that flatters a man of courage ſo much, or that carries him on to ſuch hazardous reſolutions, as to ſee himſelf courted by perſons eminent either by their dignity or their reputation. This mark of their eſteem immediately fills him with a great confidence in his own merit, and makes him think himſelf capable of ſucceeding in the greateſt affairs. The deſign which the Count had formed, muſt for this reaſon have appeared both glorious and eaſy to him, ſince he ſaw himſelf urged to it by the greateſt Prince in Europe, and by the moſt able man of his time. The one was King Francis the Firſt, who ordered * Peter Strozzi, who was to paſs with ſome troops over the mountains near Genoa, to preſs (in his Majeſty's name) the execution of it, and the other was Cardinal Auguſtine Trivulcius, protector of France at the court of Rome, from whom the Count received all imaginable honours, in the journey which he took to that city, under pretence of diverſion, but in reality, the better to communicate

* He was made a Mareſchal of France in 1554.

his design to the Pope, and to inform himself of his sentiments

That Cardinal, who was in great repute, and who was thought to have a great deal of insight in state affairs, found means to animate the Count, by exciting in him an emulation to which he was but too subject, in setting before his eyes, with all the arts that could stir up his jealousy, the present greatness of Jannetin Doria, and the future greatness which he began to assure himself of, by the deep root which his authority began to take and thus increasing his envy of the one, and his fear of the other, he represented to him how insupportable it is for a man of spirit to live in a Common-wealth, where he can find no lawful way of raising himself, and where merit and noble birth make hardly any distinction betwixt the most illustrious and the most common persons.

Having throughly confirmed him in his general design, he came to particulars by offering him all possible assistance on the part of France; and he so strongly pressed the Count, whose mind was already inclined to that side, that at last he seemed to accept with a great deal of joy, the proposal that was made to him, of giving him the pay and the command of six gallies for the King's service, a garrison of two hundred men in Montobio, a company of Gens d' Armes, and a pension of twelve thousand crowns; desiring time however, till his return to Genoa, before he gave his final answer. So true it is, that nothing is more difficult in affairs of importance, than to take at once an ultimate resolution, because the multitude of considerations which croud into the mind, and destroy each other, make people think that they never have sufficiently deliberated.

Extraordinary actions may be resembled to thunder, which never produces any violent claps or dangerous effects, but when the exhalations which it is formed of have been long struggling against each other, otherwise it is only a heap of vapours which yield nothing but a dull sound, which, far from giving us fear, is scarcely to be heard. The same thing may be said of resolutions in great affairs, when they enter suddenly into

into any one's mind, and are received there but with a weak resistance. this is an infallible sign that they make but a slight and transient impression there, which, though it may excite some trouble, can never be strong enough to produce any considerable effect

It cannot be reasonably denied but that John Lewis de Fiesque considered maturely, and with great reflection on what he had a mind to undertake, for, on his return to Genoa, though he had a violent desire to execute his design, he notwithstanding deliberated a great while, about the several means which might conduce to the end which he had proposed to himself Sometimes the aid of a great King made him incline to throw himself into the hands of the French; sometimes the natural distrust which men are apt to have of foreigners, joined to a certain itch of glory, which makes them passionately wish to owe their great actions to none but themselves, inclined him to seek, in his own strength, for means which might bear some proportion to his elevated thoughts; and perhaps these different agitations had kept his mind longer in suspense, and produced a further delay, if he had not had, at every moment, some fresh cause of just indignation against the excessive pride of Jannetin Doria, who, carrying his insolence to the pitch of contemning every body, treated the Count, after his return, with such haughty airs, that he could no longer forbear taking fire openly, and expressing his detestation of the shameful slavery of all his fellow-citizens

Politicians have blamed this conduct as injudicious, following in this the general rule of never shewing the least sign of anger against those we hate, but in the instant that we strike the blow which is to bring them down. But if he wanted prudence in this occasion, it must be owned that it is a fault common to persons of great courage, whom contempt exasperates too much to give them time to consult their reason, and master themselves This fault, however, has freed him from the imputation cast on him by some historians, that he was one of a dark and dissembling temper, that he was more covetous than ambitious, and more in love

with

with intereſt than glory. This warmth, I ſay, which has been obſerved in his conduct, ſhews that he was carried on to this enterprize by no other motives than an emulation of honour, and a generous ambition; ſince all thoſe who have engaged in the like deſigns out of a ſpirit of tyranny, and for other intereſts than thoſe which tend to a great reputation, have always begun by the moſt ſubmiſſive patience and abject cringings.

It is certain that the inſolence of Jannetin Doria was carried to an inſufferable exceſs, and that he followed in every particular that wicked maxim, that ſeverity and haughtineſs are the ſecureſt methods of reigning, and that it is uſeleſs to govern with lenity, thoſe who may be kept within the bounds of their duty, by their fear and their intereſt This conduct ſo increaſed the averſion which the Count had againſt him, that it haſtened the reſolution which he had taken, of undoing him, and gave him an opportunity of making a good uſe againſt him, of that pride with which Jannetin pretended to keep every body under

Cardinal Auguſtine Trivulcius, who knew that in theſe occaſions the minds of young people muſt not be ſuffered to grow cool again, ſent to him, immediately after his return to Genoa, Nicholas Foderato, a gentleman of Savona, and a relation of the houſe of Fieſque, to know his reſolution. That gentleman having found him more exaſperated than ever, and in the condition which we have repreſented, got him to ſign whatever he pleaſed, and immediately returned to get the treaty ratified by the French King's miniſters, who were then at Rome But by that time he had gone thirty or forty leagues, he was recalled in great haſte, the Count having reflected, that he had acted too precipitately, and that he ought not to conclude an affair of that conſequence, without conſulting with ſome of his friends, whoſe capacity he was acquainted with. He ſent for three of them, whoſe fidelity he could rely upon, and whom he very much eſteemed for their good qualities. and having, in general, declared to them the reſolution he had taken, no longer to bear with the preſent

ſent government of the Common-wealth; he begged of them to declare their opinion on this ſubject.

Vincent Calcagno of Vareſa, a zealous ſervant of the houſe of Fieſque, and a man of judgment, but of a timorous ſpirit, began his diſcourſe with the liberty which his long ſervices intitled him to, and addreſſing himſelf to the Count, he ſpoke in this manner

"I think thoſe who have the misfortune to be engaged in great affairs, are very juſtly to be pitied, becauſe they are as it were on a troubled ſea, where they can ſee no place but what is diſtinguiſhed by ſome ſhipwreck. But it is juſt that we ſhould redouble our fears, when we ſee young people whom we love expoſed to this danger, ſince they have not ſtrength enough to go through the fatigues of ſo toilſome a voyage, nor experience enough to avoid the ſhelves, and ſteer ſafely into the harbour. All your ſervants ought to be ſenſibly concerned at the enterpriſes which your courage prompts you to. Give me leave to tell you, that they are above your age, and the ſtate in which you are You dream of projects, which require ſuch a regard in the world, that the reputation of a man of your age, however great it may be, can never attain to it And you form a deſign which requires ſuch forces, as one of the greateſt kings on earth has never yet been able to ſet on foot Theſe thoughts ariſe in your mind from two errors, which are in ſome meaſure inherent to human nature. Men are apt to have too great thoughts of themſelves, that is, they act as if whatever their imagination tells them they can do, were actually within their power; and they judge with little certainty of other perſons, becauſe they judge of them only with regard to themſelves, and conſider what ſervice thoſe perſons are able to do them, and not what they ought to do or are likely to do for their own intereſt. The firſt of theſe is extremely dangerous, becauſe as no one executes a great enterpriſe alone, but is obliged to communicate it to many people, it is of the higheſt importance that they ſhould believe it reaſonable and practicable, or other-

wiſe

wise the undertaker will meet but few friends who are ready to follow his fortune. The second is more common, and no less dangerous, because it often happens that we find the greatest resistance from those very persons whose assistance we had the greatest expectation of. Be careful therefore, that the great qualities which nature has blessed you with, and which you, perhaps justly, imagine may supply your want of experience, do not lead you into the first inconveniency, and consider, that how shining soever those qualities may be, it is hard to imagine that they will procure you, even with those who have the best dispositions for that service, such a share of esteem, as is proportionate to the execution of so difficult and dangerous an undertaking. Consider, besides, that it is not credible that these qualities should so dazzle your enemies, as to prevent their making a proper use against yourself of the pretence of your youth. Take care that the greatness of your birth, and the reputation which your good qualities have acquired you the abundance of your riches, and the secret intelligence which perhaps you have secured, do not lead you into the second inconveniency, and make you believe that the assistance of those who have promised you, cannot fail you, when you have need of it. Change therefore that thought, or if you still preserve it, cease to consider others with respect to yourself, but consider them with respect to themselves, examine their interest, and think, that that is the most powerful motive of men's actions, that most of those who esteem and love you, love themselves infinitely better, and fear their own ruin much more than they wish your greatness. In short, consider that those who give you hopes of their assistance are either foreigners, or your own countrymen. The most considerable amongst the first are the French, who cannot undertake to assist you, because they are employed in defending their own country against the armies of the Empire and of Spain. And the Genoese who are capable of aiding you will not do it, because fear will make part of them apprehend the dangers which ac-

company

company affairs of this nature; and interest will make the rest afraid of hazarding their quiet and their fortunes The most part of those that are not influenced by these considerations, are persons of so mean a birth, and so little power, that nothing for your advantage is to be hoped for from them. So that Doria's too great power, and the bad state of the times, which give you these thoughts of rebellion, ought to inspire you with patience, since they have so depressed the minds of the Genoese, that they now make a glory of submitting out of gratitude to the authority of Andrew Doria, that liberty which he has restored to them, and which he snatched out of the hands of foreigners, for no other end but to usurp the dominion over them Do you not perceive that this Commonwealth has for a long time had only the image of a free government, and that it can no longer subsist without a master? Do you not see that the greatest part of the nobility are attached to the interest of the house of Doria, by the employments at sea which that house bestows on them; and that that family, under the protection of the Empire and of Spain, holds all else in fear? Do you not perceive, I say, that all the Genoese are buried in a kind of lethargy, and that the most brave do not think it dishonourable to yield to that mighty power, provided they do not adore it? I do not here pretend to justify the imprudence of the Commonwealth, who have suffered the elevation of that house, which they can no longer bear without reproach, nor pull down without danger, but I dare maintain that a private man cannot reasonably think of removing by his own power a distress which has taken so deep a root, and that all that a generous man can do on this occasion is to imitate those wise mariners, who instead of obstinately contending against the wind, to make to a harbour, steer out again to sea, and leave themselves to the mercy of the waves and winds. Yield therefore to the times, since fortune will have it so, and seek not for remedies where none are to be found, but what are worse than the disease, expect them from Providence, which disposes

poses at its pleasure of the changes of states, and which will never be wanting to this Commonwealth · enjoy peaceably that ease and those advantages which your birth intitles you to, or accept of lawful employments to exercise your valour, which the foreign wars will furnish you with opportunities enough of doing. Do not expose the great fortune which you are master of, and which would satisfy any one's ambition but yours, to the consequences of a criminal revolt, and imagine, that if Jannetin Doria has conceived any hatred or envy at your merit, you cannot oblige him more than by pursuing your present thoughts since you will give him an opportunity of concealing his private resentment, under the pretence of the general good, and of undoing you with the authority of the Common-wealth, and in short, that you yourself are working to raise upon your own ruin trophies to his glory and grandeur The greatest fortunes raised without pains most commonly fall of themselves, because it seldom happens that those who with ambition have the other qualities necessary to raise themselves to eminent stations, are at the same time possessed of qualities necessary for maintaining themselves in them; and when any one of those whom fortune has thus precipitately raised, reaches the top without stumbling, he must in the beginning have met with many difficulties, which have by little and little accustomed him to stand firm in so slippery a place Cæsar had in the highest degree all qualities necessary to a great Prince, and yet it is certain, that neither his courtesy, his prudence, his courage, his eloquence, nor his liberality, had ever raised him to the Empire of the World, had he not found great difficulties to overcome in the Commonwealth of Rome. The pretence which the persecution of Pompey furnished him with, the reputation which their contests gave him room to acquire, the advantage he made by the divisions of his fellow citizens, were the true causes of his power, and, notwithstanding this, you seem desirous of adding to the establishment of the family of Doria, the only advantage which was wanting to it, and because their happiness has

has hitherto cost them too little to be well assured, you seem desirous of settling it on a firm foundation, by endeavours, which being too weak to destroy it, will only serve to justify their undertakings, and establish their authority But for once I will give into your way of thinking, and suppose that you have happily executed your designs, imagine then the family of the Dorias massacred, all the nobility who follow their interest in fetters, imagine all your enemies overthrown, Spain and the Empire in a condition not to hurt you Flatter yourself already with your triumph in this general calamity. if you can fancy to yourself any comfort in these fatal images of the ruin of the Commonwealth, what will you do in the midst of a desolate city, which will look on you rather as a new tyrant than as a deliverer? What solid foundations will you find to build your new greatness on? Can you put any trust in the humour of the people, who the very moment that they have placed the crown on your head, if you have any such thought, will perhaps conceive the greatest horror against you, and will think of nothing but the means of taking it off again? For as I have already told you, they can neither enjoy their liberty, nor bear long with the same master. Or if you put Genoa, once again, into the possession of foreigners, if by your means the city opens its gates to them, the first time they are ill used by them, you will be considered as the destroyer of your country, and the parricide of the people. Are you not afraid that those who are now the hottest to serve you, may be the first to work your ruin by their envy at being subjected to you? And even supposing that that consideration should not induce them to it, you cannot be ignorant that those who serve a rebel, imagine they so strongly oblige him, that no reward being sufficient to satisfy them, they most commonly become his enemies. As those who roll down a mountain are dashed to pieces against those very points of rocks, which they made use of to get up to the top; so those that fall from an exalted fortune, are almost always ruined by the means which they had employed

 for

for their elevation. I am sensible that ambition continually tickles persons of your rank, age, and merit, and that it represents nothing to your eyes but pompous and splendid images of glory and grandeur. But whilst your imagination is presenting you with all the objects of that passion, which makes men illustrious, your judgment ought to make you behold it as the passion which generally makes them unhappy, and obliges them to quit the most certain advantages, for the most uncertain hopes. consider that if its just use is the occasion of the greatest virtues, its abuse occasions the greatest crimes. Imagine that it is that passion which of old mingled so many poisons and sharpened so many poniards against usurpers and tyrants, and that it is that same passion that now urges you on to be the Catiline of Genoa.

" Flatter not yourself that the design you seem to have to preserve the liberty of the Common-wealth, can be any otherwise received in the world, than as the common pretence of all factious people: and, supposing that, in reality, no other motive but your zeal for the public good should induce you to this attempt, you must not hope that any one will do you the justice to believe it; since in all actions which may indifferently be attributed to virtue or vice, when nothing but the intention of the doer can justify them, men, who can judge only from appearances, seldom make a favourable construction of the most innocent ones. But in the present enterprize, which way so ever you turn your eyes, it is impossible to behold any thing, but massacres, plunder, and such dismal objects as the best intention in the world cannot justify. Learn therefore to regulate your ambition, and remember, that the only instance wherein that passion can be justified, is where you set aside your own interest, and follow only the rules of your duty. There have been many conquerors, who have ravaged states, and overthrown kingdoms, that have not been masters of that greatness of soul, which enables us to look with an indifferent eye on the most exalted and the lowest condition, on the greatest human happiness and mise-

ry.

ry, on pleasure and pain, on life and death; and yet it is this love of true glory, this elevated state of the mind, which renders men truly great, and raises them above the rest of the world. This is the only glory that can render you perfectly happy (even though the dangers which you imagine to yourself, surrounded you on all hands) since you cannot acquire any other without disgracing yourself by the greatest crimes Embrace, therefore, this glory, as well out of prudence as generosity, since it is more useful, less dangerous, and more honourable."

The Count was extremely moved with this discourse, because it seemed grounded on solid reasons, and because the confidence he had reposed in the author of it, from his earliest youth, added to its authority. Verrina, who was one of those who were called to this council, a man of an extensive genius, impetuous, naturally inclined to great enterprizes, an implacable enemy to the present government, almost ruined by his great expences, firmly attached to the count both by interest and inclination, answered what had been said, in the following manner

"I should wonder that there were a single man in Genoa, capable of the sentiments you have just now heard, were not my wonder lost in the consideration of what the Common-wealth suffers When every body bears oppressions with so abject a submission, it is natural for them to hide their complaints, and seek excuses for their weakness This insensibility is nevertheless a sign of the deplorable condition of the state: and Vincent Calcagno has very judiciously touched upon it, as the symptom that gives the plainest proof of the violence of our distemper But it seems to me very unreasonable not to reap some advantage from the knowledge we have of our disease, since nature itself instructs us that we are obliged to make use of that knowledge, for the application of the necessary remedies However, the condition of this Commonwealth is not yet so desperate, that all its members are corrupted, and the Count de Fiesque, whom fortune has raised above the rest of his countrymen, in greatness, riches, and birth, carries his thoughts to

 those

those heights which the narrow views of the Genoese cannot reach, and rises by his courage above the general corruption. To examine whether a man be born for extraordinary actions, it is not sufficient to consider him with regard to the advantages of nature and fortune, (since there have been many persons who were possessed of both these advantages, and who have notwithstanding continued all their days to go on in the common road of life,) but we must observe, if a man of quality, when he finds himself in unhappy circumstances, and in a country where tyranny begins to take place, preserves still the principles of virtue, and the good qualities which nature has bestowed on him. For if he does not lose them on these occasions, but resists the contagion of those base maxims which infect the rest of the world, and particularly the minds of great people (because tyrants take the greatest pains to corrupt them, as those whom they are most afraid of) we may then judge, that such a one's reputation will one day equal his merit, and that fortune designs him for something great and wonderful. This being the case, Sir, I believe there never was any one from whom the Common-wealth could justly expect such great things as from yourself. You came into the world in times, which afford you hardly any example of courage and generosity but what has been punished, and which present you every day with instances of baseness and cowardice which have been rewarded. Add to this, that you are in a country where the power of the house of Doria keeps the hearts of the nobility oppressed with the most shameful fear, or engaged by the most sordid interest, and yet you are not infected with this general contagion. You maintain the noble sentiments which your illustrious birth has inspired you with, and your mind forms enterprizes worthy of your valour. Do not therefore neglect these admirable qualities, do not slight the gifts of nature, serve your country, judge by the excellency of your inclinations of the great actions they may produce, consider that there wants nothing but a man of your condition and merit to restore the spirit of the Genoese,

and

and inflame them with their first love of liberty. Persuade yourself that tyranny is the greatest evil that can befal a Commonwealth. The condition in which ours is now, is of the nature of those distempers, which notwithstanding the dejection they occasion, raise in the patient's mind a violent desire of a cure. Answer the wishes of all the people, who groan under the unjust authority of Doria. Second the vows of the most sound part of the nobility, who secretly deplore the common misfortune of their countrymen, and think that if weakness and cowardice encrease daily among them, the pride of Jannetin Doria will not be so much blamed for having occasioned it, as the want of resolution in the Count de Fiesque for having suffered it. The great esteem your good qualities have acquired you, has already done half the work: let none speak of your youth as an obstacle to the success of so glorious a design; yours is an age where the heat of your blood, and the noble impulse of your courage, can inspire you with nothing but great designs; and in extraordinary actions, we have always more need of vigour and boldness, than of the cold reflections of a timorous prudence, which shews us all the inconveniencies we have to fear. Besides, your reputation is so well established, that I may say without flattery, that with all the charms by which youth naturally acquires friends, you have gained that credit in the world which is seldom obtained but in a more advanced age. Wherefore you are under a happy obligation to keep up the high idea which the world has conceived of your virtue. Knowing your perfect disinterestedness, I know not whether I ought to add to the considerations of the misery of our Commonwealth, some motives which respect you in particular; but since there are some occasions where interest is so closely linked with honour, that it is almost as shameful not to regard it, as it is sometimes glorious to despise it. I beg of you to cast your eyes on the condition which you will be in, if the present government lasts yet a little longer. Those who join an uncommon merit to an illustrious birth have always two powerful enemies, the envy of the courtiers, and the hatred of those who are in the most considerable posts It is very difficult for those who have great fortunes not to incur the first, but it is impossible for those who have a great deal of courage and are much considered in the world, to escape the last Prudence and good manners may indeed diminish that jealousy which interest gives rise to amongst equals, but they can never entirely remove from the minds of superiors the umbrage occasioned by the care they take of their safety. There are some virtues so beautiful that they force even envy itself to do them homage. But whilst they are gaining a victory over this passion, they are encreasing the strength of the other passion which we have mentioned. Hatred grows greater as merit rises, and virtue, under these circumstances, may be compared to a ship in a storm, which has no sooner evercome the fury of one wave, than it is attacked by another more violent than the first. Can you be ignorant that Jannetin Doria is gnawed with a secret envy at your birth, which is by much superior to his? at your riches, more honestly acquired than those he possesses? and at your reputation, which far surpasses any that he can ever pretend to? What reason have you to believe that envy, raised by these considerations and animated by a violent ambition, will produce nothing in the mind of that insolent man, but weak and imperfect thoughts, and that it will not tend directly to your ruin? Have you any ground to hope, that if by your prudence and the force of your virtue, you had overcome this envy, you could avoid that hatred which the difference of your humours inspires him with against you, and that his haughty spirit (which the wisdom of his uncle has hitherto kept within some bounds) could any longer bear the man who is the only obstacle to his designs? For my part, I think the consequences of it are inevitable, because you cannot throw off those qualities which will draw his hatred upon you, nor divest yourself of your nature, and cease to be generous. But supposing it were in your power to hide, under a modest appearance, that greatness of soul which raises you so much

much above the vulgar, can you imagine that Jannetin Doria, suspicious as he is, like all his fellow-tyrants, would not be in continual distrust of your conduct? All the marks of your moderation and patience, would seem to him artifices and snares to undo him. He could not imagine that one of the name of Fiesque could be capable of so much meanness, and judging with reason of what you would be, from what you ought to be, he would make use, for your ruin, of that appearance of submission which you would assume, before him, for your safety. all the difference therefore which there would be betwixt your present condition, and that which you might then expect to be in, would be, that you would then be certainly assured of perishing with eternal infamy, whereas by following the generous sentiments which your inclination prompts you to, you are assured that the only misfortune that can happen to you is to die in a glorious enterprize, and to gain, by your death, as great a share of honour as ever fell to the lot of any private man. If you see these things, as doubtless you may see them clearer than I, it is needless for me to enlarge upon them any longer. I only beseech you to draw from them two very material consequences. The first is, to be persuaded of the falsity of those maxims, which forbid our preventing the stroke of an enemy, who designs to undo us, and which advise us to stay till he has undone himself. We deceive ourselves if we think fortune has raised those whom we hate to the highest pinacle of happiness, on purpose to give us the pleasure of seeing them fall. Grandeur is not always bordered with precipices; usurpers have not always been unhappy; and heaven is not always ready at hand, in the punishing bad men, to rejoice the good, and free them from the violence of their oppressors. Nature, more infallible than politics, instructs us to prevent the evil which threatens us, and which becomes incurable whilst prudence is considering of remedies for it. To what end should we so nicely examine the examples which have been proposed to us? Do we not know that too great a subtlety in arguing softens our courage,

 and

and is often opposite to the greatest actions? All affairs bear two different faces, and the same politicians who blame Pompey for having strengthened Cæsar's power by incensing him, have praised the conduct of Cicero in ruining Catiline The other benefit which you ought to reap from these considerations, is, that the great abilities which nature has endowed you with ought not to resemble those faint and ineffectual fires which afford only a dim glimmering of light without any heat, but ought to be like the light of the Sun, which produces what it enlightens. Great thoughts should be followed by great effects, and in the execution as well as in the forming your enterprize, nothing ought to hinder your courage from being the subduer of monsters, the avenger of injuries, the refuge of the distressed, the ally of the greatest Kings, and the umpire of Italy But if at the instant that I speak to you, the appearance of liberty which still remains in our republic makes any impression on your mind, I have reason to fear that it will stop the course of your ambition, for I know that one of so scrupulous a disposition, and so jealous of honour as you are, will hardly bear to be sullied with those terrible names of Rebel and Traitor. Yet these mighty scarecrows, which public opinion has formed to fright the minds of the vulgar, never bring any shame to those who bear them for extraordinary actions, when they are attended with success Scruples and greatness have ever been incompatible, and the narrow precepts of common prudence are fitter to be taught in the school of the people, than in that of great men The crime of usurping a crown is of so illustrious a nature, that it may pass for a virtue Every degree of men has its peculiar reputation, the common sort ought to be esteemed for their moderation, and the great ones for their am-ambition and courage. A poor pirate, who used to take little vessels in the time of Alexander, passed for an infamous robber; whilst that Prince, who took whole kingdoms from their rightful Sovereigns, is to this day honoured as a hero, and if Catiline is blamed as a traitor, Cæsar is spoken of as the greatest man that ever

ever lived. In short, I need only set before your eyes all the Princes now reigning in this world, and ask you if those from whom they hold their crowns were not usurpers. But if these maxims are any way disagreeable to the nicety of your principles, if the love of your country weighs more with you than your private glory, if you have yet any regard left for the dying authority of the Common-wealth, let us examine what honour will accrue to you from respecting it when your enemies despise it, and whether it will be any great advantage to you to run the hazard of becoming their subject. Would to God the State were in its first splendor; nobody should then dissuade you, more strenuously than I, from the design which I now excite you to. If this Common-wealth, which now retains nothing of liberty but the name, could preserve its authority, weak as it is, in the condition it is now in, I own, that there would be some reason to bear our misfortune with patience; and that if it was neither safe nor useful, it would at least be generous to sacrifice our own interests to the vain image which is left us of liberty, but now, that the artifices of Andrew Doria have confined the councils of the whole Common-wealth to his single person, and the insolence of Jannetin has put all its forces into his hands, at this instant that Genoa has reached the period of its change, by that secret but inevitable fate, which sets certain bounds to the revolutions of all states; now that the minds of the citizens are too little united to live any longer under the government of many; in this extremity, I say, when tyranny can be no longer resisted but by establishing a lawful monarchy, what are we to do? Shall we offer our throats to be cut by those murtherers who would join our ruin to that of the public liberty? Shall Count John Lewis de Fiesque look on with patience, whilst Jannetin Doria insolently ascends the throne, which his fortune and his ambition raised him to, without any one quality to deserve it? No, no, Sir; your virtue must dispute with him an advantage due to none but yourself. It is a thing as scarce as it is much to be wished for, to find one's self in such a juncture, as to be obliged, as you now are, by the

 motive

motive of the public good, and your private glory, to set a crown on your head. Do not fear that this action should acquire you the name of an interested man: on the contrary, nothing but the fear of danger, which is the meanest of all interests, can hinder your undertaking it; and nothing but glory, which is directly opposite to interest, is capable of prompting you to so great a design. If you are so nice that you cannot bear the appearance of blame, what will hinder you from restoring to your country that Liberty which you have acquired for it, and from surrendering to it the Crown which you will so well have deserved? It will then be in your own power to give a signal proof of the contempt you have for all kinds of interest, when you can part with it and preserve your honour. The only thing that remains for me to represent to you, is, that in my opinion you ought not to make use of the French. Any intelligence with foreigners is extremely odious, but in the present juncture, that which you propose cannot be useful to you, because, as Calcagno has observed, France is now sufficiently employed in defending itself against the Spanish and Imperial forces, which attack it powerfully on all sides; but supposing you could draw any assistance from thence, consider that your altering your condition would only be changing your slavery, that you would be a slave to France, whose ally you may now become. Upon the whole, determine whether it is fit for a man of your abilities, merit, and quality, to resolve to suffer every thing and be a victim to Doria's insolence, or else by hazarding every thing to shake off the yoke of tyranny, to expose yourself without necessity to the danger of becoming the slave of a foreign power, and to confine yourself as before within the bounds of a private gentleman's fortune."

Raphael Sacco, who acted as judge within the territories of the house of Fiesque, and who was the third person called to this council, seeing that the Count's inclinations were intirely conformable to to Verrina's sentiments, thought that it would be to no purpose to contradict them, and on the other hand, judging that that action was extremely hazardous, he

 would

would not advise him to undertake it, and did not declare his opinion on that subject, referring himself (as to the main design) entirely to his master's will. Wherefore he applied himself only to maintain, that if it was absolutely resolved upon, it was necessary to make use of the French, saying that it would be an extraordinary piece of imprudence for the Count not to use all his credit and his forces where he ventured his whole fortune. That he could not understand how they came to advise the Count to oppose himself singly to the arms of the Empire, Spain, and Italy, which would certainly unite against him, that it was indeed possible to take a town by surprize, but not to secure a state, that this last could not be done without a long series of years, without troops and alliances; and that the thought of seizing upon the Sovereign of Genoa, in the present disposition of the affairs of Europe, was a rash resolution, which was attempted to be coloured under the name of a glorious undertaking. Verrina opposed to the utmost of his power this reasoning of Raphael Sacco, and reminded the Count of the reasons he had urged on that subject, in his discourse, by representing to him, more strongly than before, that the friendship of Princes never out-lived their interest, and that though the favour of the house of Austria seemed inseparably united to the Dorias, because they were useful to that house, it would be at end as soon as they ceased to be so. Whereas if the Emperor saw the Count in a condition to be either useful or hurtful to him, he would soon forget the services of the others, to seek his friendship. but that if he called in the French (besides that they are easily tired with every thing, and that their application to foreign affairs is subject to be influenced by the frequent revolutions which happen within that kingdom, and depends on the genius of those who govern) he must debar himself of all means of an accommodation with the Emperor, whose Power in Italy was more considerable than theirs: that it would therefore be time enough to seek the aid of France when he should see himself entirely excluded from an alliance with the Empire; in which case the interest of the French would be so far concerned not to abandon him, that they would not fail to succour him, because the Count remaining master of Genoa, they would always be in fear of his agreeing with their enemies, if they refused him the assistance which was necessary for his defence: that as to forces, there was no need of any greater to succeed in this design, than those which he had of his own, since he knew that there were but 250 soldiers in Genoa, and that Jannetin Doria's gallies were entirely disarmed. These reasons entirely determined the Count, because they were agreeable to his natural inclination for glory, and to that greatness of soul which made nothing appear difficult to him, that was honourable. In fine, he resolved to engage in this undertaking on his own strength, and to employ none in it, but those friends and servants which his high birth, his extraordinary courtesy, his inexhaustible liberality, and his other good qualities had acquired him.

There are many persons who have merit, courage, and ambition, and who form general ideas of raising themselves and bettering their condition, but 'tis rare to meet with such, as having formed those ideas, know how to make choice of proper means for the execution of them, and who are not remiss in the continual care which is necessary to bring them to effect, or when they take that pains they generally time it ill, and act with too much impatience for the event. This is so true, that in affairs of this nature, most men are too long in taking their resolutions, but will never allow themselves the necessary time for the executing what they have resolved. They do not think early enough of disposing their actions to the end which they have proposed to themselves, to direct all their steps to the plan which they have once formed, to establish a stock of reputation, to gain friends, and finally to center all their views in the execution of their first design. On the contrary, we see them often change their views on a sudden, their mind appears disquieted and overburdened with the secret and the weight

weight of their enterprize, and amidst the changes and irregularity of their conduct, they always let slip something that may give a hold to those who watch over them, and umbrage to their enemies.

The Count de Fiesque very wisely remedied these inconveniencies, for knowing that he was naturally inclined to great things, and seeing that he should one day be able to bring these general inclinations to some particular and important design, which might tend to his own greatness, he gave himself entirely up to that thought, and as he had of himself an incredible passion for glory, and a great deal of art to increase his reputation, he lived in such a manner, that all the great qualities that were to be observed in him seemed to proceed from his native stock, and not from a studied conduct. He had always the same open, agreeable, and pleasant countenance; he was civil to every body, though with proper distinctions according to different merit and quality. His liberality was so great, that he prevented the wants of his friends; thus he gained the poor by his bounty, and the rich by his civility. He always kept his word religiously, he had an unwearied desire of obliging; his house and table were open to all comers, he was magnificent in every thing, even to profuseness, and never was any one better persuaded than he, that covetousness, stiffness, and pride, obscure the most shining qualities of great men. But what gave an extraordinary lustre to those he was possessed of, was the beauty of his person, and the graceful and noble air with which all his actions were accompanied, which were distinguishing marks of his illustrious birth, and which attracted every one's respect and inclination.

This conduct so secured him the hearts of his friends, that not one of those who promised to serve him, failed either in his fidelity or discretion, in an affair of so nice a nature, which, indeed, is very extraordinary in a conspiracy, where so many actors and so much secrecy are required, that though it should happen, that none should prove treacherous, it is hard to imagine, that none should prove imprudent. But what was

most

most wonderful in this, was, that his enemies seeing his even conduct, took no umbrage at it, because they attributed what was too shining in his actions, to his natural temper, and not to a formed design.

This was without doubt, one of the causes of the contempt with which Andrew Doria received the advices that were given him by Ferdinando Gonzague, and two or three others concerning this enterprize, I say one of the causes, because though the conduct of the Count contributed to the taking away the diffidence of this old politician, jealous of his authority, there must nevertheless have been some other reason for so great an infatuation. But it is hard to find out that cause, unless we ascribe it to Providence, which delights in shewing the vanity of human prudence, and in confounding the pride of those who flatter themselves, that they can unravel the several windings of the hearts of men, and that they have an infallible discernment for all things in the world. This presumption is never more ridiculous than in those great men whom continualy study, profound meditation, and long experience in affairs, have so raised above the vulgar, and so intoxicated with a good opinion of themselves, that they rely on the confidence of their own judgment in the most difficult affairs, and hear the advice of others only to despise it. It is certain that most of these extraordinary men, whom others go to consult like oracles, and who have so quick a penetration in things which are indifferent to them, are commonly blind in those which are of greater importance to themselves They are more unhappy than others, in that they cannot guide themselves either by their reason or by that of their friends

The act of generosity which gained the Count de Fiesque the most friends amongst the people, was his bounty to the silk spinners, who made a considerable body of the inhabitants of Genoa They were at that time extremely distressed by the misery occasioned by the late wars, the Count having learned their condition, from their Consul, expressed a great concern at their poverty, and, at the same time, ordered

dered him to send to his palace such as had most need of relief He supplied them abundantly with money and provisions, and begged of them not to make any noise about his presents, because he expected no other reward from them, but the satisfaction he felt within himself in succouring the afflicted, and accompanying these things with his natural courteousness and civility, he so gained the hearts of these poor people, that they were from that time entirely devoted to his service.

But if, on the one hand, he gained the love and esteem of the poorest amongst the people by his liberalities, he did not forget, on the other, to make himself agreeable to the most considerable of them, by the promises of liberty which he artfully insinuated in his discourses, wherein he gave them to understand, that though he was of the body of the nobility, he was too reasonable not to sympathize with a great deal of sorrow in the oppression of the people

There are some who accuse the republic of a great deal of imprudence on this occasion, and maintain that it was a piece of ill conduct in the senate to suffer the Count thus to oblige every body, and to gain with so much care the hearts of his fellow-citizens I cannot disown but the maxim on which this opinion is founded, proceeds from the most refined politics, for it seems, that aiming at the keeping private people in a state of mediocrity, its natural effect ought to be the safety of the whole But I am satisfied that it is very unjust, in that it corrupts the nature of good qualities, which by that means become hurtful or dangerous to the person that is possessed of them. I think that maxim even pernicious, because, by rendering merit suspicious, it choaks up all the seeds of virtue, and so disgusts men from the love of glory, that they never undertake great actions but with fear, and they even are diverted from those which might be useful to the Commonwealth, to avoid giving umbrage to the government It happens also, that instead of keeping men of courage within the bounds of that equality which it prescribes, it often inclines them to give a free course to their ambition, and to take violent resolutions

solutions to shake off the yoke of so tyrannical a law.

The Count did not so absolutely rely on the good-will of the common people, as to neglect the securing the soldiery, who are chiefly necessary in these enterprizes. He left Genoa in the beginning of the summer, in all appearance to visit his territories, but in reality to observe what persons fit for service might be found amongst his vassals, and to use them to warlike exercises, under pretence of the fear he feigned to be in of the Duke of Placentia He was also willing to give the necessary orders for the design he had of secretly introducing some men into Genoa when occasion should require it, and of assuring himself of the sentiments of that Duke who had promised him 2000 men of his best troops.

The Count returning about the latter end of autumn added to his usual conduct a profound dissimulation in what related to the house of Doria, expressing on all occasions a great veneration for the person of Andrew, and a strict friendship for Jannetin, in order to shew all the world that their past divisions were entirely laid asleep, and to give them all imaginable marks of an union that might be securely relied upon

If what he said on the very day that he executed his enterprize be true, that he had long before been acquainted that his ruin had been resolved on by Jannetin Doria, and that that violent and unjust man, who was only restrained by the prudence of his uncle Andrew, whom he found subject to great distempers, had ordered Captain Hercaro to rid him of all of the family of Fiesque the moment that Andrew Doria should die; that he had letters by him, which were convincing proofs that Jannetin had endeavoured to poison him, three several times, and that he was besides certainly assured, that the Emperor was ready to make him Sovereign of Genoa. if, I say, all these things are true, I cannot think that the Count's dissimulation can be justly blamed; because, in affairs where our own life and the general interest of our

country

country are at ſtake, ſincerity is a virtue out of ſeaſon; nature teaching us, by the example of the inſtinct of the moſt inconſiderable animals, that in theſe extremities the uſe of ſtratagems is lawful to defend ourſelves from violence and oppreſſion.

But if the Count's complaints were only calumnies invented againſt the houſe of Doria, to give the better colour to his deſign, and to exaſperate people's minds; it cannot be denied that theſe falſe marks of friendſhip which he ſo affectedly gave them, were artifices unworthy of ſo great a courage as his. And without doubt it would be difficult to juſtify ſuch a conduct, but by the neceſſity which the inſolence and power of Jannetin had impoſed on him to live in that manner.

The Count had bought four galleys of the Duke of Placentia, which he kept in the Pope's pay under the name of his brother Jerom. As he judged that the moſt neceſſary thing to his deſign, was to make himſelf maſter of the port, he ſent for one of them to Genoa, under pretence of ſending it a cruiſing in the Levant, and at the ſame time took occaſion to get into the city, without ſuſpicion, part of the ſoldiers which came to him from his territories and from Placentia, whereof ſome paſſed for people of the garriſon, ſome for adventurers that were ſeeking employment, ſome for ſeamen, and a great many even for galley-ſlaves.

Verrina very artfully introduced amongſt the companies of the city, fifteen or twenty ſoldiers who were vaſſals to the Count, and corrupted others of the garriſon. He obtained promiſes from the moſt conſiderable and moſt enterpriſing among the people, of all manner of aſſiſtance in the execution of a private deſign intended, as he ſaid, againſt ſome of their enemies. Calcagno and Sacco were, on their ſide, employing themſelves with no leſs diligence and induſtry, and I think I cannot better expreſs the art with which theſe four perſons conducted this enterprize, than by ſaying that they engaged in it above ten thouſand people, without diſcovering their true deſign to any one.

Things

Things being thus disposed, nothing was wanting but the choice of a day for the execution, in which there happened some difficulties. Verrina's opinion, was, that they should invite to a new mass * Jannetin and Andrew Doria, and Adam Centurione, with those of the nobility who were the best affected to that party He offered to kill them himself This proposal was no sooner made than rejected by the Count, who conceived so much horror at it, that he cried out, that he would never consent to the prophaning the most sacred mystery of our religion to facilitate the success of his undertaking It was afterwards proposed to take the opportunity of the marriage of a sister of Jannetin Doria's with Julius Cibo, Marquis de Masse, the Count's brother in-law, and they judged, that the execution of their design would be easy on that occasion, because the Count would have the pretence of making an entertainment for all the relations of that familly, and thereby be furnished with the means of cutting them all off at a blow. But the Count's generosity moved him again to oppose this black piece of treachery, as many people assure, and it may easily be believed of one of his disposition, although Doria's friends have given out, that he had resolved to make use of that way, if an affair which engaged, on that very day, Jannetin Doria to take a short journey out of Genoa, had not changed his mind At last, after several deliberations, the night of the second of January was pitched upon for this enterprize, and the necessary orders were at the same time given out with a great deal of conduct: Verrina, Calcagno, and Sacco, disposing on their side of those whom they had gained. The Count got a great number of arms secretly conveyed into his house, and sent to observe the places which they were to make themselves masters of, he introduced by small numbers, and without noise, into a part of his palace, separate from the rest, the soldiers who were destined

* A mass celebrated by some person of no e, the first time of his officiating as a Priest, to which it is common to invite people of distinction.

to begin the execution. and the appointed day being come, the better to cover his design, he made a great many visits, and even went towards evening to the palace of Doria, where meeting Jannetin's children, he took them one after another in his arms, and played with them a long time before their father, whom he afterwards desired to give orders to the officers of his gallies, not to hinder the departure of the Count's galley, which was that night to sail to the Levant. after which he took leave of him with his usual civilities, and in going home he called at Thomas Assereto's, where he met above thirty of those gentlemen who were called popular, whom Verrina had caused him to meet there, as by accident, whence the Count carried them all to sup with him. When he was got home, he sent Verrina all over the city, to the senate-house, and to that of Doria, to observe if they had no intimation of his design, and having heard that all things were as quiet as usual, he ordered the doors of his house to be shut, with direction however to let in all those who should desire it, but to let out no person whatsoever.

As he perceived that his guests were extremely surprised to find, instead of a feast prepared for them, nothing but arms, strange faces, and soldiers, he gathered them together in a hall, and expressing in his countenance a noble assurance, he spoke to them in this manner:

" We have, my friends, already suffered too much, from the insolence of Jannetin, and the tyranny of Andrew Doria. We have not a moment to lose if we have a mind to secure our lives and liberties from the oppression that threatens them, is there any one here that can be ignorant of the pressing danger of this Common-wealth? What can you imagine the twenty gallies which besiege our harbour are intended for? What is the design of all the forces and the intelligence which these two tyrants have prepared? Behold them ready to triumph over our patience and to build their unjust authority on the ruins of this State. It is now

no

no longer time to deplore our miseries in private, we must hazard all things to free ourselves from them since the evil is so violent, the remedies must be so too, and if the fear of falling into the most shameful slavery has any power over your minds, you must make a vigorous attempt to break your fetters, and prevent those that would load you with new ones, for I cannot imagine you any longer capable of bearing the uncle's injustice, or the nephew's pride I cannot imagine, I say, that there is one amongst you that will be content to serve those as masters, who ought to think themselves honoured enough with being your equals. Were we insensible to the interest of the Commonwealth, we cannot be so to our own: every one of us has but too much reason to revenge himself, and our revenge is both just and glorious, since our private resentment is joined to our zeal for the public good, and that we cannot abandon our own interests without betraying those of our country. It is now in your power to secure its quiet and your own, you want only the will to be happy, to become so I have provided for every thing which might obstruct your happiness, I have laid you open a way to glory, and am ready to lead you in it, if you are disposed to follow me. The preparations you see here, ought at this time to encourage you more than they have surprised you, and the astonishment which I at first observed in your faces, ought to be changed into a glorious resolution of employing these warlike instruments with vigour, to work the destruction of our common enemies, and the preservation of our liberty. I should offend your courage if I imagined you capable, on the sight of these objects, to deliberate about the use of them That use is certain, by the good order which I hope to put things into, it is of the greatest advantage to you; it is just, because of the oppression you suffer; it is glorious, by the greatness of the undertaking I might justify by these letters, that the Emperor has promised Andrew Doria the sovereignty of Genoa, and is ready to fulfil his promise. I could shew you by other letters which I have, that Jannetin has three times attempted to hire people to poison poſon me · it would be eaſy for me to prove to you that he has given orders to Lercaro to murder me and all my family, the moment his uncle ſhould die, but the knowledge of all theſe horrid and infamous treacheries, would add nothing to the horror you already have for theſe monſters Methinks I ſee your eyes ſparkle with the generous fire that a juſt revenge inſpires you with, I ſee you are more impatient than I, to expreſs your reſentment, to aſſure your eſtates, your quiet, and the honour of your families Let us then, my dear fellow citizens, ſave the reputation of Genoa, let us preſerve our country's liberty, and let us ſhew the world, that there are yet left in this ſtate, honeſt men, who have the heart to bring tyrants to deſtruction"

The company was very much aſtoniſhed at theſe words but as they were almoſt all of them zealous friends to the Count de Fieſque, and as ſome of them joined to that friendſhip the exalted hopes with which they flattered themſelves, in caſe their enterprize ſucceeded, and the reſt feared his reſentmant if they refuſed to follow his fortune, they promiſed him all manner of ſervice There were but two amongſt that number, which was pretty conſiderable, that begged of him not to engage them in that affair, whether their profeſſion remote from dangers, and their humour averſe to violence, rendered them incapable (as they ſaid) to be of any ſervice in an action where many dangers were to be run, and many murthers to be committed, or whether they covered, under the appearance of a diſſembled fear, the real affection which they had for the houſe of Doria, or for ſome of his party. it is certain that the Count preſſed them no farther, and was ſatisfied with ſhutting them up in a room, to take from them the means of diſcovering his deſign His gentle uſage of theſe two perſons, makes me diſbelieve what ſeveral hiſtorians, prejudiced againſt his memory, have publiſhed, which is, that the diſcourſe he made in this aſſembly was filled with nothing but threats againſt thoſe who ſhould refuſe to aſſiſt him, and I believe that we may with reaſon form the ſame judgment of the cruel and impious words which they put into his mouth on the night of the execution of his enterprize. For what likelihood is there that a man of his condition, born with an extraordinary passion for glory, should suffer himself to be transported to such expressions as cannot be remembered without horror, and could be of no manner of use to his designs? Be that as it will, as soon as he had ended his speech to those gentlemen, and had informed them of the order of his enterprize, he went into his wife's apartment, whom he found in tears, foreseeing that the great preparations which were making in the house, could not but be designed by her husband for some dangerous undertaking. He therefore thought it proper, no longer to conceal the truth from her, but he endeavoured to take away her fear, by all the reasons which he could think of, and he represented to her how far he had engaged himself, and the impossibility of retreating She did her utmost to dissuade him from that action, and made use of the power which his love for her gave her over his mind, but neither her prayers nor tears could shake his resolution Paul Pansa, who had been his governor, and for whom he had a great veneration, joined with the Countess, and left nothing untried that might bring him back to the du y of a good citizen, or set before him the hazard he ran on this occasion The Count was as little moved with his Governor's counsels, as he had been with the fondness and tears of his wife He had (as it is said of Cæsar) passed the Rubicon; and returning to the hall where he had left his guests, he gave the last directions for the execution of his enterprize. He ordered an hundred and fifty men, picked out of his best soldiers, to go into that part of the city called the Borough, whither he was to follow them, accompanied by the nobility Cornelius, his natural brother, had orders as soon as they came thither, to march (with a detachment of thirty men) to the gate of the Arch, and to make himself master of it. Jerom and Ottobon, his brothers, with Vincent Calcagno, were charged to take that of St. Thomas when they heard the cannon fired from the Count's galley

commanded

commanded by Verrina, which was ready to ſhut up the mouth of the baſon, and to inveſt that of Andrew Doria The Count was to get to that gate by land, after he had left guards in his way at the Arches of St. Andrew and St. Donatus, and at the Place des Sauvages, with the leaſt noiſe poſſible. Thomas Aſſereto was ordered to ſeize that gate by giving the word which he could eaſily know, having an employment under Jannetin Doria As this action was the moſt important point of the enterprize, becauſe if it failed, thoſe who were in the Count's galley could have no communication with the reſt of the conſpirators, it was judged proper, to render it ſtill more eaſy, that Scipio Borgognino, a vaſſal of the Count's, and a reſolute ſoldier, ſhould throw himſelf into the baſon with armed feluccas, and ſhould land on that ſide, at the ſame time that Thomas Aſſereto ſhould attack that gate on the outſide. It was alſo reſolved, that the moment that Jerom and Ottobon de Fieſque ſhould be maſters of St Thomas's gate which is near the palace of Doria, one of them ſhould force that palace, and kill Andrew and Jannetin and becauſe there was ſome reaſon to apprehend, that Jannetin, being waked at the noiſe which would be made at the gates, might get into Lewis Giulia's felucca to come and give his orders, they left three armed feluccas to prevent it. To theſe orders there was added a general one, that all the conſpirators ſhould call to the people in the name of Fieſque, and cry out Liberty! that thoſe of the city whoſe affection they were aſſured of, might not be ſurpriſed, and that ſeeing that the Count was the author of this action, they might join his people.

It is not eaſy to determine whether it had not been more advantageous and ſafe to make but one body of all theſe troops which were ſeparated in ſo many different quarters, ſo remote from each other, than to divide them in that manner, becauſe their number was conſiderable enough to make it probable, that if they had all entered the ſame way into the town, they had carried all before them, and had drawn the people to favour the victorious party, wherever they had paſſed. whereas as being divided, they could act but weakly, and ran the risk of committing mistakes, and of being all defeated one after the other For it is certain that a great deal of exactness is requisite to make the times of several attacks agree, and a great deal of good fortune for them all to succeed alike So many heads and hands are in these occasions necessary to concur in the same action, that the least fault in one of them often disconcerts all the rest, as the disorder of a single wheel may stop the motion of the greatest machine, and it is very difficult to conceive, that during the night and amidst the tumult which generally accompanies these kinds of enterprizes, either the heart or the judgment of some of the conspirators should not fail them, and that thinking danger more terrible when near than when afar off, they should not repent their engaging in such a design. But when they move all together, the example of others animates and emboldens the most timorous, who are forced to suffer themselves to be carried away by the multitude, and to do out of mere necessity what the brave do out of courage

Those who are of a contrary opinion, hold that in these enterprizes which are executed by night, in a city where the conspirators have a great deal of intelligence, and are favoured by most of the people, and where they may make themselves masters of the principal posts before their enemies are in a condition to dispute those posts with them, it is better to form several bodies, and make different attacks in a great many places, because by giving several alarms at the same time in different parts, those who would defend themselves are obliged to divide their forces, without knowing how many are to be detached; and the fright which such sudden attempts commonly create, is much stronger when the noise comes from all sides, than when they are only to provide against the danger in one single place. Besides that in narrow streets, like those of Genoa, a middling number is equally serviceable with a greater, and that ten men, by the help of a barricado, if they are attacked only in front, may stop an hundred times as many of the bravest men in the world, and give time to those who

who are behind them to rally. Lastly, those who are of the latter opinion, think that in an enterprize like this, it is less advantageous to the party of the conspirators to join their forces in one body, than to spread them in different parts of the city, having the favour of the greatest part of the inhabitants, because they raise them all at once, and the citizens are more ready to take up arms when they see themselves supported, and are more capable of serving when they have regular troops and people of credit at their head.

All these reasons being justly weighed on each side, I think that the Count acted very judiciously, for it seems to me that on this occasion, the inconveniencies which we have just now mentioned in the way of acting which he made choice of, were less to be feared than they commonly are, because his party was not only composed of the soldiery and nobility, but also of a great number of the common people whom he was assured of. So that having considerable forces in all the quarters of Genoa, he had reason to think that the garrison which was extremely weak, and those who did not favour him, could be of no great hindrance to his designs, nor make any resistance sufficient to disturb those who fought for him. Wherefore having left his palace, he divided his men according to the order which he had resolved on, and at the same time that the cannon which was ordered for a signal was fired from his galley, Cornelius surprised the gate of the Arch, which he made himself master of without any trouble Ottobon and Jerom, the Count's brothers, did not find so much ease at that of St. Thomas, from the resistance of Captain Sebastian Lercaro and his brother, who maintained their post a great while. But this last having been killed, and the other taken, some even amongst their soldiers who had intelligence of the design, having turned their arms in favour of the Fiesques, those of the guard ran away and abandoned their post to their enemies. Jannetin Doria, awakened either by the noise which was made at the gate or by the outcry which was made at the same time in the harbour, rose in great haste, and being accompanied by none but a page who carried a flambeau before him, he ran to St. Thomas's gate, where being discovered by the conspirators, he was killed as soon as he came.

This precipitancy of Jannetin's saved Andrew Doria's life, and gave him time to get on horseback, and to retire fifteen miles from Genoa; because Jerom de Fiesque who had orders from his brother to force Doria's palace as soon as he had seized St Thomas's gate, seeing that Jannetin had been killed by his own imprudence, preferred the preservation of the immense riches which were in the palace, and which it would have been difficult to save from the soldiers, to the taking of Andrew Doria, whom he no longer looked upon but as a worn-out old man, whose ruin was indifferent Whilst these things were doing about St Thomas's gate, Assereto and Scipio Borgognino executed their orders with all possible success, they killed those who made any resistance at the gate next the bason, and pushed the rest so vigorously, that they did not give them time to come to themselves, and at last they secured that considerable post.

The Count having in his passage left great bodies to guard those posts which he reckoned the most important, got into the bason, the entrance of which he found entirely open, and joined himself to Verrina, who had already attacked with his galley those of Andrew Doria He found them almost all disarmed, and made himself master of them with a great deal of ease, but fearing that in this confusion the crew would come to relieve the Captain's galley, in which he heard a great deal of noise, he ran in haste to give his orders about it, and as he was just getting in, the board on which he was happening to overturn, he fell into the sea The weight of his armour, and the mud which was deep in that place, hindered him from getting up again, and the darkness of the night, joined to the confused noise that was made on all parts, kept from his men the knowledge of this accident, so that without perceiving the loss they had sustained, they made an end of securing the harbour and the gallies.

Ottobon,

Ottobon, who was come to that place after he had executed his first design, staid to command there, and Jerom who had followed him, left Vincent Colcagno at St Thomas's gate, and left the harbour with two hundred men to stir up the populace in the streets, and get together about him as many people as he could Verrina on the other hand did the same thing, and thus a great number of persons being gathered about them, nobody dared appear any longer in the streets without declaring for Fiesque's party The greatest part of the nobility kept close at home during the noise, every one fearing the plunder of his house, the most courageous went to the senate-house with the Emperor's Ambassador, who would have run away from the city, had it not been for the remonstrances of Paul Lasagna, a man of great authority among the people. Cardinal Doria and Adam Centurione went thither also, and resolved, with Nicholas Franço, at that time head of the Common-wealth, there being then no Duke, to send Boniface Lomellino, Christopher Palavicini, and Anthony Calva, with fifty soldiers of the garrison to defend St Thomas's gate But these having met with a body of the conspirators, and being abandoned by part of their men, were obliged to retire into the house of Adam Centurione, where having met with Francis Grimaldi, Dominic Doria, and some other gentlemen, they took heart again, and returned to the same gate by a different way but they found it so well guarded, and were charged so vigorously, that they left Boniface Lomellino prisoner, who distinguished himself in that action by his courage, and happily escaped out of the conspirators hands

The Senate finding that force had been tried in vain, had recourse to remonstrances, and deputed another Jerom de Fiesque, a relation of the count's, and Jerom Canevale, to demand of the Count the reason of that commotion, and immediately after Cardinal Doria, who was allied to him, assisted by John Baptista Lercaro, and Bernard Castagno, both Senators, resolved, at the desire of the Senate, to go and speak with the Count to endeavour to soften him. But seeing

ing that things were in ſo great a confuſion, that if he went through the city he ſhould expoſe his dignity (to no purpoſe) to the inſults of an incenſed people, he would not go on, but ſtaid at the ſenate houſe. So that the Senate gave that commiſſion to Auguſtin Lomellino, Hector de Fieſque, Anſaldo Juſtiniani, Ambroſe Spinola, and John Balliano, who ſeeing a troop of armed men coming towards them, imagined it was the Count, and waited for him at St. Siro As ſoon as the conſpirators perceived them they charged them, and made Lomellino and Hector de Fieſque run away. Anſaldo Juſtiniani ſtood his ground, and addreſſing himſelf to Jerom, who was at the head of that party, he demanded of him, in the name of the Commonwealth, where the Count was. The conſpirators had juſt heard of his death Verrina, having long ſought him in vain, was got into his galley in a deſpairing condition, becauſe the news from all quarters of the town mentioned nothing of his appearing any where. This made Jerom anſwer Juſtiniani boldly, and with the greateſt imprudence, that it was now no longer time to look for any other Count than himſelf, and that he would have the ſenate-houſe immediately ſurrendered to him.

The Senate having learned by this diſcourſe the death of the Count, reſumed their courage, and ſent twelve gentlemen to rally thoſe of the guard and of the people whom they could put in a poſture of defence Some, even of the hotteſt of Fieſque's party, began to be ſurpriſed, ſeveral, who had neither the ſame affection for, nor the ſame confidence in Jerom, that they had for his brother, diſperſed themſelves at the very report of his death; and confuſion getting in amongſt the conſpirators, thoſe in the ſenate houſe perceived it, and deliberated whether they ſhould go and attack them, or treat with them. The firſt of theſe was propoſed as the moſt honourable way, but the ſecond was followed as the ſafeſt Paul Panſa, a man of the greateſt conſideration in the Common-wealth, and ever attached to the houſe of Fieſque, was choſen as the fitteſt man for that purpoſe. The Senate ordered him to to carry a general pardon to Jerom for himſelf and his accomplices. He conſented to this agreement at the perſuaſion of Panſa. The pardon was ſigned at the ſame time, and ſealed with all neceſſary formalities, by Ambroſe Senaregna, Secretary to the Republic. and thus Jerom de Fieſque left Genoa with all thoſe of his party, and retired to Montobio Ottobon, Verrina, Calcagno, and Sacco, who had made their eſcape in the Count's galley, ſteered towards France, and arrived at Marſeilles, after having ſent back to the mouth of the Vare, without doing them any hurt, Sebaſtian Lercaro, Manfredo Centurione, and Vincent Varcaro, whom they had taken at St. Thomas's gate. The Count's body was found at four day's end, and having been left ſome time on the banks of the harbour, without burial, it was at laſt thrown into the ſea by the command of Andrew Doria. Benedict Centurione, and Dominic Doria were the next day deputed to Andrew to condole with him in the name of the Republic on the death of Jannetin, and to bring him back into the city, where he was received with all imaginable honours. He went to the Senate the day after, where he repreſented to them in a vehement declamation, which he took care to ſupport with the credit of his friends, that the Common-wealth was not obliged to ſtand to the agreement which they had made with the Fieſques, ſince it had been concluded againſt all form, and ſigned (as it were) ſword in hand. He magnified extremely the danger of ſuffering ſubjects to treat in that manner with their Sovereigns, and inſiſted that the impunity of a crime of that conſequence would be a fatal example to the Common-wealth. In ſhort, Andrew Doria ſo artfully covered his private intereſts under the veil of the general good, and ſo well backed his paſſion with his authority, that although there were many perſons that could not approve of ſo great a breach of public faith, the Senate nevertheleſs declared all the conſpirators guilty of high treaſon, ordered the magnificent palace of Fieſque to be razed to the ground, condemned the Count's brothers and the principal of his faction to death, puniſhed with a fifty years banishment all those who had had the least hand in that enterprize, and ordered that Jerom de Fiesque should be commanded to surrender the fortress of Montobio into the hands of the Republic. This last point was not so easy to execute as the rest, and as the place was strong by its situation, and by its fortifications which they were continually at work upon, it was judged properest to try the most gentle means to get it out of the hands of the Fiesques, before they made use of force, the success of which is always doubtful. Paul Pansa had orders from the Senate to go thither as soon as possible, and to offer Jerom reasonable conditions on the part of the Commonwealth, but they received no other answer from him but reproaches of their breaking their faith with his friends, and a pretty haughty refusal to treat with the Genoese. The Emperor, who feared that the French might make themselves masters of that castle, which is of the greatest importance for the safety of Genoa, earnestly pressed the Senate to besiege it, and furnished them with all necessary assistance for that purpose. Augustine Spinola, a Captain of reputation, had that employment, invested the place, which he besieged for forty days, and at last obliged those who were in it to surrender at discretion.

Some historians accuse Verrina, Calcagno, and Sacco of having advised Jerom to so dishonourable a capitulation, by reason of the cold reception they had met with in France, whence they were returned, to throw themselves into that place. The taking of it created new disorders in the Common-wealth, because of the variety of opinions amongst the Senators, touching the punishment of the prisoners. Many persons inclined to lenity, and would have had a pardon for young Jerom, maintaining that that family had been sufficiently punished by the death of the Count, and the loss of all their estate: but Andrew Doria, exasperated against them, once more got the better of the Senate's clemency, and was the cause of the execution of Jerom de Fiesque, Verrina, Calcagno, and Assereto, and of the bloody arrest against Ottobon,

forbidding

forbidding his poſterity as far as the fifth generation to come near Genoa.

Let us ſtop here, and conſider exactly what happened in the execution of this great deſign. Let us, if it be poſſible, draw from the infinite number of faults, which we may obſerve in it, examples of human frailty, and let us own that that enterprize, conſidered in its beginnings as a maſter-piece of courage and conduct amongſt men, appears in the ſequel of it full of the common effects of the meanneſs and imperfection of our nature. For after all, how ſhameful was it in Andrew Doria to abandon the city at the firſt noiſe, without making the leaſt attempt to appeaſe, by his authority, that popular commotion? How great an infatuation was it in him to neglect the advices, he received on all hands, of the Count's enterprize? How great an imprudence was it in Jannetin to come alone, and in the darkneſs of the night, to St Thomas's gate, to remedy a diſorder which he had no reaſon to deſpiſe, being ignorant of the cauſe of it? How great a coward was Cardinal Doria, not to dare to leave the Senate, to endeavour to reſtrain the people by the reſpect they owed to his dignity? How imprudent were the Senate not to aſſemble all their forces, at the firſt alarm, to ſtop at once the progreſs of the conſpirators in the principal poſts of the city, inſtead of ſending only weak ſuccours, which could be of no conſiderable ſervice? And laſtly, what kind of conduct was it to endeavour to reclaim by remonſtrances a profeſſed rebel, who had arms in his hands, and who found himſelf the ſtrongeſt? But after a formal treaty, how pernicious a maxim was it in that Senate to violate the public faith and to break a promiſe ſo ſolemnly given to Jerom and Ottobon de Fieſque? For if the fear of ſuch uſage may be uſeful to a ſtate, by keeping them within the bounds of their duty thoſe who might have any thought of revolting, it may alſo be very pernicious to it, by taking away from thoſe who have revolted all hopes of a pardon. And indeed it is hard to comprehend how theſe politicians, who were reckoned very able men, were not afraid, by this example, of throwing into despair Jerom de Fiesque, who still held the rock of Montobio, which he could have put into the hands of foreigners, and the loss of which was of the greatest importance to the city of Genoa. But if those we have been speaking of were guilty of remarkable faults on this occasion, we may say that the conspirators committed still greater errors after they had lost their chief His valour and good conduct, which were in some measure the supreme intelligences which governed all the motions of his party, failing by his death, that party fell at once into a disorder, which completed its ruin Jerom de Fiesque, who on a great many accounts was obliged to conceal his brother's death, was the first that published it, and thereby gave his enemies a fresh courage, and possessed the minds of his friends with fear. Ottobon, Verrina, Calcagno, and Sacco, who had made their escape in the galley, set at liberty, almost as soon as they had left Genoa, the prisoners whom they had in their hands, without foreseeing that they might become necessary to them for making their accommodation. Verrina having heard of the Count's death, retired in his galley, and basely abandoned an affair of that consequence to the conduct of Jerom, who had neither experience sufficient, nor authority enough amongst the conspirators to finish it That same Jerom made a treaty with the Senate, and agreed to return to the condition of a private man, after having been on the point of becoming a Sovereign. He afterwards made a shameful capitulation in Montobio upon the promise of those who had already broke their word with him. Verrina, Calcagno, and Sacco, the principal actors in this conspiracy, and the most criminal of all the Count's accomplices, persuaded Jerom to that mean action, upon the hopes that were given them of impunity, chusing rather to run the hazard of dying by the hands of a hangman, than to fall honourably in a breach.

Thus ended this great enterprize: thus died John Lewis de Fiesque Count de Lavagne, whom some honour with the greatest encomiums, others load with blame,

blame, and many excuse If we consider the maxim which advises us always to respect the present government of the country we are in, without doubt his ambition is criminal If we respect his courage and all the great qualities which shone forth in the conduct of that action, it appears noble and generous. If we regard the power of the house of Doria, which gave him just cause to apprehend the ruin of the Commonwealth and his own, it is excusable But which way soever we speak of it, the most passionate tongues and pens cannot disown but that the ill they can say of him was common to him with the most illustrious men. *He was born in a small state, where all private condi*tions were beneath his courage and his merit; the natural unquietness of his countrymen, ever prone to novelty, the loftiness of his own mind, his youth, his great estate, the number and flatteries of his friends, the favour of the people, his being courted by foreign Princes, and lastly the general esteem of every one, were powerful seducers to inspire with ambition a more moderate mind than his The sequel of his enterprize was one of those accidents which human wisdom cannot foresee Had the success been as happy, as the conduct of it was full of prudence and vigour, it is to be believed that the Sovereignty of Genoa had not bounded his courage or his fortune, and that those who condemned his memory after his death, would have been the loudest in his praise whilst he lived The authors who have blackened him with so many calumnies to satisfy the passion of the Dorias, and to justify the breach of faith of the Senate, had by a contrary interest made his panegyric, and posterity had counted him amongst the heroes of his age So true it is, that good or ill success is commonly the rule of the praise or blame given to extraordinary actions However I think we may say with all the equity required in an historian that gives his judgment on the reputation of men, that nothing was wanting to that of the Count de Fiesque but a longer life and more just occasions of acquiring glory.

A

LETTER

Presented to the

COLLEGE OF CARDINALS,

In the Name of the

CARDINAL DE RETZ,

During his IMPRISONMENT.

A LETTER presented to the College of Cardinals, in the name of the Cardinal DE RETZ, during during his Imprisonment.

CATENAS meas, Ecclesiæ vulnera, cladem novissimam sacri ordinis ac publicæ libertatis, eminentissimi Cardinales, non est quod verbis prolixioribus repræsentem. Quæ me vis captivum detinet, eadem vobis profectò durissimæ servitutis jugum imposuit, & quæ immerentem oppressit calamitas, cervicibus vestris incumbit. Jam augustum purpuræ vestræ decus audacissimis hominibus ludibrium est. Nulla jam apud illos reverentia. Dumque Regium nomen, quod sacrum semper apud me ac venerationis plenum extitit, improbissimis conatibus obtendunt, non timent in Ecclesiæ Romanæ Proceres id moliri, quod in vilissimum caput nemo, nisi injustissimus admiserit; nisi fortè qui tumultuantem Galliam pacare studui, qui tranquillitati publicæ privata commoda posthabui, qui civibus Regem, Regi cives restitui, qui post redditum Lutetiæ Christianissimum Principem Ludovicum XIV. vel procul ab aula & strepitu pressi me in solitudinem domesticam, vel in suggestum publicum coram grege carissimo de rebus divinis concionaturus ascendi, dignus fui carcerem & vincula, fidelis obsequii, nec infeliciter navatæ operæ pretium referrem

Hæc sæculi nostri labes & corruptela, Cardinales eminentissimi, hæc iniquissimorum temporum conditio, sic vivunt qui neque publicum odium refugiunt, neque posteritatis judicium reformidant. Non exaggerabo atrocitatem injuriæ querelis acrioribus. erumpit ex ipso meo carcere vehementissimus clamor, nullusque ejus lapis non vocalis est. Certè si detentorum

Tranſlation of the LATIN LETTER on the other ſide.

I Need not, Moſt Eminent Cardinals, uſe many words to repreſent to you the wound that has been given to the Church, and the fatal blow that our Sacred Order and the public liberty have received by my imprifonment The ſame unjuſt power that keeps me confined, has certainly ſubjected you to the moſt grievous ſlavery, and the yoke of oppreſſion, under which I undeſervedly groan, hangs heavy on your necks. The auguſt glory of your purple is now become the ſcorn of the moſt inſolent among men, who have quite forgot the reſpect which is ſo juſtly due to it. And whilſt they make uſe of the royal name, always ſacred and venerable with me, to cover their wicked deſigns, they are not afraid of undertaking againſt the Princes of the Church of Rome, what none but the moſt unjuſt of men would ever attempt againſt the vileſt offender. But what are my offences? Unleſs, perhaps, my endeavours to ſettle peace in a nation diſtracted with tumults and ſeditions, my preferring the public tranquillity to my own private intereſt, my reſtoring the King to his people, and the people to their King, and, after the return of his moſt Chriſtian Majeſty, Lewis XIV. to his capital city, my retiring from the noiſe and buſineſs of the Court, to my domeſtic privacy or to the public exerciſes of my office, and the care of my deareſt flock, unleſs theſe things, I ſay, have merited a dungeon and chains, as the reward of my ſteady loyalty, and my honeſt and not unſucceſsful endeavours for the public good

Such, moſt eminent Cardinals, is the degeneracy and corruption of our age, ſuch is the ſtate of theſe wicked times, ſuch is the conſtant way of acting of thoſe who neither fear the public hatred, nor dread the impartial judgment of poſterity I will not pretend to aggravate the barbarity of the injury that has been done me, the very walls within which I am confined proclaim my wrongs, and there is not a ſtone in them but rum carcere Cardinalium aliquot fortassè leguntur exempla, præterquam quod longè hic dispar occasio, tam grave vulnus Ecclesiastico ordini nunquam inflictum est, illorum manu qui sacræ libertatis hostes esse nequeunt, quin simul propriæ dignitatis proditores evadant Alios ira Principis, alios vexatæ plebis odium, quosdam nutantis Coronæ necessaria visa defensio conjecit in carcerem; nullos, quod sciane, illorum conspiratio profligavit qui Ecclesiæ illud ipsum debent, quod vivunt. Mihi longè aliter contigit, neque jam violatam purpuram conquerer, si in debitoribus nullos hostes haberet. Sed quàm mihi citra noxam pati honorificum est, Cardinales eminentissimi, tam vobis gloriosum erit illatam ordini vestro, totique Ecclesiæ injuriam vindicare Eminentiam vestram interpellat, vel in ipso carcere, liber animus ferreisque cratibus evolans, inde auxilium expectat, unde mihi collatam dignitatem æternum recordabor Agnoscite ergò in fratre vestro calamitatem propriam, parem injuriæ zelum induite, & apud Sanctissimum Dominum, communem patrem efficite, ne una eademque clades, afflictam innocentiam, concultatam Ecclesiæ libertatem, triumphantem nequitiam diutius exhibeat.

Eminentiæ vestræ

Humillimus Cliens &

Addictissimus Frater.

Nomine & jussu Eminentissimi Domini nostri, Domini Cardinalis de Retz, qui has literas jussit, sed ob strictissimam custodiam subsignare non potuit.

but ſpeaks my complaints aloud. We may read of ſome Cardinals detained in priſon, but, beſides that the occaſion was widely different, ſure ſo great a wound as this was never given to our ſacred Order, by men who cannot be enemies to our liberty, without becoming at the ſame time betrayers of their own dignity. Some of the Sacred College have been thrown into priſon by the anger of their Prince, others by the hatred of an incenſed people, others out of a ſeeming neceſſary care for the defence of a tottering crown, but none, that I know of, have as yet been undone by the vile contrivances of thoſe who owe their very lives to the high character they bear in the Church To me it has happened far otherwiſe, nor ſhould I now complain of the violence offered to the purple, were not thoſe who are the moſt indebted to it, its greateſt enemies. But as it is an honour to me to ſuffer without deſerving it, it will be ſtill the more glorious in you, Moſt Eminent Cardinals, to avenge the injuries done to your Order, and to the whole Church My mind, free even in a priſon, and deſpiſing the reſtraint of grates and bars, flies to your Eminences to implore relief. Thence I expect my ſuccour, whence I ſhall ever remember that I received my dignity View therefore your own misfotune in that of your brother, let your zeal be equal to the injury, and uſe ſuch effectual endeavours with his Holineſs, our common Father, that we may be no longer preſented with ſo diſmal a ſcene, as innocence oppreſſed, the liberties of the Church trampled under foot, and iniquity triumphant

Your Eminences

moſt humble ſervant, and

moſt devoted Brother.

In the name, and by the command of our Maſter his Eminence the Cardinal de Retz, who ordered this letter to be written, but could not ſign it by reaſon of the ſtrictneſs of his confinement.

Some

Some short OBSERVATIONS on a Book, published in French since the foregoing sheets were sent to the press, intitled, MEMOIRS towards writing the History of ANNE of AUSTRIA, wife to LEWIS XIII. King of France, written by Madam de MOTTEVILLE, one of her Favourites.

WHAT has been said in the preface to the foregoing translation, about the Memoirs of Joli, and those of the Duchess de Nemours, may likewise be said of these, that is, that they probably would never have been published, if the Memoirs of the Cardinal de Retz had not first appeared; the curiosity of the public being chiefly excited in respect to them, because of the mention which is made there, and of the character which is given of that Cardinal

This is visibly the case in respect to Madam de Motteville's Memoirs, as may be seen by the advertisements put out by the French booksellers in our newspapers. They have taken great care to acquaint the public, sometimes that these Memoirs will be of great help for the better understanding those of the Cardinal de Retz, sometimes, that they are written in opposition to his, hoping by this means to make the Lady's Memoirs the more reputable and the more saleable.

I shall leave these last Memoirs (as I have done the others) to the judgment of those who have the patience to read over the five volumes which there are of them. What the Lady says in respect to the Cardinal de Retz, is much of the same stamp with the others, for though she allows him to have been a man of the greatest parts and courage, she taxes him with an unbounded ambition, and with views altogether destructive to the peace and welfare of the kingdom As I do not pretend to set up for his apologist, I shall say nothing in excuse of his actions, many of which, as I have said in the preface, he himself condemns, though, if he is to be believed, he was led into what related to the state,

ſtate, by better motives than thoſe which are attributed to him.

As to any difference in relation to matters of fact, between the Lady and the Cardinal, I can obſerve but very little, except in one place, where indeed they differ very much. It is towards the end of the ſecond volume of the Cardinal's Memoirs, where that Prelate excuſes himſelf to the Queen from entering into the meaſures of the Mareſchal d'Hoquincourt againſt the Prince of Condé, which probably would have ended in the Prince's death. What the Cardinal ſays about this matter, and the particulars he brings in to ſupport his relation, have certainly in them a great air of ſincerity The Lady however is pleaſed to ſay that the Cardinal was directly for having the prince of Conde murthered, which ſhe is in the right to exclaim at as much as ſhe does, if the fact is true. But that Lady ſays ſo many things upon ſlight grounds, and was ſo little in the Queen's ſecret (though ſhe is ſtyled one of her favourites) that it is very probable that ſhe may be miſtaken. I cannot find out by her Memoirs what place ſhe had in the Queen's family, but it muſt not have been of very great importance by the ſlight penſion that was allowed her, and by her not being obliged to attend on the Queen in any of her journeys. This is not ſaid in the leaſt to undervalue that Lady's merit and good qualities, which for ought I know might be very great, though perhaps ſhe will not be reckoned amongſt the firſt rate writers of Memoirs The character ſhe gives of Cardinal Mazarin agrees perfectly with what the Cardinal de Retz ſays of him, and ſo do moſt of her other characters, excepting that of the Queen, whom ſhe repreſents as much milder and better than ſhe appears in the picture which the Cardinal de Retz gives of her. It is probable enough that as the Lady may have ſomewhat flattered her, ſo may the Cardinal have been too hard upon her What he ſays however in relation to her coquetry in her younger years, is altogether confirmed by what we read in the beginning of Madam de Motteville's Memoirs, and as there is ſomething curious

curious enough in the particulars she gives of what passed between the Duke of Buckingham and the Queen, I believe it will not displease the reader to find these particulars mentioned here.

I shall first take notice that according to the accounts, both of the Cardinal de Retz, and of Madam de Monteville, Queen Anne of Austria had been beloved by others before the Duke of Buckingham entered the lists. The Duke de Montmorenci, brother to the Princess of Condé, and one of the finest gentlemen of that age, had been one of her profest lovers, as had likewise been the old Duke de Bellegarde The Queen hearkened to these gentlemen's courtship, without any appearance of being displeased, but she treated Cardinal Richelieu in his addresses to her in another manner

" The Duke of Buckingham was the man who appeared to have attacked her heart with the best success. That gentleman came on the behalf of the King of England, his master, to marry Henrietta Maria of France, sister to Lewis XIII He was (says Madam de Motteville) handsome, well shaped, high spirited, generous, liberal, and favourite to a great King He had all his treasures to spend, and all the jewels of the crown of England to adorn his person with. No wonder then, if with so many lovely qualities, he had such high thoughts, such noble, yet such blameable and dangerous desires, and no wonder if he had the good fortune to persuade those who were witnesses of his addresses that they were not troublesome

" There was (according to Madam de Motteville) a great deal said about an adventure which happened in the garden of the house where the Queen lay, when she went to accompany the Queen of England as far as Amiens As she was one day taking a walk in that garden with the Duke of Buckingham, in the presence of the retinue which usually attended her, that Duke expressing a desire to have some private conversation with her, she was left alone with him, Puange, her Gentleman-usher, thinking that he was obliged

obliged out of respect not to hearken to what that nobleman was saying to her. Chance having led them into a by-walk, which was hid by a pallisade from public view, the Queen at that instant surprised to find herself alone, and it is likely (says the Lady) importuned by some too passionate expression of the Duke's sentiments, cried out, and calling to her Gentleman-usher, she blamed him for leaving her. By this crying out (continues the good Lady) the Queen shewed her prudence and her virtue, in preferring the preservation of her inward innocence to the fear of being censured, and of the trouble she might be put to if this story reached the King's ears. If on this occasion she shewed that her heart was susceptible of a tender impression, which invited her to listen to the fabulous talk of a lover, it must be owned at the same time that her virtuous sentiments, and her love of purity out-weighed every thing else, and that she preferred to a reputation liable to some suspicion a true and real glory.

" At the Queen of England's leaving Amiens, the French Court accompanied her Majesty a little way out of that city, and the Queen of France (says Madam de Motteville) has done me the honour to tell me that when the Duke of Buckingham came to kiss her gown, she being in the fore-seat of the coach with the Princess of Conti, he hid himself with the curtain as if he had something to say to her, but in reality to wipe away the tears which then came into his eyes. The Princess of Conti, who had an agreeable way of raillery, and, as I have heard, a great deal of wit, said on this occasion, speaking of the Queen, that she would be answerable to the King for her virtue, but that she could not say so of her cruelty, since without doubt the tears of that lover which she had seen on this occasion ought to have touched her heart, and that she had suspected her eyes to have looked on him at least with pity.

" The Duke of Buckingham's passion (continues the Lady) prompted him to a bold action, which the Queen has informed me of, and which has been confirmed

firmed to me by the Queen of England, who had it from Buckingham himſelf. That illuſtrious ſtranger having left Amiens, in order to return to England, whither he was to conduct the Princeſs of France, now Queen of England, to the King her huſband, being overcome by his paſſion, and unable to bear the pains of abſence, reſolved to ſee the Queen of France again, though it were but for a moment. He formed that deſign when he was come almoſt to Calais, and he executed it under pretence of news which he had received from the King his maſter, that obliged him to return to Amiens. He left the Queen of England at Boulogne, and came back to Mary de Medicis, then Queen-mother, to treat about ſome pretended affairs, which he took for the pretext of his return. After having done with his chimerical negotiation, he came to the reigning Queen, whom he found in bed almoſt alone. That Princeſs was informed, by a letter from the Ducheſs de Chevreuſe, who accompanied the Queen of England, of Buckingham's coming back. ſhe ſpoke of it before Nogent in a jeſting manner, and was not ſurpriſed when ſhe ſaw the Duke. But ſhe was ſo when he came freely to kneel down by her bed-ſide, kiſſing her ſheet with ſuch uncommon tranſport that it was eaſy to perceive that his paſſion was violent, and of that kind which does not leave the uſe of reaſon to thoſe that are ſeized with it. The Queen has told me that ſhe was troubled at it, which trouble, joined with a little indignation, made her continue a long time without ſpeaking to him. The Counteſs de Lannoi, then her Lady of Honour, an old, diſcreet and virtuous Lady, who was at the bed's head, not being willing to ſuffer the Duke to continue in that condition, told him with a great deal of ſeverity, that what he did was not cuſtomary in France, and would have made him riſe. But the Duke, without appearing ſurpriſed, diſputed with the old Lady, ſaying that he was no Frenchman, and not bound to obſerve the laws of the kingdom. Then addreſſing himſelf to the Queen, he ſaid aloud to her the moſt tender things imaginable, which ſhe anſwered only

with

with complaints at his boldneſs, and perhaps (ſays the Lady) without being very angry, ſhe ordered him ſeverely to riſe and be gone. He did ſo, and having ſeen her the next day in preſence of all the Court, he went away fully reſolved to return into France as ſoon as poſſible, and the two Queens returned to Fountainbleau.

" All matters relating to Buckingham were told King Lewis to his Queen's diſadvantage, ſo that ſome of her domeſtics were turned off; Putange, her Gentleman-uſher, was baniſhed, and Datal, La Porte, and the Queen's phyſician were ſerved in the ſame manner.

" The Queen of England (continues Madam de Motteville) has ſince related to me, that quickly after her marriage with King Charles the Firſt, ſhe had ſome diſlike to the King her huſband, and that Buckingham fomented it, that Gentleman ſaying to her face, that he would ſet her and her huſband at variance if he could He ſucceeded in it, and the Queen in her affliction was deſirous of returning into France, to ſee the Queen her mother; and as ſhe knew the paſſionate deſire which the Duke had of ſeeing once more the young Queen of France, ſhe ſpoke to him of her deſign, he embraced it with eagerneſs, and he ſerved her powerfully in obtaining leave from the King her huſband to execute it. The Queen of England wrote about it to the Queen her mother, deſiring leave to bring the Duke of Buckingham with her, without whom ſhe could not undertake that voyage. She was refuſed both by the Queen her mother, and by the King her brother, her deſign coming to nothing by reaſon of that of the Duke of Buckingham, which was not to be wondered at conſidering the noiſe which his intrigue with the young Queen had made, which could not but be an invincible obſtacle to his being ſuffered to come again into France

" This gentleman, (ſays the Lady) who, according to the deſcriptions I have heard of him, had as much vanity as ambition, raiſed a diviſion betwixt the two crowns, that he might have an occaſion of returning

turning into France; by the necessity there would be for a treaty of peace, when he had satisfied his desire of acquiring a great reputation, by his victories over the French nation. On this foundation, he came at the head of a powerful navy, to succour those of Rochelle, who were besieged by Lewis XIII. expressing publicly his passion for the Queen of France, which he gloried in. but this ostentation of his was at last punished by an unfortunate success, and by the shame of having been disappointed in all his projects. Madam de Chevreuse, who zealously seconded his inclinations, and who loved the Earl of Holland, a friend of the Duke of Buckingham's, being at that time returned from England, saw with some satisfaction the Duke of Buckingham's fleet, and his return into France, which, at first, was accompanied with a great reputation; and she never ceased to speak of it to the Queen. The mistress and her favourite hated Cardinal Richelieu, because he was a creature of the Queen-mother's, who had placed him in the Ministry Nothing, therefore, was more pleasing to them than to vex him, the Queen, besides, being persuaded that he did her ill offices with the King, so that she made no scruple of hearing with pleasure the wishes which her favourite made for the prosperity of the English. She herself has often told me this, wondering at the errors which she was then led into by her gaiety of temper, and the folly of her unexperienced youth, which was yet unacquainted with the extensiveness of the duties enjoined to women, by reason, virtue, and justice."

Madam de Motteville, continuing to speak upon this subject, says a great deal in justification of the Queen, and yet I do not find by the sequel of the Lady's Memoirs, that she became afterwards much better acquainted with these duties, at least so far as to the year 1644 This will appear by the following account, taken likewise out of her Memoirs

" During the Queen's stay at Ruel, in 1644, (says the Lady) as she was taking a turn in the garden in a chariot, she saw Voiture walking there, seeming to be intent

intent on ſomething He was a man of wit, and by the agreeableneſs of his converſation he was become the darling of the beſt aſſemblies of Ladies who made it their buſineſs to keep viſiting-days The Queen, to oblige the Princeſs of Condé, who ſat by her, and who loved Voiture, aſked him what his thoughts were employed upon. In anſwer to the Queen's queſtion, Voiture made ſome extempore verſes, which were both pleaſant and bold. The Queen was not offended at his raillery, and ſhe thought them ſo pretty, that ſhe kept them in her cloſet a long while She has ſince done me the honour to give them me, and by what I have already ſaid of her, it will be eaſy to find out the meaning of them

Je penſois que la deſtinée,
Après tant d' injuſtes malheurs,
Vous a juſtement couronnee,
De gloire, d'eclat & d' honneurs.
Mais que vous eſtiez plus heureuſe,
Loiſque vous eſtiez autre fois,
Je ne veux pas dire amoureuſe,
La rime le veut toutefois,

Je penſois que ce pauvre amour,
Qui toujouis vous prêta ſes armes,
Eſt banni loin de vôtre cour,
Sans ſes traits, ſon arc, & ſes charmes:
Et ce que je puis profiter,
En paſſant près de vous ma vie,
Si vous pouvez ſi mal traiter
Ceux qui vous ont ſi bien ſervie.

Je penſois, car nous autres poetes,
Nous penſons extravagamment,
Ce que dans l' humeur ou vous êtes,
Vous feriez ſi dans ce moment,
Vous aviſiez en cette place
Venir le Duc de Buckingham,
Et lequel ſeroit en diſgrace
De lui ou du Pere Vincent.

As

As I dare not pretend to translate these lines into English verse, I shall only give the English reader the true sense of them.

"I was thinking, that after so many undeserved *misfortunes, fate has, at last, deservedly* crowned you with glory, splendor, and honours; but that you were formerly happier, when you were———I will not say, in love; though the rhyme will have it so.

"I was thinking, that the poor god of love, who was always ready to serve you, is banished your court, after being stripped of his bow and arrows, as well as his charms, and I was thinking what advantage I may expect, by spending my days with you; if you can resolve upon treating those so ill, who have so faithfully served you.

"I was thinking (for we poets are apt to think extravagantly) what you would do, if in the humour you are now in, you saw the Duke of Buckingham advancing towards you; and which of the two would be out of favour with you, either he, or father Vincent *."

I have, perhaps, dwelt too long upon these passages which I have extracted out of Madam de Motteville's Memoirs; but besides the reason I have alledged for speaking of them, I have been likewise induced to do it, because they serve to confirm and explain something said by the Lord Clarendon, in the account he gives of the Duke of Buckingham, which seems but darkly expressed

Having met in that Lady's Memoirs with some original pieces, which are but just mentioned in the Cardinal de Retz Memoirs, and which, in my opinion, are very well worth reading I thought it better to insert them at length here, than to fill up this fourth volume with some other things, which the French bookseller has made up his with. These pieces are,

* Vincent de Paul, mentioned in the preface, who had been Preceptor to the Cardinal de Retz, and who was, at that time, Almoner to the Queen-Regent.

1. The

1 The King of France's Anſwer to the deputies ſent by the Parliament of Paris, in relation to their giving audience to an Envoy ſent to them from the Arch-duke of Auſtria

2 A Declaration in writing, by the King's Order, to the Deputies of Parliament of Paris, &c.

3 A Declaration of the Duke of Orleans, ſent to the Parliament, for the Juſtification of the Conduct of the Prince of Condé

4 The Prince of Condé's Anſwer to the King's Declaration againſt him.

Beſides theſe four pieces which are genuine, I find in theſe Memoirs ſome pretended Articles of Agreement between Cardinal Mazarin, the Lord Keeper Chateau-neuf, the Coadjutor of Paris, and the Ducheſs de Chevreuſe, which are there ſaid to have been found upon the road going to Cologn, in a pacquet carried by an expreſs belonging to the Marquis de Noirmoutier, Governor of Charleville These pretended articles having been ſecretly handed about at Paris, were in the beginning of September, 1651, printed, and diſperſed there, by order of the Princes. and though they appear to me to be ſpurious, I have thought fit, however, to inſert them likewiſe in this volume.

The King's ANSWER to the DEPUTIES, sent by the Parliament of PARIS, in Relation to their giving audience to an Envoy sent to them from the Archduke of AUSTRIA.

THE King being in council, by the advice of the Queen regent his mother, there present, together with his Royal Highness the duke of Orleans, his Highness the Prince of Condé, and other persons of note of his Majesty's said Council, upon consideration of what has been represented to him by the deputies of the company pretending to hold the court of Parliament of Paris, hath ordered the following answer to be delivered to them

His Majesty might, with a great deal of reason, have refused admittance to the said deputies, having every day new occasions of being more incensed at their conduct, and at that of their company, chiefly, in respect to what they have now given him an account of, and of which his Majesty was before informed. their having given admittance to an Envoy sent from the enemies of the state

His Majesty is, besides, very well informed of the journeys taken from Paris to Brussels, and from Brussels *to Paris*; and *of the occasion of the* coming of St Ibal, and Sauvetat, (the first of whom is with the Duke de Longueville, and the second a prisoner here) after their having had interviews with the Duchess de Chevreuse, and with the Ministers of Spain.

His Majesty knows, that Laigues, who was sent to Brussels by some private persons that have conspired the ruin of the state, as far as their malice was able to effect it, was the man who solicited and persuaded the Archduke, and the Count de Pigneranda, by whose advise he is governed, to send a person on purpose to the said company with a blank letter, which was to be filled up at Paris by the very man who had sent Laigues, with such credentials as the present state of affairs should require the said Laigues not being satisfied with assuring the Spanish Ministers, that they would

would draw great advantages from it for the benefit of the King their master, but even having assured them (a thing horrible to say) that those measures would occasion a total confusion in France, if they knew how to make the proper use of that opportunity, by such means as he should suggest to them.

As those who gave Laigues these instructions, without the knowledge, and contrary to the intentions of the said company, are the same people, who, before the King's leaving Paris, kept up a correspondence with the enemies of the state, for seizing his Majesty's person, as they are the same who were then labouring to excite seditions in Paris; the same, who had their several shares both within and without the city, in treating with Princes who are since come into their party, the same, who, (after the accommodation made at this place, in the month of October last, by the declaration which his Majesty caused to be dispatched for that purpose, and which seemed to have cut off for ever all roots of division) finding that the enemies would, perhaps, resolve upon making peace, after having lost all manner of hope of seeing troubles arise within the kingdom, immediately gave them notice, that they should not be concerned at that accommodation, for that they would play their part so well, that before six weeks were at an end, the Parliament would stir afresh, and cut out more work for the Queen than ever; and even assuring them, that their party would then be strengthened by the uniting to them divers Princes and other persons of quality As these are the same persons who, to the great affliction of all good men, have had credit enough with that company, to induce it to take so many extraordinary steps since the King's leaving Paris, there is no reason to be surprised, that these people have had the power to get the Parliament to exercise such an act of Sovereignty, as the receiving an Envoy from a foreign Prince, and, what is more, from a Prince who is an enemy to this state, at the time that they had but just refused to hear those who were sent to them from the King, their master, and their sovereign.

The Sieur de l'Isle, Lieutenant of his Majesty's life guards, who was going from his Majesty to the said company, was refused admittance, under pretence of their forms and yet they find it consistent with these forms to receive the Envoy of the Archduke, who is armed against the King, though no precedent for it appears in their registers, or even in those of the Parliament of the League

The company refuses entrance into Paris to a herald sent on the behalf of the King, taking for their pretext, that those of whom it is composed not being Sovereigns, they had, by admitting him, been wanting to the respect which they owe his Majesty but they forget that they are subjects and take upon them to act like Sovereigns; when the matter in question is, the receiving an Ambassador from the enemies of the state, who is a monk, Almoner to the Count de Garcies, Governor of Cambray, who had long held correspondence in Paris, and who gave and received advices, to and from thence every week, having resided there a long time since the death of the late King, and managed several intrigues extremely prejudicial to his Majesty's service, with some Spanish prisoners of war, which obliged his Majesty to take the resolution of arresting him, which his flight prevented the effect of

It is easy to perceive that his credentials were made at Paris, by the very people who sent for him thither, otherwise the artifice of the Spanish Ministers would have been too palpable, in making the Envoy say to the said company, that every thing has been offered those Ministers to conclude a peace speedily, provided they would assist the King with the Spanish forces, to oppress the company and ruin Paris at the same time, that the Count de Pigneranda, writing to this court, on the 12th of February, complains, that nothing precise or particular has been made known to him, by the return of the Sieur Friquet, concerning the interests of the King his master, and those of the Duke de Lorrain, and that, by the same letter, the said Count desires, that an express should

be

be dispatched to him, with some better information concerning the King's intentions which evidently shews, that he has not received such advantageous offers for a peace, and that he does not refuse to treat of it here, as judging it neither safe nor honest, as the monk has falsly suggested to the company And in reality, since that letter, his Majesty has chosen the Sieur de Vautorte, a Counsellor of State, to go to Brussels, where he is now negotiating, having met with a safe conduct from the Archduke at Cambray, that he may go thither in safety

His Majesty, who is willing to give the said company all the information that he is able, to keep them from being imposed on by that artifice, has been graciously pleased to order, that the originals of the said letters of the Count de Pigneranda shall be shewed the said Deputies, wherein they will also see how that Count was preparing to come this way to confer with the King's Ministers, and put the last hand to the treaty of peace: and he would already be in France, if the hopes he has conceived, of drawing greater advantages from these divisions, and the instances which have been made to him at Brussels, by those who there sollicited the Archduke to send to the said company, had not obliged him to seek out pretences for deferring his journey They may also observe in the said letters, that what the Envoy says, as from his Catholic Majesty, is manifestly suppositititious, since it was impossible for his Majesty to give orders concerning affairs of which he had, as yet, no knowledge.

All these, and many other circumstances here omitted, seemed to oblige his Majesty not to admit the Deputies; but considering that there are in the said company a number of good Frenchmen, well-affected to the state, and whose hearts bleed to see at every moment such practices, as the greatest malice could with pain conceive, his Majesty has been willing to act like a good father of a family, who, however great his children's faults may be, is never weary of lending them a helping hand, to endeavour to bring them back into the right way, and hath resolved to give them this further mark of his goodneſs, at the time that he has the greateſt reaſon to be offended Thus all France will ſee, that his Majeſty has not left untried any way to bring the company back to their duty, and to oblige them to put an end to the miſeries of Paris, and to prevent thoſe with which the kingdom is threatened by its enemies, foreign and domeſtic. And at all events, if their hearts ſhould be ſtill ſo hardened, as not to pay the King that obedience which is due to him, they only would be anſwerable before God, before his Majeſty, before the Royal Family, and before all orders and conditions of men in the realm, for the evils which will neceſſarily enſue.

As to what concerns the peace, the conſtant pretence of thoſe who are the moſt afraid of it, and who are the moſt deſirous to bring things to confuſion; there is no one, ever ſo little verſed in affairs, who is ignorant, that as the imperialiſts have been obliged to conſent to that of Germany, which has been concluded with ſo much glory and advantage to this crown; and in which it has had occaſion to ſhew its moderation, by reſtoring a great number of important places, and ſome entire ſtates. the Spaniards had been alſo forced to come to an accommodation, if the conduct of ſome factious people had not made them conceive ſuch great hopes of theſe diviſions and commotions in the kingdom, that they thought it proper to wait for the event, in order to turn them to their advantage.

For as to the offer which was made by the monk, as from the Archduke, to make the ſaid company the umpire of that great affair; ſuppoſing this propoſal to be as ſincere, as reaſon and probability ſhew it to be otherwiſe, it is not an honour which the Spaniards do them, but an injury and affront to their whole body

France has often offered the Spaniards to ſubmit all the undecided points which remain in conteſt between them, to the arbitration and deciſion, either of the United Provinces, with the Prince of Orange; or of

I the

the ſaid Prince of Orange, calling to him ſome of the Miniſters of the States, or of the Queen of Sweden, or of the Princes or States of the Empire, jointly or ſeverally, as they ſhould like beſt, which they have conſtantly refuſed. and they now addreſs themſelves to the ſaid company, to refer themſelves to their judgment, for the determination of the greateſt intereſts depending betwixt the two crowns.

Would it not be a ſtain to the company, that being entirely compoſed of Frenchmen, the King of Spain ſhould judge them more inclined in his favour, and ſhould promiſe himſelf a better treatment from, them, than from the Queen herſelf, who is his ſiſter; or from ſo many foreign Princes and Potentates, with whom the crown of Spain is in peace, and even in alliance?

The Spaniards have ſhewn, by their conduct at all times, that they wiſh for nothing ſo much as the diminution of his Majeſty's power, grandeur, and authority: and yet they have recourſe to the Parliament preferably to all others, and declare, that they chuſe that company for the umpire of all their diſputes. Can they more ſenſibly wound good Frenchmen and Officers of the crown, than to think them capable of being, under a ſpecious pretence, proper inſtruments for the abaſement of their King, and the weakening their monarchy, which is the Spaniards principal aim in all their actions?

Thoſe who drew up the monk's inſtuctions, reaſoned very ill, not to perceive that they made him pull down with one hand what he was building up with the other The Spaniards, ſays he, are paſſionately deſirous of peace, and for a proof of it, they are willing to ſubmit to the judgment of the ſaid company, but if that paſſion was true and ſincere, would they refuſe ſo many places, and entire provinces, which, they ſay, the King has offered them; to addreſs themſelves to others, from whom all that they can flatter themſelves with expecting, can be nothing but the promiſe of the ſame thing, without hope of the execution of that promise, since that can never depend but on the King's orders?

Can any one be simple enough to persuade himself, that they are willing to spare France? They will enter into it with their forces, and take advantage of all these commotions, as soon as they have the means of doing it, and as they see any way left open to do us harm; but the particular interest of the company will neither put them forwards, nor retard them a single instant. their resolution will depend merely upon the condition of their army; and if they do not do it, we shall be obliged for it only to the season of the year, to their incapacity, and to their fear of exposing their troops inconsiderately.

Could they injure the company in a higher manner, than by believing them easy to be imposed on, and altogether disposed to leave France a prey to its enemies, than by addressing themselves to that body, under the specious pretences of peace and assistance; when they have no other design than that of kindling a civil war within the kingdom, and of burying it in its own ruins?

Their affairs, on all sides, are in a worse condition still than they appear to be, and it is next to a certainty, that if these intestine disorders can be quickly appeased, as his Majesty contributes all that he can to that end, they will be quickly forced to come into such terms of peace as will be advantageous to this crown.

It is to this that his Majesty applies himself, and this he will continue to do, with all possible care, without omitting any of the means which may the soonest conduce to this great end.

But if, contrary to all appearance, the enemies refuse to come to a just and equitable accommodation, and continue obstinate in demanding unjust and exorbitant conditions, such as the Envoy supposes to have been offered them; in this case, as the strongest passion which the Queen has, and her principal view is the good of the State, and the greatness of the King her son; that she may one day give him such an account of her

her administration, as may be no occasion of reproach to her; her Majesty will not, indeed, be bold enough, though to the advantage of a brother, to dispose of what she finds a King in his minority possessed of, by virtue of a just war; and chiefly, seeing that Spain now holds several kingdoms, which France has formerly enjoyed under a just title. She will not make so ill an use of the blessings which God has so abundantly bestowed on this kingdom, as to abandon, in one day, to the Spaniards, the fruit of so many years labours, which have been all crowned with success, and what has cost his late Majesty so much pains, and so much care to his Royal Highness the Duke of Orleans, and his Highness the Prince of Condé, who have so freely exposed their lives to a thousand dangers, to maintain the conquests of the late King, and to augment them, as they have done, with abundance of important places, and a great extent of land; which both those Princes have declared they would never dare advise her Majesty to relinquish. Wherefore, in that case, her Majesty must think herself obliged to take the advice of the States General of the kingdom, who are already summoned, and who will shortly be assembled, about the resolution which it was proper for her Majesty to take; not doubting but that that will be the best, since it will be taken by the general consent of all orders and conditions of men in the kingdom.

As to the instances which the said deputies have made to his Majesty, when, at his leaving Paris, he removed the seat of the said company; it was with no design to punish them, either for their past excesses, or to touch either the persons or the goods of any of those of whom that body is composed: his Majesty's end was only to endeavour to remedy the disorders under which the State has laboured, by the continuance of their assemblies, to restore to them the liberty of voting, which was interrupted by continual threats, and by notes in writing which were scattered among the people, in order to render odious to them those who were willing to live within the bounds of moderation: to stifle the faction that was then springing up in Paris, and which hath since appeared so powerful; to re-establish the tranquillity of the city, and put it into such a condition, as that his Majesty might reside there in safety.

His Majesty had, since that, sent a herald to the said company, to assure them of the safety of the persons and estates of all those who should repair to him, without excepting any one. his Majesty again confirms that gracious offer to all those who shall come to him before the sixth of the next month.

And as to what concerns the Archduke's envoy, as it had been to be wished, for the honour of the company, that the advice of the seventy-two, who were against introducing him, and for sending him to the King, had prevailed, so the best answer, and that which his Majesty expects shall be made him, is to give him none, that his master may be made to understand, that if the company has been too easy in giving him audience, yet they are incapable of entering into any correspondence or negotiation with the enemies of the crown.

As to the instances which the said deputies make to his Majesty, to withdraw his troops from the neighbourhood of Paris, and that he would leave open the passage for the coming in of provisions; the performance of what they desire depends intirely on the company, and on the resolution which they will take, to repair to his Majesty, upon the assurances which he gives them.

This is what his Majesty expects from the fidelity which the deputies are come to assure him of, and, that the Company, by a ready obedience, will put an end to the sufferings of the city of Paris, and to the miseries of the distressed people, that tranquillity being once restored, may quickly produce the conclusion of the general peace, and the quiet of Christendom.

Done at the King's council of state, held at St. Germains en Laye, the 25th day of February, 1649.

Signed, DE GUENEGAUD.

A DECLARATION in writing, which, by Order of the King and the Queen-regent, was read in their Presence, and in the Presence of his Royal Highness the Duke of ORLEANS, and of the Princes, Dukes, Peers, Officers of the Crown, and great Men of the Kingdom, to the Deputies of the Parliament, Chamber of Accounts, Court of Aids, and Town-house of PARIS, in relation to their Majesty's Resolution of keeping Cardinal MAZARIN for ever removed out of the Kingdom, and likewise in Relation to the present Conduct of his Highness the Prince of CONDE.

The 17th of August, 1651.

IT is with the utmost concern, that after all the declarations which we have heretofore made in so solemn a manner against the return of Cardinal Mazarin, we see that the enemies of the public quiet are still making use of that pretence to foment the divisions which they have kindled in the state. This is the reason which has obliged us to send for you, to declare again to you, that our will and intention is to exclude, for ever, the said Cardinal, not only from our councils, but from our kingdom, and the countries and places under our obedience and protection, forbidding all our subjects to hold any correspondence with him; expresly declaring, that all persons who shall act contrary to this our will, shall incur the punishments directed by the ancient ordinances of the Kings our predecessors, and by the late arrests of our sovereign courts; and ordering all necessary declarations for that purpose to be dispatched.

After having given these assurances to all our subjects, we can no longer, without wounding our authority, be silent about what is now acting. Every one knows the favours which the House of Condé, and this Prince of Condé in particular, have received, from the late King our most honoured Father of glorious memory, and from the Queen regent our most honoured Lady and Mother. After having granted the Prince of Condé his liberty, at the earnest desire of our most dear and intirely well-beloved uncle, the Duke of Orleans, and at the most humble request of the Parliament of Paris; after having restored him to the rank he used to bear in our council, and to the government of the provinces and places which both himself and those who belong to him hold in our kingdom in so great a number, that it is easy to judge that he that desired them, sought rather to make himself feared than beloved, after having re-established the troops raised in his name, which are sufficient to compose an army; after having given him leave to exchange his government of Burgundy for that of Guienne, with the liberty of keeping in his hands the places which he had in his first government, which was never practised before; after having caused payment to be made to him of the immense sums which he pretended to be due to him, for arrears of his pensions, allowances, and equivalents for the non-payment of his troops, both in the field and in garrison, upon the foot of his muster-rolls; which demands of his have been such, that to satisfy him, the funds appropriated to the maintenance of our own houshold, and for the subsistence of our armies, have been forced to be diverted; in fine, after having done every thing that might have satisfied him to the full, and inclined him to employ the good qualities which God has given him, and which he has formerly made use of for our service, we were in hopes that he would have acted accordingly, when, to our very great grief, we have found ourselves deceived in our expectation, by his acting in a manner very contrary to the protestations which he had solemnly made to us in the assembly of our Parliament

We shall say nothing of what the eagerness of his pursuits obliged us to do, immediately after he had recovered his liberty, in relation to the change which you have seen in our councils Having succeeded in that attempt, he became so bold as to complain of, and to accuse, three officers belonging to us, or to the Queen

our

our moſt honoured Lady and Mother, who thereupon commanded them to withdraw themſelves, not only from our Court, but from our good city of Paris, with a deſign thereby to take away from our ſaid couſin all pretences of complaint, and to ſtifle the tumults which *he was ſtirring up* We flattered ourſelves that all theſe favours would have inclined him to comply with us in ſomething, or would at leaſt have prevented him from continuing his evil deſigns, when, to our very great regret, we found effects quite contrary to thoſe which we had endeavoured, by our good uſage, to excite in him We have obſerved, that after our moſt dear and intirely well beloved uncle, the Duke of Orleans, had been the bearer, both to him and our Parliament, of our royal word, whereby we offered him all manner of ſureties which he required or could have deſired, he yet continued ſome days without taking the reſolution to ſee us, though he once met us as we were riding along *; at laſt being preſſed by our moſt dear and intirely well beloved uncle the Duke of Orleans, and by our Parliament, to pay us that duty and reſpect which is due to us, he reſolved upon ſeeing us, for once only, on which occaſion he was received both by us and by the Queen regent, our moſt honoured Lady and Mother, with all the demonſtrations of ſuch a perfect good-will as might have been ſufficient to cure him of all his apprehenſions, if thoſe apprehenſions did not rather proceed from his own conſcience, than from the ill offices which he is willing to believe have been done him

We are obliged to acquaint you with what is come to our knowledge in reſpect to his practices, as well within as without our kingdom. To begin with things that are public, every one has ſeen that our ſaid couſin has for theſe two months abſented himſelf from our councils, that he has ſpoken ill of them at the Parliament and *every where elſe*, alledging that he could not confide in us, nor in thoſe who approach our perſon; that he hath written letters to all our Parliaments, and

* At the Court.

to some of our good cities, to misrepresent to them our intentions, that at the same time he hath engaged in all our provinces, many gentlemen and soldiers to take up arms, as soon as they should be required in his name to do it. He hath likewise caused evil reports of our intentions to be spread in our good city of Paris, whose motions all other cities follow We have likewise learnt that he is reinforcing the garrisons of the places which we have intrusted to him, that he is furnishing them with all necessary things, and setting people at work, without our order, to fortify them with all diligence, making use for that purpose of our subjects, and forcing them to abandon their harvest. He has caused our two cousins, his wife and sister, to retire into the strong castle of Mouron. He hath gathered together from all parts considerable sums of money In short, he publicly practises all that may give us room to believe his evil intentions We have been confirmed in our belief by certain advices, which we have received from divers parts, of the intelligences which he is forming with our enemies, as well at Brussels with the Archduke, as in the camp with the Count de Fuensaldagre, causing expresses to be guarded to the very gates of Cambray, by some horse taken out of the troops which pay obedience to none but him These practices being carried on without our knowledge, without any passes from us, and against our will, who can doubt of his intelligence with those, against whom we are in open war? He hath likewise refused to cause the Spaniards to withdraw out of the town of Stenay, as he had engaged to do, it being the only article that was required of him when he was released out of prison He is the cause, by his conduct, that Don Estevan de Gamarre is come near the Maeze with his army, that he has supplied Mouzon with provisions, and has preserved in his hands the passage of Dan, which enables him to lay under contribution part of Champaign, and whereby he has furnished our enemies with better means of making attempts against us, and of putting a stop to the progress which our army, more powerful than theirs, might make in the Low Countries. By an attempt

tempt unheard of before in our kingdom, those who commanded the Prince's troops, notwithstanding the express orders which were given them, have constantly refused to obey the commands they have received from us, to join their forces to the body of troops which they were designed for, both by us, and by our uncle the Duke of Orleans, this hath hitherto overthrown all our designs, as well by reason of the just diffidence we have had of those of our cousin, as because he has given time to the enemies to discover them, and to put themselves in a condition to oppose our forces, the courage of our enemies being besides increased, by the hopes, or rather certainties, which he hath given them of some commotions within our kingdom.

We cannot forbear mentioning all the desolations, which the forces under our said cousin's command have committed, and continue to commit, whilst they are maintaining themselves in Picardy and Champaign, which provinces they make an end of ruining, instead of entering into the enemies country to wage war with them. The liberty which his troops take in pillaging our subjects, is likewise the cause that many of our soldiers desert our camp to go and join him.

We have been willing to impart all these things to you, although the greatest part of them was already known. We believe that you will judge by these public deportments of our said cousin, that his secret practices are not less dangerous. The knowledge we have of them will no longer suffer us to dissemble, without abandoning the helm of this state which God hath put into our hands, and which we are resolved to hold firmly. We know that if we do not apply a speedy remedy to the confusion which he will throw our state into, we shall not be able to oblige our enemies to hearken to the peace which we are desirous to conclude, nor to reform the abuses which have crept into our kingdom, which is agitated with so many designs and enterprizes, if we do not prevent or stop their course, as we are resolved to do, by all the means which God has put into our hands, upon the assurances which we have,

and

and which you haved always expressed, of your loyalty and affection in maintaining our authority, in keeping our subjects in the obedience they owe to us, and in continuing, as we assure you we will ourselves, to do all that lies in your power, to pursue our good intentions for the welfare and tranquillity of our kingdom.

Given at Paris,
the 17th of August, 1651.

Signed LEWIS,

and countersigned,

DE GUNEGAUD.

A. DE.

A DECLARATION sent by the Duke of ORLEANS to the Parliament for the Justification of the Conduct of the Prince of CONDE.

WE Gaston, son of France, uncle to the King, do declare that it is only since Wednesday last at seven at night, that we have been informed by Mr de Brienne, of the Queen's resolution of sending for the Sovereign Courts of judicature, and for the Officers of the Town-house, to declare to them that she had no thoughts of recalling Cardinal Mazarin, and that she would cause all the declarations necessary for that purpose to be drawn up, and likewise to inform them of her sentiments in relation to the Prince of Condé's not having been at the Palais Royal since our carrying him thither.

The next day, which was Thursday, when we came to the Palais Royal about eleven in the morning, the Queen caused a declaration to be read, of which we had had no communication before, and in which we found many things which we did not approve of, chiefly in what relates to the Prince's intelligence with Spain, for which reason we thought it unfit to be read, but the queen would absolutely have it read, saying that it was necessary for her discharging herself of her Regency, the King's Majority happening in twenty-two days time.

We likewise declare, that the Prince hath proposed to the Queen in our presence, and hath since done the like at the Council-board after the return of the Marquis de Sillery from Brussels, to which place he had been sent by his Majesty, two ways for the evacuating Stenay; one of which was a negotiation, the Spaniards having offered to the said Marquis de Sillery to evacuate that place, provided the king would agree to a suspension of arms, and that they should be allowed to keep possession of the places in the county of Luxem-

Luxembourg during the rest of the campaign. Which first way the Queen having absolutely rejected, the Prince gave us to understand, that with two hundred men which were in the citadel, he could not drive out five hundred that were in the town, and which might be recruited at every instant by the enemy's army, but that if her Majesty would give him but two thousand men, he would force the Spaniards to leave the town.

We likewise certify, that all the troops which go under the name of the Prince, and which have been designed by us for the army in Picardy, are there at this present time excepting the regiment of horse, and the company of light horse of Anguin; and as for the said regiment, as well as the other troops which were designed for the army in Champaign, we declare, that his highness the Prince not having judged those troops to be under the command of the Mareschal de la Ferté, because that gentleman is attached to Cardinal Mazarin, whom he hath guarded in his journies, and has received in the towns under his government since the arrests of the Parliament against him; his highness hath desired us to send a person belonging to us to command the said troops, assuring us that they should punctually obey the orders of such person. We accordingly named Mr. de Vallan to his Majesty for that employment, who being just upon the point of going, received a contrary order from his Majesty, which is the reason that the said troops have continued where they were, in expectation of the said Mr. de Vallan who was nominated to command them.

We further declare, that the jealousies and mistrusts of the Prince are not without foundation, as we have already acquainted the Parliament, having had information of several negotiations which have been carried on to his Highness's prejudice, so that since the time that we carried him to the Palais Royal, where he met but with a cold reception, we have not invited him to return thither.

We

We likewise certify, that we do not think the Prince capable of having ever entertained any ill designs against the service of the King, and the good of the kingdom

Given at Paris,
the 18th day of August, 1651.

Signed GASTON,

and countersigned

DE FREMONT.

The Prince of CONDE's ANSWER to the King's DECLARATION against him.

Gentlemen,

IT is with the greatest regret, that after having so many times declared to your company and to the public, the sincerity of my intentions, justified by a conduct approved of by the whole kingdom, and which leaves me nothing to reproach myself with, I am yet obliged to explain myself to you concerning a declaration which I respect, because it bears the name of the King, but which is defamatory of my person and my actions. No one can think it strange, that with all the respect I owe his Majesty, who has been imposed upon by the artifices of my enemies, I should justify my reputation, considering besides that that declaration carries with it none of the marks which distinguish those writings whereby Kings usually disclose their thoughts to their subjects concerning Princes of my birth and quality.

It seems as if I were charged with making use of the name of Cardinal Mazarin as a pretence to foment the divisions which are said to be in the state All France knows that I had no hand in what was said or done against him, before my imprisonment, that he was proscribed before I was set at liberty; and that if I have since

since united in my sentiments, with all the Parliaments in the kingdom, and with the wishes of the whole people, it has only been, to maintain the quiet and tranquility of the state, which his return might have disturbed. And if the King's council had taken as much care as they ought to have done, to remove on that occasion the jealousies and distrusts, which so many journies taken to Cologne have given room to, the Parliament would not have been put to the trouble, in order to dissipate the fears which people had of his being restored, to ask for a declaration from the King that should confirm the arrests of the company, which declaration seems to have been shifted off, by means of the writing now delivered against me, but that writing not being in any of the usual forms ought in no manner to be regarded.

This would be sufficient to shew that I stand in no need of answering it, were it not that, as it has been read in the presence of your company, and of all the other Sovereign Courts, and even in the presence of the officers of the Town-house, and has afterwards been printed, it is fit that I should undeceive the public in respect to all the calumnies that are contained in it against me.

I am reproached with the favours conferred on my house by the late King, as if the Prince my father had merited no favours by his services. For as to the places of Stenay and Clermont, which have been given me since the Regency, as an equivalent for the post of Admiral held by the late Duke de Brezé my brother-in-law, and which I lost by his death, I think that I ought not to be envied them, considering what I have done for the state; neither do I think that the employments and government I hold ought to be envied me, since I could not have been deprived of them without injustice, the late Prince my father having been possessed of them.

I have publicly acknowledged that I owed my being freed from my imprisonment, to the goodness of their Majesties, to the Duke of Orleans's instances in that behalf, which he made with all the marks of affection that

that I could have expected from a Prince of his generous temper, and to the supplications of the Parliament, to whom I have returned my thanks for it. But I shall not think I act against gratitude, if I say that justice had a share in that action And the declaration of my innocence, which it hath pleased his Majesty to grant me, being a proof of the oppression I have suffered, it is strange that after an imprisonment that has lasted thirteen months, without any cause or foundation, the name of favour should given to the setting me at liberty.

It is said in the writing delivered against me, that I have been restored to the post I had in the King's Council, which having belonged to the late Prince my father, I am intitled to by my birth which right has been since confirmed to me by the will of the late King of glorious memory, and since by your arrest in the time of the Regency. And I think it cannot be called a favour to let me enjoy the right which I have as Prince of the blood, and of which, no more than of my governments and towns, I cannot be deprived without injustice. It is ridiculous for the new confidents of Cardinal Mazarin, who are in all likelihood the authors of the writing sent to this company against me, to publish that by the great number of towns, which, say they, I have in my possession (although I have only Stenay and Clermont, besides those that were before in my family) I have affected to make myself rather feared than beloved, since not one complaint has ever been made of any violence committed by those who commanded in the said towns. And I should not now be put to the trouble of excusing myself in respect to the hatred which I am reproached with, if I had not in some measure sacrificed my interest and glory. to the obedience which I thought I owed the King, and of which however use is made at present to discredit me. I leave it to the Parliament to judge, whether these new friends of Cardinal Mazarin's ought to reproach me with the number of my governments, considering that the Cardinal, under the name of his servants, is in possession of Pignerol

in

in Italy; of Salses, Perpignan, and Rose, in Roussillon; of Brest, Dunkirk, Mardyke, Bergues, Dourlens, Bapaume, la Bassée, Ipres, and Courtray; besides Portolongone and Piombino, which he has since lost, without reckoning an infinite number of other towns, of which the Governours are his dependants By this it is easy enough to know, whether other things besides words are not necessary to secure the removing out of the kingdom a man who has so many doors to return into it, and one whose chief policy is known to be, by too fatal an experience to France, the making himself feared

The King is made to say in the writing sent to this company against me, that he has again set on foot the troops which were and are still under my name, and which are numerous enough to compose an army, as if those troops by the use they have been of, and the manner in which they have performed their duty, had not deserved that piece of justice, when it is notorious to all the kingdom, that the advantages which his Majesty has gained over his enemies are in a great measure due to their labours and fatigues, and as if his Majesty could have too many regiments like those that have on all occasions maintained the glory of his arms with a success that might have given peace to all Europe, if Cardinal Mazarin had not rendered their efforts useless by his ill and pernicious conduct. That Cardinal ought to have remembered that he has had belonging to him, two Italian regiments of foot, two regiments of German and Polish foot four regiments of horse of the same nation, besides his companies of Gens d'Arms, of light horse, and of guards, which by an unparalleled insolence he has had with him in the Palais Royal, without mentioning twenty other regiments which he had for the guard of his strong places, or under the name either of his domestics or of persons devoted to him He ought not to have caused his creatures to reproach me, as if I had troops enough to make up an army, since I never made use of those troops but for the service of his Majesty and the good of the kingdom, when on the contrary there is all the reason possible to fear, that he will make an ill use of his forces, and do by his arms, what he has already done by his intrigues, that is, disturb our quiet and tranquility.

I own that I have accepted of the government of Guienne, in the room of that of Burgundy, which the King has given to Mr d' Epernon; and I have done it upon the instances which were made me in the Queen's name, more out of a desire of restoring peace to that province, and of satisfying Mr d' Epernon by that agreement, than out of any other regard. I have even begged of her Majesty not to proceed in that matter; and one of the Ministers * that was present when I said those words, having asked me whether they came from my heart, and I having answered that they did, the Queen said that she would absolutely have me accept of that government, it being a thing necessary for the tranquillity of Guienne, and for the satisfaction of the Duke d' Epernon, who could not return into that province with any success in respect either to the King's service or to his own safety I think it strange that my condescension on that occasion should be made use of to calumniate me with the public

As for my keeping in my hands the towns in Burgundy which I have the command of under the King, it is because I have no place given me in Guienne, and that having bought the government of the towns in Burgundy, it would not be just to take them away from me, without giving me others in exchange; or without reimbursing me the sums which the late Prince my father paid to the late Duke de Bellegarde for them

As to the immense sums which are said to have been paid me for the arrears of my pensions, allowances, and equivalents for the non-payment of the troops under my name, and in my garrisons, upon the foot of the muster rolls, the person that has drawn this writing against me has not been furnished with good instruc-

* Chavigni.

tions,

tions, it being certain that I have received nothing but assignments payable in 1652 and 1653, out of the imposts laid for the years 1651 and 1652; and which consequently cannot have been the cause of the laying down the expences of his Majesty's tables, for the keeping up of which it is known what contests I have had with those of the Council, neither could it have been the occasion of a want of a fund for the subsistence of his Majesty's troops, which require to be paid immediately and regularly. and I can sincerely assure your company, that of all these assignments I have not received in money fifty thousand livres, and that what remains still due to me, ought for the most part to have been paid me before my imprisonment; which would indeed have been done, if the greatest part of the money had not been diverted, by order and for the use of Cardinal Mazarin, and of those who belong to him, as I can shew the company by the papers I have in my hand It is strange that I should be charged with being burthensome to the state, for having been paid in paper what I should have received in ready money, if I had not had more regard to the necessities of the state than to my own interest; chiefly when I have made it appear that I am indebted to my creditors above two millions of livres, for expences made for his Majesty's service. In this manner are my enemies willing to shift off upon me the disorders which the public revenues are in, as if that disorder did not proceed from the Cardinal's profuseness, and the innumerable sums issued out in ready money, which the Parliament may require an account of, that they may be satisfied for whose use they have been paid What is certain is, that none of that ready money is come to my hands for the discharge of what is due to me, and that the Queen is still indebted to me in the sum of two hundred and fifty thousand livres, which the late Princess my mother and I lent her at the time she wanted it most, and for which I have still her promissory notes in my hands

The unjust imprisonment under which I was detained for the space of thirteen months, prevented, to my my great ſorrow, my making uſe of the good qualities allowed me by the writing which has been ſent to this Company; and if the intentions of thoſe who drew up that writing tended as ſincerely to the good of the ſtate as mine do, there would quickly be an end of all thoſe diffidences, which prevent my acting as I could wiſh for his Majeſty's ſervice.

I have taken no ſteps in reſpect to the change which has been made in the council, and if thoſe who charge me with taking any ſuch ſteps, had ever ſo little conſidered the terms on which I have ſince been with the firſt preſident, and all that paſſed on that occaſion; they would hardly have been of opinion, that I had expreſſed any eagerneſs in demanding things to be ſettled in that manner; or that I had had any other ſhare in that change, except in oppoſing, jointly with his Royal Highneſs the Duke of Orleans, the propoſal made by Mr de Montreſor, and ſupported by the Coadjutor, to cauſe arms to be taken up in the city, to take away by force the ſeals from the Firſt Preſident, and to go directly to the Palais Royal, which propoſal was made in the preſence of the Duke de Beaufort, and of many perſons of quality, who may certify the truth of what I now ſay.

The ſteps which I have taken for the removal of Meſſieurs Servien, le Tellier, and Lionne, are nothing like continuing to attempt againſt the royal authority, ſince the Parliament have juſtified my conduct by their remonſtrances; as the public have likewiſe done by their approbation of a demand not only juſt, but neceſſary for eſtabliſhing the ſafety of all good people, and mine in particular.

If that removal had been executed, as the good of the kingdom required it, the deſire of all France had been accompliſhed by my ſubmiſſion to the Queen's will But having perceived, that at the ſame time that this ſatisfaction was ſeemingly given me, my diffidence was, in effect, renewed, by a continual correſpondence with Cardinal Mazarin, and with my greateſt enemies; I thought myſelf obliged to provide for my ſafety, without being wanting, however, to the respect I owe the King from which I shall never depart, whatever efforts those who design to disturb the state may use to excite me to a contrary conduct And if I have done myself the honour to wait on their Majesties but once, I protest to you, that I have for it all the sorrow that can be imagined in a Prince of my birth, who thinks himself extremely obliged to the King for the kindness he has ever expressed for me, and of which I should have endeavoured, by my submissiveness, to deserve the continuance, if my enemies, with a view of depriving me of this advantage, had not made it their study to fill me with new jealousies, by the expresses which are continually sent to the Cardinal, and by the new regulation which they are about making in the council, without my participation or consent, by placing there persons newly engaged in affection and interest with Cardinal Mazarin, since it is by his means they are to be admitted there this has, therefore, obliged me no more to hazard my liberty in the hands of those, who have no other rule to conduct themselves by than their ambition, and who have, consequently, give me just cause to be afraid of their counsels for which reason, I think fit to declare to you, that whenever those persons shall be admitted to the council-board without my consent, it will be impossible for me ever to confide in them, and that I shall not think myself safe there

I own, that the continuance of these distrusts has made me abstain from assisting at the King's council, though I have all along preserved, in respect to it, the same sentiments that his Royal Highness has expressed in that assembly, and the resolutions taken there would not have been exposed to public censure, if the Court had affected to render them as useful and glorious to the state, as they are *submissive to the will* of the Cardinal, whose advice, as every one knows, has hitherto always been expected before any resolutions were taken, either concerning the distribution of favours, or the general orders in respect to the government of the whole kingdom, as his Royal Highness

neſs has ſeveral times expreſſed. If I have written letters to the Parliaments of the kingdom, and to ſome towns, it has only been to give them an account of my conduct and actions, and to diſſipate the report that was ſpread, of my willingneſs to begin a civil war, my letters being occaſioned by thoſe which were written in the King's name throughout all the provinces, ſince my retiring to my houſe at St. Maur: and I wonder that my enemies ſhould, in the paper written againſt me, endeavour to repreſent as blameable and criminal, a proceeding which has been approved of as juſt and lawful by your company, to whom I owe the juſtification of my whole conduct on this occaſion, by the favourable reception you have given to my letters What is alledged, of my ordering extraordinary levies of men to be made, as well as my reinforcing the garriſons of the towns of which I am Governor, of my fortifying them a-new, and of my obliging the country people in the neighbourhood to work about them, is altogether againſt truth, it being certain, that *thoſe garriſons do not exceed the* number ſpecified in the eſtabliſhments of the army; and that I have received both orders and money from his Majeſty for the fortifying thoſe towns, and it were to be wiſhed, that all Governors of frontier places would follow my example in doing it

As to the retreat of my wife and ſiſter into my caſtle of Mouron, it being an effect of the obligations I am under to do my beſt for the preſervation of my family, which after ſo many juſt cauſes of diffidence, I have not thought fit to leave all expoſed in one place, none but thoſe who wiſh its ruin can find fault with my proceeding but if they were better informed, or leſs malicious, knowing that my ſiſter is in the convent of the Carmelite nuns at Bourges, and my wife in one of my houſes which had, even during my impriſonment, been allowed her for a retreat, they would not take hold of a conduct not only lawful, but altogether indifferent, to ſow diſtruſt among the public, neither would they give a malicious interpretation to my collecting my revenues for the payment of my debts, and the subsistence of my family

At the time of my being released out of prison, not a single article was required of me in relation to Stenay, and it will be easily judged that I entered into no such engagement, since it was out of my power to do it his Royal Highness the Duke of Orleans giving sufficiently to understand by his declaration, that I have not been wanting to what I owe, either to the King, or to my birth. for, after the return of the Marquis de Silleri, who was gone to Brussels by order of his Majesty, his Royal Highness having, in some measure, offered to cause the Spaniards to evacuate Stenay, by way of negotiation, provided he were promised that the King's forces should make no incursions between the town of Stenay and the country of Luxemburg; or else, that if I was furnished with two thousand men I should force them to retire, and the Queen having refused to accept these offers; it ought not to be laid to my charge, that the garrison of the citadel of Stenay, which is composed but of two hundred men, does not expel five hundred Spaniards that are in the town, and that may be recruited by the troops of the Archduke as often as he pleases

As to the pass of Dun, it is so inconsiderable that three hundred men will force the enemy to abandon it, and they would not be in a condition to preserve either that pass, or the town of Mouzon, and the other places which they took from us last year during my imprisonment, if the army had been employed as it might have been from the beginning of the campaign, and if that army had not been kept from the field, for some designs which time will shew to be extremely different from what is alledged in the writing against me.

As to the troops that go under my name, and their staying upon the frontiers, my conduct cannot be better justified than by his Royal Highness the Duke of Orleans, who declares, that I have, in that, done nothing but by his orders, and to prevent the wasting of thoſe forces, which may be very uſeful to his Majeſty; and the ruin of which would infallibly have followed their joining with other troops commanded by generals and officers entirely in the dependance of Cardinal Mazarin. And it is plain enough, that the clamour that is raiſed againſt the ſtaying of thoſe forces in France is only an artifice to diſcredit me, ſince nothing is ſaid of thoſe commanded by Meſſieurs de Turenne and de Vendôme, nor of the regiments of Chack, and of Mettencourt, which are quartered near the others, and which have no orders to join the army

The diſorders that are imputed to my ſaid troops are not peculiar to them, but are a general evil, againſt which the Parliament having provided by their arreſts, I have declared, and do ſtill declare, that I ſhall always take care that thoſe amongſt my troops that have committed faults, ſhall be puniſhed according to the rigour of the ordinances.

If I had not ſo openly declared againſt Cardinal Mazarin, by what I have expreſſed both among the public, and before this company, and by my oppoſing, as I have done, the going and coming of his expreſſes to and from Cologn, I ſhould not need to juſtify myſelf, in reſpect to the intrigues which it is ſaid that I manage both within and without the kingdom, and when it comes to be conſidered that Cambray is the place through which the expreſſes that are ſent to the Cardinal muſt paſs, as appears by the letter from the Mareſchal d' Hocquincourt, of which Metayer was the carrier, it will be hard to imagine that I have made uſe of the ſame road to have a communication with the Archduke, and that I have expoſed thirty men for guarding my pretended expreſſes, which men would have been ſo many witneſſes againſt me, which is ſo ridiculous that it does not deſerve an anſwer

I ſhall conclude at laſt what I am now ſaying, with what is moſt important in the writing againſt me, the charge of holding intelligence with the Spainards, which is a calumny falſly invented by my enemies I therefore require ſatisfaction for it, as the greateſt injury that can be done to my rank and dignity of Prince of the blood, and I beg of this company to interpose its authority for procuring me such satisfaction, and to beg of the King and Queen to name the authors of this calumny, and to send hither immediately those papers and advices which are said to be certain, as well concerning that intelligence as the listing soldiers in the kingdom, in an extraordinary manner, and for my private service, being willing to submit myself to your judgment, in case I have done any thing against my duty and the honour of my birth.

A R-

ARTICLES of AGREEMENT pretended to have been made between Cardinal MAZARIN, the Lord Keeper CHATEAUNEUF, the Coadjutor of Paris, and the Duchess DE CHEVREUSE, said to have been found upon the Road going to Cologn, in a Pacquet carried by an Express belonging to the Marquis DE NOIRMOUTIER, Governor of CHARLEVILLE; and secretly printed and dispersed in Paris by the Prince of CONDE's Orders, in the beginning of September, 1651.

THAT the Coadjutor, the better to preserve his credit with the people, shall be at liberty to speak in the Parliament and elsewhere against Cardinal Mazarin, till he meets with a favourable opportunity of declaring in his favour, without running any risk, and that in the mean while, Mr de Chateauneuf and Madam de Chevreuse shall appear as if they were on ill terms with the Coadjutor, that they may thereby have room to make a separate treaty with the Cardinal, and remain masters of the Queen's mind, preserving at the same time a power among the people by means of the Coadjutor

That Madam de Chevreuse, with the said Lord-keeper and Coadjutor, shall do their utmost to take off his Royal Highness the Duke of Orleans from the interest of the Prince of Condé; but without obliging him however to break entirely with him, knowing that it would be impossible for them to effect it, and that by their undertaking it they should lose their credit with his Royal Highness, to whom they durst not propose any thing directly tending to favour the Cardinal; being conscious as they are of his Royal Highness's affection for the people, and his aversion for Cardinal Mazarin, in whom he can put no trust after what is past It will be sufficient for the fulfilling their engagement, if they do what lies in their power to prevent his Royal Highneſs from puſhing the Cardinal too far

That Mr de Chateauneuf ſhall be firſt miniſter; that the only thing required of him, is the ſurrendering the ſeals for ſome time to the Firſt Preſident, who on his part ſhall yield him the precedency.

That the Marquis de la Vieuville ſhall be ſuperintendant of the finances, he paying the ſum of four hundred thouſand livres to the ſaid Cardinal Mazarin, and fifty odd thouſand livres to the Sieur Bertet who negotiated for him at Cologn, as a help towards buying him the place of Secretary of the Cabinet, which Bertet has leave to buy.

That the ſaid Cardinal Mazarin ſhall give Mr de Chateauneuf all the ſureties that are neceſſary for his being made Chancellor, if that poſt becomes vacant whilſt the ſeals are in other hands than his.

That the ſaid Cardinal ſhall procure all the neceſſary promiſes and diſpatches, for the King's nominating to the Cardinalſhip, and giving the poſt of Miniſter of State to the Coadjutor of Paris, which he is to be put in poſſeſſion of, immediately after the Aſſembly of the States of the kingdom is over, it not being convenient that it ſhould be done before, becauſe the ſaid Coadjutor will be the better able to ſerve the ſaid Cardinal effectually during that aſſembly, by not being known there for his profeſſed friend; and if it is propoſed in that aſſembly (as the Coadjutor hopes) to petition the King to call him into his councils, the ſaid Cardinal promiſes to procure him, at the entreaty of the States, the poſt of Miniſter, that thereby appearing indebted for it rather to the public than to the Cardinal, he may be the better able to ſerve him uſefully in that poſt. The ſaid Coadjutor promiſes likewiſe to uſe his intereſt in the aſſembly of the ſtates, for annulling the declaration which the Parliament put out againſt his advice, for the excluſion of French Cardinals from the King's councils. That the ſaid Cardinal Mazarin ſhall from henceforward procure to the Marquis de Noirmoutier, all honours and advantages granted to Dukes, as a conſequence of the patent of Duke

Duke which he has caused the Queen to grant him That the said Cardinal shall cause the sum of one hundred thousand livres to be paid to Mr de Laigues out of the money which Mr. de Nouveau is to pay for the place of Secretary of State; which the Cardinal has promised Laigues out of gratitude for the good offices in furnishing men of trust to be sent express to him for the negotiation set on foot between the said Cardinal, Madam de Chevreuse, and Mr. de Chateauneuf

That the said Cardinal shall give to Mr. de Mancini, his nephew, the Duchy of Nevers, or that of Rhetelois, with the government of Provence; and shall oblige him to marry Madamoiselle de Chevreuse, as soon as he shall be put into possession of the said duchy and government, and of an employment in the King's houshold, the said gentleman and lady promising to favour, with his Majesty, the Cardinal's return, and re establishment in his post.

That the said Cardinal shall hinder Mr de Beaufort from having any share in the King's or Queen's confidence, and shall come to no accommodation with him, but shall look on him as his enemy, as shall likewise the above named gentlemen and lady, because in forsaking them he has attached himself to the Prince; notwithstanding that he obtained the post of Admiral, at the solicitation of the said lady and gentleman, and by the power of the said Cardinal

That the said Cardinal shall support with the Queen, the said Mr Chateauneuf, and Coadjutor, as likewise Madam de Chevreuse, and shall place an entire confidence in them, in consideration of the promise which the said Mr. de Chateauneuf enters into with the said Cardinal, as well in his own name, as in the names of the Messieurs de Villeroi, d'Estrees, de Senneterre, and de Jars, that these last will be sureties for him that he shall be altogether attached to the said Cardinal's interest, and shall endeavour to procure his return whenever he has an opportunity of doing it, the said Mr. de Chateauneuf and Madam de Chevreuse promising the like in the name of the said Coadjutor, for which they bind themselves as sureties, the said

Coadjutor not signing the present treaty, for the reasons abovementioned, and being left at liberty to disown whatever may be said of him upon this account, in case the said Cardinal should insinuate or say that he had promised him any thing All these articles are agreed, upon condition that no mention shall be made of any thing that has passed before, during, or since the war of Paris; nor of any thing since the present accommodation and treaty has been set on foot, or since the imprisonment of the Princes, against whom the present union is chiefly made, the common interest of the said Cardinal Mazarin, Lord keeper Chateauneuf, Coadjutor, and Madam de Chevreuse, being founded on the ruin of the Prince of Condé, or at least upon his being removed from Court The said Cardinal likewise promises to hinder the Duke of Orleans from having any knowledge of the present treaty, or of the conferences or negotiations which the said Madam de Chevreuse, or Mr de Chateauneuf, have had, or may henceforwards have with the said Cardinal Mazarin.

ADVICE

ADVICE to the Cardinal MAZARIN concerning the Affairs of the Cardinal DE RETZ

My Lord,

YOU will doubt, perhaps, of my true intention in thus addressing myself to your Eminence, and of the occasion which obliges me to speak to you after a manner so little conformable to your conduct, and so contrary to the sentiments of all those that are about you. The apprehension which I am under, as well as many other persons, to see those troubles and divisions arise again in Paris, which have so long and so unfortunately disturbed the general quiet of all France, is the only true reason which made me despise all others, and which at last made me resolve to shew your Eminence the almost inevitable dangers, to which you expose the fortune of the state and your own, in giving way to a schism in the metropolis of the kingdom, the consequences of which cannot but be fatal; since all that we see in our history that bears any resemblance to it, presents to our view at the same time the image of the public desolation, which is the constant effect of the fury that is commonly raised in people's minds by a zeal for religion, for which all other regards of honour, life, and fortune are slighted and despised.

Do not imagine me, my Lord, to be one of the partisans of the Cardinal de Retz. I protest to your Eminence that I never had any share in his past concerns, and if I reflect on his conduct and on his great qualities, it is only from the fear I have that they may yet help him in his present designs, and contribute to the putting us once more into that deplorable condition which I apprehend for the public, for myself, and for my friends.

I do not pretend, my Lord, to examine the question nor all the reasons that have been written pro and con, about the deprivation of the Cardinal de Retz. I refer myself to the determination of your most intimate confidents, and to your own reflections. Neither will I put your Eminence in mind of the dictates of conscience and of the church, I know that these sort of reasons are of the least weight with politicians and Ministers of State. It suffices me to make it appear to your Eminence, that all the opposition which is formed in his Majesty's name to the return of the Cardinal de Retz to his Archbishoprick of Paris, is a manner of acting which puts arms into his hands, which will doubtless prove of the worst consequence to the kingdom, and to yourself in particular; and that on the contrary, by granting him, on this occasion, what cannot be justly denied him, you will take from him all manner of pretence, and you will avoid all the ill steps which a contrary conduct must necessarily occasion in the sequel of this affair: and lastly, that those who advise your Eminence to act in the manner which I am speaking against, are the same people who for their private interest have plunged your Eminence into all your former disgraces, and that they now, perhaps, seek to give in this juncture the last blow to your fortune, which they hope to be the successors of, and that they do it with the more advantage and security, because they do it under the pretences of advice, of succour, and of friendship.

I therefore beseech your Eminence to consider the present state of the kingdom, and the disposition of the people who constitute that great body. It may certainly be said that there is scarce one amongst them, but preserves some remains of that ill temper and that hatred to your ministry and person which appeared at the time of the siege of Paris, and if we now see, since the King's return to Paris, some appearance of quiet in people's minds, there is no one but very well knows, that the true cause of this seeming calm, which is rather a lethargy than a true sleep, is rather people's weariness of their past calamities, than their being satisfied with their present condition.

There have been very few campaigns these three or four last years, in which the public wishes have not been for the prosperity of the arms of the Prince of Condé. And indeed, who, that judges impartially, can

can but believe that all Frenchmen bear a ſecret grudge to a foreign miniſter, whom they ſee, contrary to their wiſhes and deſires, the tyrant of their lives and fortunes? Whilſt the Princes of the Blood bear no part in the adminiſtration; whilſt they are exiled, or obliged to ſeek for refuge with the enemies of the ſtate, and whilſt five or ſix raſcals, who abuſe the ſacred name of the King, are ſuffered with impunity to triumph at Paris over the ſpoils of the kingdom, laughing themſelves at the eaſineſs of the Miniſter who ſuffers them

I will not enlarge on all the occaſions of people's diſcontent. I will only ſay by the bye, that there is ſcarce a family in Paris that (beſides the general grievances) is not concerned by the baniſhment or the perſecution of ſome of their family The caſe being ſo, can your Eminence imagine, that that great city, whoſe motion governs that of the whole kingdom, can long keep their uneaſineſſes and troubles from diſcovering themſelves. and that the fire which now lies hidden under the aſhes will not at laſt break out into a fatal conflagration? What fairer occaſion can be given to the male contents, and what more reaſonable pretence can they have for their taking up arms, than the violence which is offered to their conſcience and their religion? This motive ſo ſtrongly affects mens minds, that the more they reſiſt it, the ſtronger impreſſion it makes. Who is there in Paris that can at this time doubt that the Cardinal de Retz is the true and lawful paſtor of that city? Can any ſcruple remain, after the public declarations of a Pope*, who is known by all people for ſo great a lover of juſtice and peace? The Pallium which his Holineſs has given the Cardinal de Retz, and the prohibitions given by his Nuncio to the Chapter to intermeddle in the ſpiritual juriſdiction of his dioceſe, are unanſwerable determinations I dare even to add, that on this occaſion, the people are not ſatisfied with paying a bare and ſimple obedience to the commands of the Holy See, but that they do it with joy, and that

* Alexander VII.

they are induced to it by the natural inclination they have for the Cardinal de Retz

All the libels which they see every day pasted up or published in the streets against the honour and the conduct of that Prelate, only shew them the more effectually the injustice of the violent proceedings which are used against his person and his dignity. And if it be true that the division betwixt the Prince of Condé and him suspended for a while the credit which he had in Paris; it is now certain, that the hatred and persecution of the Minister abundantly restores him to that first favour with the people, and strengthens him in the esteem which his great qualities and merit never suffered him to lose.

Paris being thus inclined, it may be said, my Lord, that there needs nothing but a blast contrary to the torrent of your good fortune to stop the course of it yet it seems to me that you are tired of it, and would willingly contribute to its destruction. What other effect can be produced by those arrests of the Council, so full of the encroachments of the secular jurisdiction on the ecclesiastical authority? To what intent are so many endeavours used to make the Chapter of Paris resume an authority which they had abandoned, and which they held only in the absence of their bishop, and under his sanction? Does your Eminence imagine that when you have compassed your designs against the prohibitions of the Pope's Nuncio, his Holiness will suffer that violent establishment, that he will not make use of all the thunderbolts of the church to vindicate his despised authority, and that he will not chuse to make examples of the criminal chiefs and first authors of this schism in the kingdom of Jesus Christ, so injurious to the honour of his Papacy? And should it be otherwise, will the censures, the interdictions, and other spiritual arms which are in the hands of the Cardinal de Retz, and which become necessary by your resisting them, fall upon Paris without effect? Will they not at least trouble the consciences of people, and perhaps produce one of those sudden and dangerous revolutions, which leave no no way of guarding one's ſelf from them, by remedies or means which one had foreſeen.

Your Eminence may poſſibly imagine, that length of time will bring the Cardinal de Retz to what you deſire of him, and that his want of neceſſary means to ſubſiſt will oblige him to yield to what you deſire of him But is there any likelihood, beſides the help of ſo many friends, and other perſons intereſted in his preſent fortune, and in his hopes of a better, that he will not receive from the new Pope the ſame aſſiſtance that he had from the late Pope Innocent the Tenth, as ſoon as he entered the city of Rome? And can your Eminence, who every day accuſes the Cardinal de Retz of holding intelligence with the enemies of the ſtate, imagine that if what you ſay is true, they cannot at leaſt ſupply him with a moderate annual ſubſiſtence, after having in his paſſage through their territories made him immenſe offers, which it was only through his own fault that he did not accept?

I imagine that your Eminence is every day told, that the continuance of the injuries done to, and the violent methods of proceeding uſed againſt the Cardinal de Retz, will at laſt give him ſome unquiet and impatient thoughts, which will oblige him to yield to your deſires, and that at worſt you will come off with leaving him, when you think fit, in the quiet poſſeſſion of his Archbiſhoprick, beyond which you know that he has no intereſts or pretenſions But can you believe, my Lord, that this man, of whoſe firmneſs and obſtinacy you have had ſo many marks on other occaſions, and whom you believe to be the moſt ambitious man in the kingdom, can be capable to yield up a title which neither impriſonment nor threats could ever get from him, but involuntarily and againſt his own inclination? Do you think that he will part with the only thing that makes him conſiderable, and throw away the only weapons which he has left againſt your perſecution, when he muſt run the riſk of ſeeing it renewed with more violence, when he ſhall no longer have the ſame help to reſort to as before? Beſides, can your Eminence imagine, that ſucceſs having once favoured in the leaſt the

the deſigns of the Cardinal de Retz, he will keep within the bounds in which they ſay he now contains himſelf, and that he will not take all advantages of the juncture of time to make uſe of againſt the man, whom he believes to be the author of his impriſonment and of his paſt diſgraces? There will even be ſome inſtants wherein the popular fury can no longer be reſtrained by any one; and God grant that the pretence of religion may not draw after it an infinite number of complaints and clamours, which the public and private diſcontents uſually produce on theſe occaſions.

If it is true then, my Lord, that the conduct which your Eminence follows cannot bring the Cardinal de Retz to what you deſire, if he is reſolved, as all thoſe of his party give out, not to part with his Archbiſhoprick but with his life; if he has given too many aſſurances of it to the public, and has tied his own hands on that occaſion, if it is alſo true, that the way which you take increaſes the ſtrength of the Cardinal de Retz, if it is impoſſible, how ſlow ſoever the Pope may be in giving his final reſolution, that he ſhould at laſt forbear coming to the laſt extremity, and if all the advantage you can pretend to, is the creating a ſchiſm which cannot but be pernicious to you; on what foundation can you ground the advice which is given you? and how can your Eminence find your account in adventuring to raiſe again in the kingdom the fire and the confuſion, which the pernicious advice of thoſe who are near your perſon had formerly cauſed there?

I ſay nothing to your Eminence but what is perfectly known to all thoſe of your party, and to thoſe who call themſelves your true friends and ſince they will not ſubmit to ſuch clear and apparent reaſons, your Eminence ought, I think, to judge better of their intereſts and their true intentions, and not ſubject yourſelf ſo much to thoſe petty tyrants of your miniſtry.

I mean thoſe who under pretence of ſerving you, uſed during your abſence to ſay every day to the Queen, that ſhe muſt not be intirely governed by you, that you were not deciſive nor bold enough, and many other ſayings which perhaps had ſome more ſecret end than

than that of your service, though they would have it imagined that they acted by no other motive. These are the same persons, who sometimes seeing themselves farther from the honour of your good graces than their competitors, whom they keep up divisions with, to your prejudice, get libels against your Eminence, which bear the name of the Prince or of the Cardinal de Retz, pasted up in public places, and afterwards make a merit of having them taken down publicly, and present them to your Eminence, as a proof of the diligence with which they exercise the employments which you have bestowed upon them of superintendants of all the spies in the kingdom. In the mean while, they regard much more their own interest than the safety of your Eminence's affairs, and as the division betwixt you and the Cardinal de Retz, is what they say touches you the most nearly, they keep no bounds on that occasion, not for your service, but to salve the appearances of serving you, caring little for the success, and carrying their hopes beyond your fortune, and forming still greater hopes from the secret engagements and the private cabals which they have entered into For this reason there are many amongst them who speak so indifferently of your Eminence, who refuse to acknowledge the favours and benefits which they have received at your hands, and who are insolent enough to think themselves the sole makers of their own good fortune

In fine, my Lord, these are the people who advised you to the siege of Paris, to the imprisonment of the Prince, and to that of the Cardinal de Retz These are they who would turn to their own advantage the retrenchment of the Town house rents, who invent a thousand new edicts, against which they themselves stir up the Parliament by the cabals which they have there, who oblige you to bring the King thither in a warlike habit, to do an action without example, and for which his Majesty must make some kind of satisfaction to his subjects. These are the people who make you treat with Cromwell in a manner so mean and injurious to the French nation; who advise you to lower

our

our flags before his ships, and who are willing to allow him the title of Protector of the Protestants of that kingdom. These are the persons who drew up that arrest of the Council, whereby the ten millions which it is pretended you have laid out for the service of the crown are adjudged to your Eminence, and lastly, these are the persons who flatter your Eminence with the marrying one of your nieces to his Majesty, and who would almost make us believe that you can be rash enough to mix your blood with that of the Gods, and to pretend to an alliance with our empire.

Certainly, my Lord, all these things, and an infinite number of others which it would be too long to recollect, are what have occasioned the general hatred and contempt which all Frenchmen bear you. Your pretended advisers endeavour to make you on this occasion also take an ill step; but I give you notice, that there is no retrieving your error, and that it has never been with impunity that arms have been put into the hands of the people of France on account of religion.

Consider also, that an accommodation with the Cardinal de Retz about his Archbishoprick cannot hurt you. Do you think that being peaceably in the enjoyment of his benefice, he will venture a second imprisonment by his returning to Paris? Do you fear that his title will give him some advantage over the place which you are possessed of, and can restore him, to your prejudice, to his Majesty's good graces? Do you fear that he will make use of the power which his character gives him, to embroil affairs at Paris? As if it was not certain that you would then have justice on your side, that you might oppose to the extraordinary orders of his Vicars-general, or to his own, all the authority of the secular arm, which in that case has but too much power, and too many ways to make use of, to curb those things which are against public order and tranquility. Whereas at present the resistance which is made against his indisputable title authorises all the orders which come from him, more and more incenses the Pope, and the people, who are always angered by the opposition

opposition which is given to things which they have wished for, and which they thought reasonable

Give therefore, my Lord, no longer an ear to the pernicious advices of those treacherous confidents. fear that the hand of God, which has miraculously saved you from so many precipices which they would have thrown you into, will at last prove an avengeful hand, and arm itself against you for the defence of its altars, and the protection of its ministry.

It signifies nothing to object to the Cardinal de Retz, the crimes and the revolts which you accuse him of. As those commotions were common to him with all the people of the kingdom, with the Parliaments and the other Sovereign Courts of the kingdom, your reproaching him with it turns rather to his honour and advantage than to his shame and confusion.

Take the advice which I give you, shew that your private resentments are less than your passion for the public good and if the evil counsels of those who surround you have drawn on the kingdom the war, and all past curses, let a wiser and more prudent conduct divert the second storm which it is threatened with, and which is likely to be more grievous than the first In fine, give no room, by despising the reasons which I represent to you, to the just complaints of all honest men, who would in the sequel look upon you as the author of the evils into which you had suffered France to be plunged, after you had had such particular notice given you of it

Forgive, my Lord, the liberty which I have taken to speak to you in this little discourse, in terms which may not be all of them pleasing to your Eminence. The necessity of the subject, and of representing to you the true state of affairs, has emboldened me to it, not doubting but that your Eminence will take well whatever is laid before you for the good of the state, and your particular advantage, especially when it comes from one who is, as I am, with respect,

My Lord,

Your Eminency's

Most humble, &c.

The ACCOUNT which the Lord CLARENDON gives of the Cardinal DE RETZ, in his History of the Rebellion Vol. vi. p 511, 512, of the OCTAVO Edition.

THERE was an accident fell out, that administered some argument to make those complaints appear more reasonable. The Cardinal de Retz had always expressed great civilities towards the King, and a desire to serve him , and upon some occasional conference between them, the Cardinal asked the King, " Whether he had made any attempt to draw any assistance from the Pope, and whether he thought, that nothing might be done that way to his advantage?" The King told him, " Nothing had been attempted that way, and that he was better able to judge, whether the Pope was like to do any thing for a man of his faith?" the Cardinal smiling, said, " He had no thought of speaking of his faith?" yet, in short, he spoke to him like a wise and honest man . " That if any overtures were made him of the change of his religion, he must tell his Majesty, it becomes him as a Cardinal to wish his Majesty a catholic, for the saving of his soul, but he must declare too, that if he did change his religion, he would never be restored to his kingdoms But he said he did believe, though the Pope was old and much decayed in his generosity (for Innocent X. was then living) that if some proper application was made to the Princes of Italy, and to the Pope himself, though there would not be gotten wherewithal to raise and maintain armies, there might be somewhat considerable obtained for his more pleasant support, wherever he should chuse to reside " He said, " He had himself some alliance with the Great Duke, and interest in other Courts, and in Rome itself, and if his Majesty would give him leave, and trust his discretion, he would write in such a manner in his own name to some of his friends, as should not be be of any prejudice to his Majesty, if it brought him no convenience." The King had reason to acknowledge the obligation, and to leave it to his own wisdom what he would do In the conclusion of the discourse, the Cardinal asked his Majesty a question or two of matter of fact, which he could not answer; but told him "He would give a punctual information of it the next day in a letter," which the Cardinal desired might be as soon as his Majesty thought fit, because he would, upon the receipt of it, make his dispatches into Italy. The particular things being out of the King's memory, as soon as he returned, he asked the Chancellor of the Exchequer concerning them; and having received a punctual account from him, his Majesty writ a letter the next day to the Cardinal, and gave him information as to those particulars. Within very few days after this, the Cardinal coming one day to the Louvre to see the Queen-mother, he was arrested by the Captain of the guard, and sent prisoner to the Bastile*; and in one of his pockets, which they searched, that letter the King had sent to him was found, and delivered to the Queen-regent; who presently imparted it to the Queen of England, and after they had made themselves merry with some improprieties in the French, (the King having, for the secrecy, not consulted with any body) they discovered some purpose of applying to the Pope, and to other catholic Princes; and that his Majesty should enter upon any such counsel, without first consulting with the Queen his mother, could proceed only from the instigation of the Chancellor of the Exchequer.

* This is a mistake, for the Cardinal was sent to the Castle of Vincennes.

Some

Some ACCOUNT of the Court of BRUSSELS, and of the Count DE FUENSALDAGNA, so often mentioned in the preceding Memoirs, taken from the Lord CLARENDON'S History, Vol v p 310, of the OCTAVO Edition.

THERE were two Spaniards, by whom all the councils there * were governed and conducted, and which the Archduke himself could not control, the Conde of Pignoranda (who was newly come from Munster, being a Plenipotentiary there, and stayed only at Brussels, in expectation of renewing the treaty again with France; but whilst he staid there, was in the highest trust of all the affairs) and the Conde of Fuensaldagna, who was the Governor of the arms, and commanded the army next under the Archduke, which was a subordination very little inferior to the being General. They were both very able and expert men in business, and if they were not very wise men, that nation had none. The former was a man of the robe, of a great wit, and much experience, proud, and if he had not been a little too pedantic, might very well be looked upon as a very extraordinary man, and was much improved by the excellent temper of le Brune (the other plenipotentiary) who was indeed a very wise man, and by seeming to defer in all things to Pignoranda, governed him The Conde of Fuensaldagna was of a much better temper, more industry, and more insinuation than Spaniards use to have. his greatest talent lay to civil business, yet he was the best General of that time to all other offices and purposes, than what were necessary in the hour of battle, when he was not so present and composed as at all other seasons.

* At Brussels.

A LET-

A LETTER from Mr. PATRU, Advocate at the Court of Parliament of PARIS, to the Cardinal DE RETZ, on his Return into FRANCE.

My Lord

MY ill ſtate of health not permitting me to wait on you, you will forgive me if I acquit myſelf by a letter, of the reſpect I owe your Eminence. I have learned from Mr Joui and from Mr Matharel, the honour you have done me to remember me it is a goodneſs in you for which I can never be ſufficiently thankful, and I ſhould be very unhappy if your Eminence could have entertained the thought, that upon this occaſion, a groundleſs reſentment had made me wanting to my duty I have no manner of ſhare in the requeſt which my friends, out of affection, made you in my behalf. Had they communicated their thoughts to me, I had certainly eaſed you of a great trouble, for I know what burden it is to a magnanimous ſoul, to be obliged to refuſe. my intereſt, if I am believed, ſhall never ſet any body at variance. I could wiſh to be rich, if it were only to give, but I diſlike all the ſteps that one muſt take to become ſo and beſides, at my age, that little time I yet may live is not worth troubling myſelf to provide for Wherefore, my Lord, Mr de —— is ſtill alive in reſpect to me, or at leaſt I look upon what has paſſed in the dividing his ſpoils, as ſome remains of the tempeſt of your fortune When I liſted myſelf in your ſervice, I had no regard to what I might expect from you. that courage which nothing can overcome, that goodneſs which can never be enough admired, all thoſe precious gifts which heaven has ſo happily endowed you with, made me entirely yours It is, my Lord, neither your purple, nor the ſplendor of the coronets of your family, it is ſomething greater, it is your perſon, it is your virtue that binds me to you, which bonds can never be broken but by the

loſs

loſs either of life or reaſon. I have therefore ſhared the joy which your Eminence has lately given all Paris, the whole Court, or rather the whole kingdom. In that unhappy retreat where the misfortune of my ears detained me, I have bleſſed an hundred and an hundred times the happy day that has entirely given you back to France, to your friends, to your ſervants; and your Eminence will do me juſtice, if you are perſuaded that amongſt the croud of perſons, who have had the honour of kiſſing your hands, no one is more truly or with greater reſpect than I,

My Lord,

Your Eminency's, &c.

A LET-

A LETTER from the Cardinal DE RETZ written the Day of his Escape out of the Castle of NANTES, to the Chapter of the Cathedral Church of PARIS.

Gentlemen,

THE condition which I have been in till this hour having obliged me to forbear expressing the just sense I have of my obligations to you, I make use of these first moments of my liberty, to assure you of my true sentiments. Since I had the happiness to be brought up amongst you, and that that was the first step by which I rose to the dignity of your Archbishop, which you have so generously laboured to preserve me in, even to the exposing yourselves to all kinds of dangers for my sake; I am resolved to live and die in that quality hoping, that as your affections will continually encrease, my thankfulness and gratitude will likewise be immortal. This I intreat you to believe, and to give me a part in your remembrance and in your prayers, which are earnestly wished for by,

Gentlemen,

Your most hearty and affection servant,

Signed The Cardinal DE RETZ.

From near Beaupreau,
8th Aug 1654.

Superscribed, To the Deans, Canons, and Chapter of the Church of Paris.

A LETTER from the Cardinal DE RETZ to the Curates of PARIS.

Gentlemen,

AS ſoon as I found myſelf in a place of ſafety, and at liberty to make known the ſentiments of my heart concerning the affection which you have univerſally expreſſed for my perſon, I would no longer defer returning you my juſt thanks, and giving you aſſurance that I ſhall, for the reſt of my days, be inſeparable from a clergy which henceforth ſhall ever be as dear to me as I have experienced it to be generous. My removal has been the effect of your ſteddineſs, and my liberty that of your prayers. I return you all poſſible acknowledgements for it, and in hopes that you will continue your good offices to me, I remain,

Gentlemen,

Your, &c.

Signed, The Cardinal DE RETZ.

From near Beaupreau,
the 8th Aug. 1654.

Superſcribed, To the Curates of PARIS.

MANI-

MANIFESTO of his Highneſs the Prince of CONDE, containing the true Reaſons of his leaving PARIS the 6th of July, 1651.

I DOUBT not but my leaving the city has given a great deal of trouble to thoſe who are not acquainted with my reaſons for haſtening my departure, even at a time when that departure could not but be neceſſarily followed by the ſurprize of the public, conſidering the general opinion that I am the firſt mover of all the ſtate machines, and that I have ſo powerful an influence over affairs, that they never take any other turn than that which I give them, guided ſolely by my own inclination

If thoſe who are of that opinion, found their judgment only on the great reputation which I have acquired on an infinite number of occaſions, where I have thought it the greateſt pleaſure to be laviſh of my blood, to cement with it the glory and the quiet of France; I muſt acknowledge that having had that happineſs in all my enterprizes, which have conſtantly ſucceeded, both to the ſatisfaction of my own juſt ambition, and to the advantage of the crown, for the defence of which I ſhall never be ſparing of my honour, my fortune, or my life, there is no one, truly zealous for the good of the Monarchy, that has not always ſubmitted to me, as to a perſon who having no other end than the intereſt of the ſtate, could not for that reaſon fail of juſtifying all the ſteps of thoſe who ſhould be willing to regulate them by the level of my conduct

And I can with truth proteſt to all France, that I never had any other enemies than thoſe who were enemies to that kingdom, and that I had never fallen into the misfortune which occaſioned, two years ago, injuſtice to triumph over my generoſity, if the diſturbers of the public quiet had not foreſeen that I ſhould never be weak enough to comply baſely with the deſign which they had formed to traverſe the quiet of the

 ſtate.

state, and that far from favouring them, I should be the first to countermine their ill practices, by invincible obstacles which my honour and dignity of first Prince of the blood would oblige me to form against them for the interest of the people

That hatred which seemed to have been fully satisfied by a cruel imprisonment of fourteen months, and which the exile of the Cardinal made me henceforwards look upon as incapable to hurt me, hath shewn me by clear indications, that it was only by force that it submitted to the enlargement of three Princes; and that the Cardinal's creatures, supported by the Sovereign authority, still kept it in their hearts, to let it break out upon the first occasion; which design would have succeeded without doubt, if their imprudence had not obliged me to escape their snares.

I own, that since my enlargement I have never lived without secret apprehensions of the second enterprize, and that I have all along suspected, that that happy calm which my liberty had restored to France, being incompatible with the impatience of my enemies, could not fail of being disturbed by those who have aggrandized themselves to so great a degree, only by the troubles of the state. But I thought that they would not be so imprudent as to execute so bold a stroke at the latter end of a minority, and that they would have staid at least until the authority of a King at age might have made them hope for a favourable success, in seconding their design of arresting me.

This precipitancy inclines me to believe that they foresaw, that the innocence of my intentions and the fidelity of my services could never be discredited in the idea of our young Monarch, who being perfectly well informed of the treasons of their monopolists, and of the sincerity of my proceedings, instead of favouring them, would justify me by his authority in the good opinion of the public. and for that reason, they judged that they ought to prevent that time, fatal to their perverse intentions, and endeavour to seize my person, before the King was in a condition to signalize himself by his first act of justice, in the condemnation of their

their iniquity, and the entire justification of my innocence.

And indeed since the time of my enlargement, and the pursuit which has been judicially commenced against the Cardinal, the upholders of his tyranny have so cautiously disposed matters to the execution of this second attempt, forcing to that end the gracious intentions of the Queen-regent, that France was upon the point of having the Cardinal again upon its hands, and of falling again into the same inconveniences which occasioned the late wars, if by the advice of my friends I had not preferred a prudent flight to a vigorous resistance, to obviate the troubles which might have ensued from following this last conduct

I believe there is no subject so ignorant in affairs of state, as not to be fully informed of the continual intrigues which the enemies of our quiet have never interrupted for the re establishment of the protector of all their practices; and to endeavour to make me condescend to that bloody cabal, whose propositions have always seemed to me highly criminal, and which I judged to be no less disadvantageous to the good of the state, than the party which is every day forming at Brussels or Madrid.

It is true, that the motive of those propositions seemed at least supported by a specious pretence, which the emissaries of Mazarin borrowed from the marriage of the Duke de Mercœur with the Cardinal's niece Madamoiselle Mancini, pretending, that after this alliance of the blood of Vendôme with that of an unknown stranger, the reasons for opposing the re-establishment of the new uncle were nothing more than obstinacies artificially disguised; and that his return was no longer to be hindered, unless it was with a design to kindle a civil war, by the efforts which his partisans would use against the most just resistance of those who should refuse to agree to it.

If his Royal Highness the Duke, whom I have always looked upon as the standard of my conduct, had not constantly protested against the seditious proposal which was made for restoring the Cardinal, I believe so so many importunities would at least have shaken my conscience, and that it would have been difficult for me to resist so many instances; but besides that my consent would have been altogether useless, I thought I ought never to yield after that illustrious example to the contrary, and that I owed that piece of resolution to the weakness of a minor, whose throne would infallibly have been shaken by the troubles which the return of that enemy would infallibly have excited in the kingdom.

These oppositions, which my quality of Prince of the Blood would never let me discontinue, have at last made the Cardinal's emissaries conclude on the horrid design of arresting me, upon the belief which they had, that if they had once tied my hands up, they should be at liberty to labour with more success for the re-establishment of that proscribed person, and that they had nothing to do but to secure my person to shelter themselves from all manner of dangers.

The design was upon the point of being executed when I perceived it, and when those who carefully observed my enemies countenance, gave me notice, that it was time to look to my own safety, and that the violent state of affairs gave those who had formed that design, no longer time to defer it, for fear it should miscarry by my readiness in preventing the execution of it. This is the only motive that obliged me to leave Paris, which I hope will not be disapproved of by those who consider, that neither my imprisonment nor Mazarin's return could happen without the manifest danger of seeing the monarchy relapse into the convulsions it is but just recovered from.

My enemies might indeed make this reason pass for a specious pretence to cover the true motive of this action, if I did not establish my suspicion of what I thought likely to happen to me by evident reasons, and if I did not make it appear by the proofs I have of the most secret transactions of the state, that there is a design of recalling Cardinal Mazarin at what rate soever, to put him again at the helm of this monarchy, and

and that consequently there is something intended against the state, and against my person.

The unknown designs which the Coadjutor of Paris and Mr. de Lionne secretly manage, in so strict a correspondence that it is a sign of an intimate friendship, which cannot be renewed after so great a breach as has happened, but out of a motive which may reasonably be suspected, make me justly apprehend the effects, which I leave to the political judgment of every one, since the one of them being my most mortal enemy, and the other the most zealous partisan of the Cardinal, it seems to me that it is not without reason that I mistrust the success of their negotiation.

Those who are acquainted with the names of the people whom my imprisonment had united to the Coadjutor, by the false pretence of a principle of friendship, and whom the ill success of a premeditated alliance has mortally exasperated against my house, cannot condemn the just fear which I have, that their reunion, supported by the Sovereign power which I respect, would not end in the disposing things a second time to my undoing, experience having taught me, that at this time one cannot be too mistrustful of any one's conduct, nor of the tricks which Cardinal Mazarin has introduced into the politics of France

I should yet be willing to impute this great correspondence of Mr de Lionne's with the Coadjutor, to the renewal of an innocent friendship contracted upon other motives, if the journey of the Duke de Mercœur, who went some days since for Cologn, with a design of going to see his uncle the Cardinal, did not give me still more ground to suspect, that this really is a design of recalling this out-law, against my will. Politicians may judge, if they please, of the sincerity of my way of acting since the said Duke's journey, and may consider whether it is not with a great deal of reason, that I have been alarmed at the prospect of the return of that common enemy, who, absent as he is, governs this monarchy more absolutely than ever.

If France considered Cardinal Mazarin as the real enemy of the state, it is not true that the most ordinary politics would forbid, not only this so visible correspondence with the disturber of the nation's quiet, but would also oblige all its subjects to give some public offence both to him and his party, to undeceive entirely those who had or might have conceived an idea that there was some secret intelligence still held with him. But this is so far from being the case, that people are not satisfied with keeping up their friendship with him constantly by expresses which are secretly dispatched to him, but they have at last consented that no less than a Prince should undertake that journey, and that in the face of all the subjects of this state, whom the tyrannies of that stranger had unanimously stirred up, he should go to carry him the news of the certain assurances that were given him of his speedy re-establishment

It is in vain to disguise that journey of the Duke de Mercœur's, and to make it pass for the rashness of a young Prince, whom a sudden start of fancy inclined to escape out of the hands of those who narrowly watched him. This pretence is fit only to amuse weak minds, or those who are unacquainted that that journey happened in a conjuncture, which induces me to too reasonable a suspicion of the design there was, either to recall Mazarin, or to give him a place of safety within the dependance of the Crown, if I had power enough to make the designs of my enemies upon my liberty miscarry.

All France is but too well informed of the Cardinal's extravagant importunities, who having been condemned to leave the kingdom for misdemeanours sufficient for condemning to death an hundred prime Ministers, has nevertheless had the boldness to make all his creatures act vigorously for the obtaining him an asylum in some strong place dependant on the Crown. Though that proposal was hissed at in the council, it has had its secret agents, who wickedly seducing the natural goodness of the Queen regent, have inclined her mind to such counsels as she would never have consented to, if she had not been unfortunately be-

sieged

fieged by thofe, who fubfift only by their cringings and frauds.

To this end, thefe fecret enemies of the ftate having caft their eyes on Brifac, that is, on one of the ftrongeft places in Chriftendom, have imagined, that their mafter would be fheltered from the threats of all the good fubjects of France, if they could find the means of opening the gates of it to him, by procuring the government of it to one of his creatures. The defign has fucceeded perfectly to their mind, by the favour of Charlevoy, the King's Lieutenant in Brifac, who, allured by the Mazarinians with the hopes of a higher fortune, fo fecretly managed his treafon againft Mr. de Filladet, Governor of that place, that he drove him from thence, without any other order than the fecret intelligence which he held for that purpofe with the emiffaries of that outlaw.

What makes me believe without any doubt, that my enemies and thofe of the quiet of France defign Brifac as the harbour where Mazarin will gather up the remainder of his fhipwreck, is, becaufe I fee that the government of it is given to Vardes, a profeffed partifan of the Cardinal's, and a treacherous deferter of his Royal Highnefs's fervice. And as this is done juft at the juncture of the Duke de Mercœur's departure for Cologn, it is not without reafon, that I fufpect that Prince to be going as his convoy, to bring him thither with more fplendour, for the reparation of his honour fullied by fo many arrefts

What elfe can I think of this affurance given to my greateft enemy, and the incendiary of the commotions which trouble this monarchy? May I not fay, without being accufed of rafhnefs, that there is a defign againft my perfon, againft the quiet of France, againft the throne of my King and the tranquility of his people? fince notwithftanding the oppofition of the council and in fpite of all Frenchmen, they make ufe of all the artifices poffible to find him out a place of fafety.

All thefe reafons would ftill be but pretences, which I fhould have much ado to put off but as flight fufpicions, that the Mazarinians defign a fecond attempt on my person, if two or three hundred armed men, who were roaming all the night of the 6th instant, in the Fauxbourg St Germain, and the doubling of the regiment of Guards at the same time, had not given me good reason to suspect the enterprize which was then going to be executed, after having been concerted ever since the time of my enlargement. This conjecture, strengthened by the advice of all my friends, no longer suffered me to defer my departure, that I might provide for my safety by a speedy retreat, which I have even been obliged to hasten, for fear of seeing myself forced to a resistance, which I could not have made without troubling the public tranquility And after all, I should have been forced to come to blows, by my meeting as I went from Paris two hundred armed Mazarinians, if my very presence had not defeated them, or at least hindered them from opposing my departure, by the apprehension they were under that my resistance would make all their attacks miscarry shamefully

These are a great part of the reasons and motives which induced me to retire to St Maur, till such time as justice should lay the storm which my enemies were forming against me Has it been possible, or would it have been just for me to act with greater precaution? Could I more prudently preserve the public quiet, which I had certainly very much troubled if I had armed for my defence all those whom the justice of my cause might have interested in my quarrel, let any one judge of my proceeding, let them weigh my reasons, I will refuse no disinterested judge, and I protest to all France, that had I not a sincere passion for the glory of serving my native country, I should not now be reduced to the condition I am in, by the unjust pursuits of my enemies

Having nakedly exposed the motives of my departure, I think it will not be amiss, to shew the reasons for persecuting me, after my enlargement, so generously procured by the courts of justice, had, I thought, put me into a condition to be no more blackened by the efforts of calumny.

The

The first, or rather the only general reason, is nothing, but the aversion which the partisans of the Cardinal have constantly entertained against me, since they were forced to consent to my liberty, and to dissemble their hatred, till some other occasion should put them into a condition of shewing it, or of extinguishing it entirely, supposing that they could alter the resolution I had taken, of never quitting the design of being Cardinal Mazarin's most irreconcileable enemy. And indeed I doubt not, but the importunate applications which have been constantly made to me to endeavour to bring me into his party, and which I have always rejected as criminal suggestions, have been the causes of the designs formed against my person, and it has been impossible for me to confirm myself in the idea which I was endeavoured to be made conceive, that my imprisonment had entirely taken away all the ill will which some had against the innocence of my conduct, because I saw that the Cardinal's mind still animated and governed the whole Court, that his creatures were better heard than the Princes of the Blood; and that no dispatches relating to affairs of moment were ever made, unless they were authorized by the consent of one who has been shamefully expelled as a criminal of state

There is no need of much intelligence in state affairs, to know that the Court put off so constantly the giving me the government of Guienne only because the Cardinal did not think it proper; and that his politics made him forge chimeras rather than reasons, to support the injustice of that refusal There is no need, I say, of much penetration into the secrets of state, to see that the negotiation of Sedan, which has been given in exchange for the Duchy of Burgundy to the Queen-regent, is one of the most visible effects of his intrigues, and of the design which he has to open himself a way to return to the government of this kingdom.

This invincible obstinacy in the Court to pursue the return of Mazarin, and to distrust my conduct, because I formed the most powerful opposition to it,

 obliged

obliged me to intermit the visits which my duty made me often pay at the Palais Royal; till by the favour of his Royal Highness, who interposed, to give the Court a better and juster idea of the sincerity of my behaviour, I should know that I was no longer looked upon there with so evil an eye, and that I might hope to be no longer treated there with so much mistrust.

But that illustrious interposition has been no less useless to me, than the endeavours which I constantly used to make it the more effectual; and the calumnies of my enemies having prevailed over the good offices of the Lieutenant-general of the kingdom, it has been impossible to delay the design of undoing me, to save, at the expence of a Prince of the Royal Family, the shattered remains of the fortune of an obscure fugitive. It is true, the execution of it has been hastened, only because the Duke de Mercœur's marriage being discovered, it was no longer time to comply with the oppositions of France, and that this alliance of Cardinal Mazarin with the house of Vendôme would thenceforwards justify all the efforts which should be made to dispose the matters for his return.

So that it may easily be concluded, that my disgrace is only an effect of the opposition which I have constantly made to the re-establishment of that enemy of the public, and that it is in my power to bring myself again into the highest favour, with a full assurance that my utmost ambition might be satisfied, if I would second the pernicious design of recalling the Cardinal to the government of this state But God forbid that I should descend to that base action, which would doubtless render me a state-criminal, considering the perfect knowledge I have, that that return cannot be procured without giving a dangerous shock to this monarchy God forbid that I should load the people once more with this intolerable burthen, whom their former loss of blood, which that leech has perpetually fattened himself with, has reduced to the last necessity; God forbid that I should give his Majesty occasion to reproach me (when he comes to be of age) that I have in anywise contributed to the return of him,

him, who cannot come back without bringing with him all the troubles which may disturb this kingdom

I know too well what I owe to his Majesty during his infancy, what I owe to his Royal Highness, who has so vigorously interposed to break the chains of my captivity; what I owe to the Parisians, who do me the favour to look upon me now as the fatal shelf of that foreign tyranny, and as the restorer of their just and ancient liberty; what I owe to all France, which having so generously interested itself in my liberty, justly claims of my gratitude that I should not at least consent to the return of its capital enemy.

These motives are too just not to influence all my actions; these reasons are too pertinent, not to make them the rule of my conduct. in fine, I am resolved to sacrifice all my interests to the glory of the King, the advantage of the Princes, the defence of Parliaments, the progress of state affairs, and the ease of the people.

A LETTER from Cardinal MAZARIN, during the Time of his Removal out of FRANCE, to the Count DE BRIENNE, one of the Secretaries of State.

I Have been informed, that her Majesty believed that you had only sent me the King's letter in the usual form, as it is sent to all the Cardinals of the nation, when news comes from Rome, that the Pope is in danger But for my part, I was distinguished from the rest, since, besides the King's first letter, and the duplicate of it, I received another, and three of your dispatches, all of them in such pressing terms, to oblige me to take, without any delay, the way to Rome, that I own I was surprised as much as I ought to be, not being able to find out how I had been wanting to the respect I owed their Majesties, that they should press me to take a journey with so much disgrace, so much hazard, and so little means to subsist That they should think, that a letter of recommendation to the Pope would satisfy every thing, as if they were such novices at Rome, as not to know how to infer what sort of protection they ought to give me there, since I was abandoned to the persecution of my enemies in France, where the King is master With all this, if I had had the honour to receive a short word from the Queen, to let me know it was the King's intention and hers, that I should go thither, as she was pleased to let me know it when she would have me leave the kingdom, and remove myself as far as the Rhine, I assure you, that after having placed my nieces in a monastery, and discharged my family, I would have gone thither with two servants only, to give their Majesties new proofs on all occasions, that my obedience is blind, and that my fidelity will stand any test And I am still ready to do, without disputing it in the least, whatever the Queen shall order me on that head, though nothing can be a greater mortification to me, than

than the taking that journey in the condition I am in; which besides cannot but be very prejudicial to the dignity of the King. As to what Madam de Aiguillon has let me know by Rouzereau, I proposed it myself, asking for the conditions which you know, and the whole negotiation ended in orders to go thither without speaking of any thing else The greatest misfortune in this affair is, that some people have had the art to make it pass with her Majesty for a favour done me, that I might yet feel some of the good effects of the King's majority. All these things have overwhelmed me with grief, seeing to what degree my enemies took advantage of my disgrace; and with how much success they made use of their address, to oblige the Court to treat me in so harsh a manner, at a time when I might with justice have hoped, that I should have had some relief from the violent persecutions which I suffered during eight months, with so great disadvantage to the Royal authority

But all this is not comparable to the excess of my grief, in seeing in all the letters of many of my friends at Paris and elsewhere, the pleasure which has been occasioned by the King's declaration, which has been registered at the Parliament, and which was cried about the city, all of them, without having concerted together, agreeing, that since the establishment of the monarchy, so violent a proceeding was never had against any one, whatever crime he might have committed No body has dared to send it me and I can swear to you, that I have never seen it But it is sufficient for me to know that his Majesty has declared that I have hindered the peace, and encouraged all the depredations against the allies of France, to be persuaded, that my master will have me known for the most infamous and most villainous of men, and for the scourge of christendom. After this I must be sent to the place of my nativity, to make a shew before my relations and friends of the glorious titles which I have brought away with me, as the reward of three and twenty years, as faithful and as useful ser-

vices,

vices, as ever were rendered by the moſt diligent and moſt diſintereſted Miniſter.

All my enemies have laboured theſe ſix months, with the application which every one knows, ſending Commiſſaries every whither, and making all poſſible enquiries . ſome of them ſetting up falſe witneſſes, to ſee if it was poſſible to blacken me with any crimes, which by juſtifying in the minds of the people the oppreſſion which I was under, might ſtill increaſe their hatred againſt me; and all this has produced no other effects but what may be of great uſe to undeceive them, and to ſhew my innocence and the injuſtice with which it was attacked. At that time my ſaid enemies deſpairing of ſucceſs in any other way, found means to calumniate me with their Majeſties, to get a declaration iſſued out againſt me in as public and authentic a manner as againſt a common robber.

After this, I think that I ought rather to be adviſed to hide and bury myſelf for ever, than to go to Rome; ſince I have not only the people of France to fear, but all thoſe who are troubled at the continuance of the war, and who have the greateſt reaſon to throw ſtones at the man, who is declared to be the cauſe of it.

I know very well, that their Majeſties cannot have been informed of all the particulars which are contained in the King's declaration, for I know them to be too equitable, to imagine, that they would have conſented to the declaring me the worſt and wickedeſt man in the world. And it is a great misfortune to the King's ſervice, that there was none who would ſhew what advantage it was of to the enemies of France, that by this declaration all Europe ſhould be perſuaded, that the King's principal Miniſter had hindered the peace The Spaniards could obtain nothing more advantageous, than the being able to caſt off upon France the hatred of chriſtendom for the evils which it ſuffers by the war; and the allies of the Crown would have a right to demand ſatisfaction for the depredations committed againſt them, which amount to

millions;

millions; and in case of refusal, to fall out with France; since it is certain, that the King and the State are answerable for the conduct of those who have the management of affairs

I know also that my interest was not strong enough to oblige any one to speak in my favour, but the interest of the King, of the State, and of the Queen herself, was engaged upon so many other accounts, besides those which I have mentioned which are of the greatest consequence, that it must be owned, that it was a great misfortune that no one durst speak of them to their Majesties; and my particular misfortune is so much the greater, that besides what I suffer myself, the passion I have for their Majesties and for the State, makes me feel the reflection of the blow which they receive.

You see that after the crimes which his Majesty hath been obliged to delare me guilty of, I am no longer in a condition to take any part in the management of affairs Wherefore, you need not take the trouble to communicate any to me; and if my enemies have not the satisfaction of seeing me go to Rome, they will at least have that of seeing me hide myself, without intermeddling with any thing whatever, until his Majesty is pleased to do me justice. most humbly begging of him, that I may surrender myself a prisoner to what place he shall order, and even into one of the places of the Duke of Orleans; that if I have failed, I may receive an exemplary punishment for it. And to take away the difficulties which may arise from the dignity which I am honoured with, I shall take it as a singular favour if I am suffered to send my resignation of it, since it cannot in my person be of any further use to the King I shall be very much obliged to you, if you use your endeavours so effectually that that favour may be granted me, and so much the more, because it may contribute to the reparation of my honour; and I beg of you this last time, to excuse my importunity.

ARTI-

ARTICLES and CONDITIONS, agreed upon between his Royal Highneſs the Duke of ORLEANS, and his Highneſs the Prince of CONDE, for the Expulſion of Cardinal MAZARIN, in purſuance to the King's Declarations and the Arreſts of the Parliaments of FRANCE.

I.

THAT his Royal Highneſs and the Prince are ready to lay down their arms, and to come again to attend his Majeſty, to partake in his councils, and to contribute all that ſhall depend on them, to procure the general peace, to re-eſtabliſh affairs, and reſtore the King's authority, if his Majeſty is pleaſed to command, bona fide, Cardinal Mazarin to leave the realm, and the places under his Majeſty's obedience, and to remove from his councils, and from about his perſon, the Cardinal's friends and adherents; and finally to execute the declarations which his Majeſty has made upon that ſubject, ſo that his ſaid Royal Highneſs and his Highneſs the Prince may have room to be perſuaded, that the public faith will be no longer violated.

II.

If on the contrary, the Cardinal ſhould prevail by his artifices, over the King's mind, and if, contrary to the wiſhes and ſentiments of all France, and in breach of the declarations, the Court ſhould perſiſt in ſupporting him; his Royal Highneſs's quality of uncle to his Majeſty obliging him to be careful of the good of the kingdom, and to oppoſe whatever may diſturb it during the King's minority, and the Prince not being able to diveſt himſelf of the ſame ſentiments, conſidering the honour he has to be of the Royal blood, and conſidering alſo, that they can find no ſafety for their perſons, whilſt Cardinal Mazarin continues the maſter

master of affairs, his said Royal Highness and the Prince have promised and have mutually engaged themselves, and hereby do engage, as well for themselves as for the Prince of Conti, brother, and the Duchess de Longueville, sister to the said Prince of Condé, who they promise and oblige themselves shall ratify this treaty, when his said Highness does, as also for all those who are in their interests and united with them, to join their forces, and use their credit and their friends, to procure the expulsion of Cardinal Mazarin out of the kingdom, and the removal of his creatures and adherents who have declared themselves to be such, by the continual correspondence which they have had with him since his leaving the Court.

III.

They promise not to lay down their arms till they have obtained the effect above mentioned, and not to hearken directly or indirectly to any accommodation, but under that condition, and by the common consent of each other.

IV.

The shall maintain and augment the forces they have on foot, as much as it is possible for them to do, and make them act jointly or separately as they shall judge most expedient; promising likewise to use all their endeavours to subsist those troops with the least inconveniency to the people.

V.

They promise to accept voluntarily of all reasonable expedients, which shall be proposed to them for the pacifying of the kingdom, on the condition of the exclusion of Cardinal Mazarin, declared in the second article, and to labour incessantly towards making a general peace, which is one of the principal ends of the present treaty; to which, doubtless, there will be no obstacle, when he that has occasioned the continuance of the war, shall be removed, and when the re-union

union of the Royal family which he has so long hindered shall be accomplished.

VI.

His Royal Highness and the Prince promise to maintain the Parliaments, the Sovereign Companies of the kingdom, the principal Officers of State, the nobility, and all persons of condition, in all their privileges, and to do them justice in relation to the lawful pretensions which they may have; to make no treaty without their participation, and until satisfaction shall be made for all the injuries and losses which they may have suffered in pursuance of this agreement; and particularly to hinder any infringement of the declaration of the 22d of October, 1648, and for that purpose they are invited to enter into the present union, and to concur in the ends for which it is established.

VII

Cardinal Mazarin, who has always governed in effect, thought he was in appearance banished, having hindered the assembly of the States General of the kingdom, which the King had promised should be called together on the 8th of September last, and having obliged the Deputies, who were come to Tours on the day prefixed, to retire with shame and confusion, and it being known besides, that he will not alter the conduct which he hath holden, but will hinder, by all sorts of means, the effect which is expected from their deliberations; or that if he is capable of giving his consent to their assembling, it will only be to put them into a place where he is master: his Royal Highness and the Prince, to obviate these two inconveniences, promise and oblige themselves to labour incessantly that they may be called together at Paris, or in the nearest and most commodious city, so that they may act with full liberty; in which case they declare, that they heartily and willingly submit all their interests to the determination of that assembly, having no other views than the good of the King and king-

Kingdom, of which a perpetual and irrevocable edict shall be drawn up to be verified in the Parliament of Paris, and in all those which have entered into this present union.

VIII.

His Royal Highness and the Prince not holding for lawful, or acknowledging the council established by Cardinal Mazarin, one of those who constitute it having bought his place with a large sum of money which he gave the Cardinal; and being each of them, according to the different degrees of blood in which they are related to his Majesty, obliged to take care of his affairs, and to do their utmost that they may be well governed, promise to hearken to no accommodation, till the creatures and public adherents of Cardinal Mazarin are excluded from the Council of State, and upon condition that the said Council shall consist only of such persons as cannot be suspected to have any thing to do with Mazarin.

IX

And for as much as the Prince's enemies are capable of endeavouring to cry down his conduct, by publishing, that he has some intelligence with foreigners; his Royal Highness and the said Prince declare, that they never will have any correspondence with them but for the settling a general peace, and that they will henceforwards have no communication with any foreign Prince, but as far as the Parliament and the principal persons who shall enter into this union shall think it advantageous for the good of the King and the State.

X.

And that those who have evil intentions and are most attached to the person of Cardinal Mazarin, may have no reason to doubt of the good intentions of his Royal Highness, and his Highness the Prince, they have thought it proper to declare expressly by this particular article, that they have no other interest than the

the entire ſafety of their perſons, and whether they make any progreſs whilſt the misfortune of the State obliges them to uſe their arms for the expulſion of the ſaid Cardinal Mazarin, or whether matters are accommodated by his excluſion, as has been above explained, they will pretend to no new ſettlements, and will find their entire ſatisfaction in that which France will have, in ſeeing an end of its troubles, and the public tranquility aſſured.

XI.

His Royal Highneſs and his Highneſs the Prince have nevertheleſs thought fit, for good conſiderations, to agree that they ſhall contribute to the utmoſt of their power, in the accommodation which may be made, to the juſt and reaſonable ſatisfaction of thoſe who are now engaged in the common cauſe, or ſhall hereafter join in it, ſo that they ſhall receive effectual marks of their favour and protection as far as their power extends.

Two parts of this treaty were ſigned by his Royal Highneſs, and by the Counts de Fieſque and de Gaucourt, for, and in the name of their Highneſſes the Princes of Condé and Conti, and the Dutcheſs of Longueville by virtue of the power given by his Highneſs the Prince to the ſaid Count de Fieſque, which laſt mentioned parties are bound to furniſh his ſaid Royal Highneſs with their ratifications within a month at fartheſt. Dated at Paris the 24th day of January, 1652.

Signed GASTON.
CHARLES LEON DE FIESQUE,
JOSEPH DE GAUCOURT.

ADVERTISEMENT.

AS some mention has been made, in the preface to this work, of Joli and his Memoirs, I thought the remaining sheets of this volume could not be better filled up, than with the following piece taken out of those Memoirs; which being an entire relation of the transactions in the Conclave wherein Alexander VII. was elected Pope, and being different in the manner of relating, and in some circumstances of the facts, from the account which the Cardinal de Retz gives of that Conclave in the last book of his Memoirs, I hope will not be unpleasing to the reader.

A LETTER to Mr. ——— concerning what passed in the Conclave wherein ALEXANDER VII. was elected Pope.

SIR,

IF I had not writ you word at the very beginning of the conclave what I thought would be the event of it, I should not now pretend to speak to you of the several ways and means by which that great Assembly was at last brought to elect Cardinal Chigi, as I had foretold to you. But finding myself not mistaken in my conjectures, I own that I am inclined to believe that the general and particular dispositions of people's minds, which I endeavoured to observe carefully, were really the chief reasons which contributed most to the completing that work. This makes me, Sir, the more willingly yield to the request you made me, to send you a relation of what passed at that Assembly, which I cannot warrant the exactness of, but for such things as came to my particular knowledge, for there is none perhaps that can justly boast of his having the knowledge of all the intrigues, cabals and secret negotiations which are formed on these occasions

I suppose first that you are not unacquainted with the manner of electing Popes, which several persons have written of. I shall only desire you to observe that the notes in which the Cardinals votes are written are folded up in ſuch a manner that the authors of them cannot be diſcovered, nothing but the name of the Cardinal for whom the vote is given appearing at the firſt opening. Thoſe who are authoriſed to open thoſe notes are obliged to go no farther till the election is over, for then liberty is given to unfold them intirely, which unveils many myſteries and much treachery

It is proper alſo that you ſhould be acquainted with the difference between the Scrutiny and the Acceſſit, which are two ſeparate acts, but which have a ſtrict relation together. As to the election, the ſcrutiny is firſt made by a note in this form, "Ego Cardinalis," &c. which firſt words are not ſeen till the ſeal is broke open, "eligo in ſummum pontificem Dominum N——" which is ſeen at the firſt opening. And at the bottom, "Sic me Sancta Dei Evangelia adjuvent" To which every one adds a ſentence of ſcripture according to his own diſcretion, which is alſo folded and ſealed up in the ſame manner as the beginning, ſo as not to be ſeen

If upon this firſt act, which is called the Scrutiny, any one had the number of votes which is requiſite, he would be Pope without proceeding to any other formality, but that ſeldom happens. Uſually they alter and correct the Scrutiny by what they call Acceſſit, every Cardinal giving a ſecond vote for another perſon, with this only difference, that inſtead of the word "eligo," they ſay, "accedo Domino N." or elſe "accedo nemini," if they ſtick to their firſt choice. After this the votes of the Acceſſit are joined to thoſe of the Scrutiny, and if it happens that any of the Cardinals has two thirds of the votes and one over, the election is complete, but if it is otherwiſe they are to begin again; which is done twice a day, morning and evening.

As to what paſſes in the inſide of the Conclave, if you would have a perfect intelligence of it, you muſt not mind what is ſaid of it in the world, there being many people who ſeek for marvels and myſteries where there are none, and others who do not ſufficiently obſerve the actings of Providence, which always rules and governs the fancies of men.

Therefore

Therefore though the external figure of the Conclave be surrounded with pomp and majesty as much as any Assembly whatever, the necessary consequence of this appearing grandeur is not always a more than ordinary elevation of the minds of those who compose it. Men are there, as every where else, subject to passions and weaknesses, full of inequality, of contradiction and caprice Not but that a wise and prudent conduct has in that place, as well as elsewhere, a great advantage over others, and that a superior genius may often find means there to manage artfully the minds of others and make them conduce to his ends, but it must also be owned that we may often observe there an invisible power which actuates the will, and which forces the consent of men in a very astonishing manner, which often confounds the best concerted projects, and the intrigues of the most able politicians This has appeared manifestly in the Conclave which I am giving you an account of, where we have seen old men, contrary to their custom, concur in the choice of a person whose less advanced years must extinguish all their hopes, and the young ones sollicit for a very regular man who probably will have no great indulgence for their natural weaknesses We have seen France return to a candidate whom they had excluded, Spain, contrary to its custom, desire a Pope who appears firm resolute, and Cardinal Barberini leave his partisans, the creatures of his uncle Urban the VIIIth, and chuse for his master the man whom he used so ill the last days of the life of Pope Innocent the Xth. All the tongues of the Court of Rome being untied, the city changed its face on a sudden on the first news of Pope Innocent's being past recovery. It is true this is no uncommon thing at the end of every Popedom, but in this the revolution was more sudden and more sensible, because there was no nephew to support the memory of the deceased, and that people's minds being penetrated with a lively sense of the scandals and disorders of the late government, gave a loose to the first impulse of their passions with too much licentiousness and violence

Though this passion was carried to excess it was however founded in reason It may even be said that it was the principal cause of the choice which was made in this Conclave, by shewing that every one expected and desired a new Pope, whose good conduct should remedy what had displeased them in the preceding government. The late Pope's attachment to, and his unbounded complaisance for the Signora Olimpia, was what had given most offence. The Electors endeavoured to make choice of one the most remote from that failing: besides, the interest of all the christian world was to be considered, and as they were persuaded that the inactivity of Innocent the Xth, and his too great parsimony had made him defer too long and even neglect the war against the Turks, which gave uneasiness to all Europe, and that the war which was then carried on between the Christian Princes wanted a more effectual and vigorous mediation, they aimed at finding out a successor who had the necessary qualities, to provide for the public exigences.

In these almost general dispositions, no one more advantageously offered himself to satisfy the desires of the people than Cardinal Chigi, who, in their opinion and in that of the public, was reckoned to be master of all the perfections requisite to secure the Romans against the fear of falling again into their past disorders, and to make all the christian world entertain the hopes of more happy times for the future

Not but Cardinal Sachetti had his share of the good opinion and good wishes of the people, the sweetness and evenness of his manners, joined to pretty long experience in affairs, drew on him the eyes and hearts of a great many. besides he had for him the advantage of age, which was made up in Chigi only by dubious signs of an uncertain health and a tender constitution. However, as Cardinal Sachetti left in people's minds some occasions of mistrust in respect to his relations, and particularly of a sister in-law who was not indifferent to him, and that his competitor seemed more remote from any occasions of shewing that inclination, this consideration was of great help to determine the Cardinals. not to speak of the great reputation which Cardinal Chigi had acquired at Munster. of the authority which his employment of Secretary of State had given

given him, the functions of which he had exercised with great humanity, and lastly of the recommendation of the late Pope on his death-bed. This recommendation, though it came from no very commendable person, had however its effects on people's minds. But besides these two Cardinals, there were others who in some respects drew on them the public attention, though not very strongly. All that can be said of them is, that they had rather been approved of than desired, unless it were perhaps by some of their particular friends or for some private interests.

The Conclave was, as it always is, divided into several factions, which were dependent on the principal potentates of Europe, which it is proper to give you a general idea of. That of France was then inconsiderable as to the number of votes, and was not capable, upon its own strength, of excluding any one. But let the Italians say what they will, the name of that kingdom and the reputation of its arms gave it weight enough to keep the Electors within the bounds of respect, and to hinder them from naming a Pope for whom that Crown had owned an open distrust and aversion. I cannot let you into the secrets of that party, the Cardinals of which it was composed, * Barberini, Bichi, Grimaldi, d'Este, and Ursini, having refused to suffer the Cardinal de Retz to join with them, or to have any communication with him as he had offered. What appeared outwardly was, that France continued in favour of Cardinal Sachetti the same good offices which they had used for him in the preceding Conclave; because he was an intimate friend of Cardinal Mazarin's and that, on the contrary, they openly rejected Cardinal Chigi, whom they had even excluded.

But this so positive declaration of France for Cardinal Sachetti, was every way advantageous to Cardinal Chigi, because it attached him more firmly to the Spanish party, and took off from the party of France all the other old Cardinals who had any pretensions to the Popedom. He also drew great assistance from Cardinal Bichi, his relation and friend, who omitted no oc-

* Antonio Barberini.

caſion of ſerving him, without having any regard to the King's orders.

‡ The Spaniſh faction was beyond compariſon more numerous, and could, if they remained united, give a certain excluſion. But all the Cardinals which it was compoſed of were not ſo dependant on, and aſſured of each other, that their votes could be reckoned on, without fear of miſtaking. the only thing which they agreed in was their conſtant and unanimous oppoſing Cardinal Sachetti, which was not to be overcome. On the contrary, they always declared their true inclinations in favour of Cardinal Chigi, becauſe of the excluſion which France had given him, of the enmity which he profeſſed againſt Cardinal Mazarin, and of the conduct which he had followed with great reſolution, with relation to the vacant benefices of Portugal, having all along kept the Pope from determining any thing on that account, by giving him to underſtand that it would be a new obſtacle to the genaral peace. However, theſe diſpoſitions of Spain in relation to thoſe two Cardinals were concealed with ſo much diſſimulation, and ſo impenetrable a ſecrecy, that many people believed that not only that Court did not deſire the election of Cardinal Chigi, but even that they would not have agreed to the excluſion of Cardinal Sachetti; but out of condeſcenſion to the Cardinals de Medicis, who had ſupported the intereſt of that Crown in the preceding Conclave; grounded upon a kind of miſunderſtanding which appeared between the two Cardinals de Medicis, and the Spaniſh Ambaſſador, who avoided on many occaſions to declare himſelf touching the excluſion of Sachetti, which he affected to lay upon the Cardinals of his faction: whilſt on the other hand, thoſe of the houſe of Medicis let fall ſome words which did not appear favourable to Chigi

But it is likely that theſe feigned miſunderſtandings and contradictions were politic pieces of management, the better to cover their deſigns, and ſecure the votes of ſome private perſons who would have left the faction, if they had declared themſelves more openly in

‡ Carlo di Medicis, J. Carlo di Medicis, Trivulcio, Colonna, Caraffa, Ceſi, Aſtalli, Brancaccio, Capponi, Burozzo, Coſtugali, Filomarini, Harach, de Heſſe, Ludoviſio, de Lugo, Montalto, Maldachini, Roſetti, Raggi, S. Sforza, Savelli.

favour of one, or against the other: for example, that of Cardinal Rosetti, who certainly had not remained one moment in their party, if he had believed that their design was to elect Cardinal Chigi, for whom he had a natural antipathy, and those of many other persons of worth, who esteemed Sachetti too much to consent to the excluding him formally.

*The faction of the Barberini's was composed of a number of votes, almost equal to that of Spain, and consequently could give as certain, or a more certain exclusion, considering that it was made up of old men, who had each of them their pretensions to the Popedom, and their particular reasons for excluding those who were the most likely to attain to it. They seemed, for some time, strongly determined in favour of Cardinal Sachetti, exclusively of any other, but the persons of the best sense judged, that they gave him their votes only because they judged that they would be useless to him, because of the exclusion of Spain: and in hopes that after having long balotted for him in vain, another Cardinal might be found out amongst them who should be less displeasing to the Court of Spain. There is even reason to believe that this was particularly the view of Cardinal Barberini, because after there had been for several days together thirty-three votes for Cardinal Sachetti, there appeared on a sudden thirty-one for Cardinal Barberini, which gave a violent alarm to the other factions, and obliged them to observe with greater attention his steps, and the discourses of his conclavists, or other partisans, who let slip no opportunity of setting forth his good qualities, and of suiting them to the taste and disposition of the conclave. But after all, they remained persuaded that the chief view of the Barberini's was always in favour of Cardinal Sachetti, as the person who was the most fit for the purpose, either in obtaining the release of their goods, which Spain had caused to be seized in the kingdom of Naples, or in securing the fortune of

* Francis Barberini, Carlo Barberini, Bragadini, Cherubini, Carpegna, Cesa, Lechini, Casarolli, Facquinetti, Franciotti, Gabliel, Ginetti, Giorio, Gualtieri, Mantulano, Palotta, Rapaccioli, Spada, Santa Suzanna, Sachetti

their houſe, and that of the Signora Olimpia, who ſince the Pope's death had abſolutely put herſelf into their hands, in purſuance of the alliance which ſhe had contracted with their houſe.

They had no inclination for Cardinal Chigi. And it may even be ſaid, that there was a kind of antipathy betwen him and Cardinal * Antonio Barberini. Not only he avoided to explain himſelf, in relation to him, to the Cardinal de Retz, and rejected the propoſals which he made him in favour of that Cardinal, as being diſagreeable to him, but he often endeavoured to take away the good opinion he had of him, by touching on ſeveral ſubjects on which he thought the Cardinal de Retz more tender than he really was, as for example, upon Janſeniſm. He uſed to ſay that the Cardinal de Retz would do well, before he went farther, to aſſure himſelf of Chigi's ſentiments on the ſubject of grace. Chigi on his part was not better diſpoſed in relation to Cardinal Barberini, and he never failed to admoniſh the Cardinal de Retz not to truſt him too much, repreſenting him as one of an artificious and malicious ſpirit. It was not the ſame with the young Cardinal Carlo Barberini, who expreſſed on all occaſions a great deal of affection and conſideration for Cardinal Chigi, as did Cardinal Sachetti, and ſeveral others of the ſame party.

† The faction of the Flying Squadron, though not ſo numerous, was perhaps neither leſs conſiderable, nor leſs powerful than the others, being compoſed of young Cardinals who were ſkilful, vigilant, and always ready to take hold of every opportunity. They appeared from the beginning all of them extremely in the interests of Cardinal Sachetti, ſaying on all occa-

* This ſeems to be a miſtake of Joli's, for this muſt be Francis Barberini, who was the head of the faction that bore that name, and Cardinal Antonio Barberini was of the French faction, which had no communication with the Cardinal de Retz.

† Aquaviva, Albizzi, Azzolini, Borromeo, Chigi, Corrado, Homodei, Imperiale, Lomelino, Ottoboni, Pio, de Retz, Santa Crocé.

Theſe names differ from thoſe which the Cardinal de Retz ſaith that this party conſiſted of, the Cardinal leaving out ſome of thoſe here mentioned, and adding others, ſome of which Joli afterwards mentions under the name of the Little Squadron, which the Cardinal does not diſtinguiſh from the Flying Squadron. See page 8, and the following, of this volume.

ſions, Sachetti o Cataletto. But in reality, a great part of them had nobody in their thoughts but Cardinal Chigi, and the reſt gave him at leaſt the ſecond place; which made them declare without heſitation in his favour, when they ſaw that the excluſion of the other was certain. This difference of ſentiments in the Cardinals of that party was known but to few perſons, and the ſecret friends of Cardinal Chigi kept themſelves concealed from Cardinal Barberini, by joining as they all did with him in favour of Sachetti. But they had not the ſame reſerve for the Cardinal de Retz, for though he was not one of their council, as they knew that he was intirely well inclined towards Cardinal Chigi, there was always ſome one among them that joined him at the entrance of the Chapel, or elſewhere, to give him notice to give his vote for Sachetti, when they knew that it would be of no ſervice to him, and not to give it, when they had room to fear his being elected; and if they could not give him that notice themſelves, they took care to let him know it by Monſignor Febei Maſter of the Ceremonies. It is not known whether Cardinal Chigi was informed of this management, but he pretended always to be ignorant of it, and the Cardinal de Retz, who was ſeated near him in the Chapel, has ſaid, that he had hindered him from giving his vote for Cardinal Sachetti, in ſeveral occaſions where he wanted but very few votes.

* The faction of the Little Squadron was compoſed only of ſix Cardinals, whom Prince Pamphilio and the Princeſs Rozane his wife had united together ſo ſtrongly in favour of Chigi, that they looked on thoſe of the Great Squadron as their declared enemies, ſuppoſing that they were all ſtrongly attached to Cardinal Sachetti. This obliged them to concur with the Spaniſh faction, the better to ſecure his excluſion. The Princeſs Rozane was particularly in the intereſt of Chigi, because he had had a great regard for her during the laſt papacy, and that he had ſeveral times taken her part againſt the Signora Olimpia, in the quarrels which they often had together.

Beſides theſe factions, which comprehended all the

* Cibo, Aldobrandini, Odeſchalchi, Bondaccini, Vidman, D[illegible]

votes of the Conclave, there was one less sensible, which intermixed itself with all the others This was that of the Jesuits, who have not indeed all the power which is generally ascribed to them on these occasions, but who are always a kind of *Conditio sine qua non* It being almost impossible to make one's way at the Court of Rome, and to rise to great dignities, without their approbation and consent This invincible cabal was not opposite to Cardinal Sachetti, but was properly attached to Chigi, for whom chiefly they laboured without doors by their intrigues, and within by the Cardinal de Lugo, and some others: but chiefly after a very effectual and imperceptible manner, by the sermons of Father Quoechi, preacher to the Conclave; in which there was always some particular character which agreed only with Chigi that Father very artfully describing his manners and conduct, as one who was to be a model for the Conclave to guide their choice by

Things being thus disposed, all these different factions began to act more closely, and to take their measures as well as every one's genius would permit, to arrive at their desired ends. The Spaniards with their usual phlegm, and without discovering their true designs, were satisfied in the beginning with keeping closely united together, to secure the exclusion of Sachetti, by giving their second votes to no-body, in the form Accedo nemini They constantly followed this practice for two months together; two or three and twenty notes in this form being, during that time, constantly found amongst those of the Scrutiny: whilst the French Cardinals, with the Barberinis, and the Squadron, made useless efforts in favour of Cardinal Sachetti, who had every day thirty-three votes, and sometimes thirty-five, though he ought to have had thirty-eight or thirty-nine, if they had all been sincerely well-affected towards him. But as I have already said, a part of the Squadron betrayed him. However that was, this uniform and constant observation gave room to a jest of Cardinal Cesi's, who was called in the Conclave la Vecchia, the old woman, he having the look of a battered eunuch. He said one day, going out of the Chapel, that there would be no Pope elected, unless Cardinal Nemo and Cardinal Thirty-three agreed.

The treachery of the Squadron continued long undiscovered by Cardinal Barberini, whose suspicions rather fell on the old Cardinals of his own faction, whom he used in his fit of anger to call le mie Bestie, when he found that he almost wanted six votes out of thirty-nine, which he thought he might reckon upon, and which would probably have set Cardinal Sachetti on the throne, if they had all faithfully answered to what they outwardly professed, since the number requisite to make a valid election was but forty-one or forty two votes, and when any one is so near the requisite number, it often happens that some out of the other cabals detach themselves, to follow the stream, for fear they should be found in the list of opponents, under the new papacy, which every one endeavours carefully to avoid.

Besides the ambiguous manner in which the Spanish Ambassador explained himself, in relation to Cardinal Sachetti, and a kind of misunderstanding which was observed between that Minister and the Cardinals de Medicis, might give him some ground to hope for a favourable turn of some of the Spanish faction, whom they knew to be but weakly attached to that party. Amongst others, of Cardinal Rosetti, who had not failed to join them, if he could have foreseen the election of Chigi, as he would have done afterwards when it was too late.

Lastly, it is very probable that Cardinal Barberini stuck so obstinately and so long by Cardinal Sachetti (though that Cardinal begged of him every day to abandon his pursuit, the impracticableness of which every one was at length convinced of) only to give a check to the Spanish party, and to engage the King of Spain to give him a favourable answer to a letter which he wrote to him at his going into the Conclave. He complained in that letter of the injurious treatment he had met with from that King's ministers, who had caused all his goods to be seized in the kingdom of Naples, offering however to serve his Catholic Majesty, as much as lay in his power

Not but from time to time there were some other intrigues in favour of different persons who threw themselves in the way, hoping to succeed to the extinguished hopes of Cardinal Sachetti. But all these vain attempts did nothing but afford diversion to the Conclave, which made Cardinal Celsi who laughed at those little intrigues say, Per Dio gli Sacchettano tutti

The first that entered the lists was Cardinal Caraffa, who, after the Cardinals Sachetti and Chigi, was certainly the person who had the greatest share in the public esteem, and if he had not died at the beginning of the Conclave, no body knows what would have happened; though his illness, which obliged him to keep always sitting, ought to have excluded him from a dignity which requires action on a great many occasions.

Cardinal Rapaccioli was also balotted for more than once, but to no purpose, because of the exclusion of France, of the secret opposition of Spain, which looked upon him as a creature of the Barberini's, and of the open enmity of Cardinal Spada

Much the same reasons might be urged for the opposition given to the Cardinals Capponi, Ginnetti, Bragadini, Franciotti, Cherubbini, Carpegna, Lecchini, Palotta, Durasso, Brancacio, Santa Suzanna, and Corrado, who were proposed one after the other with the same success Cardinal San Clemente, otherwise Fiorenzola or Matulano, drew on him a little more the regard of the Conclave, being strongly supported by the Cardinals Trivulcio and Grimaldi, who were each of them capable enough of re-uniting the factions of France and Spain, and even of securing the concurrence of Cardinal Barberini But the irreconcileable enmity of the Cardinals Montalto, de Lugo, and Altieri, and above all, the formal opposition of the Jesuits, whom none of the parties durst directly affront, made his hopes miscarry, which otherwise appeared well grounded

At last, after all these fruitless attempts, the friends of Cardinal Chigi, who during all these intrigues had neglected nothing to gain him votes, judged that it was time to declare themselves, seeing the patience of the greatest part of the Cardinals worn out, and that they had at last brought it about that France should no longer exclude him.

For

For you are to know that Cardinal Bichi, after having convinced Sachetti of the little probability there was of his pretensions succeeding, had artfully wrought upon him to write to Cardinal Mazarin in favour of Cardinal Chigi, to remove the aversion which Mazarin had for him, by engaging for his future conduct as well to him, as in respect to France. And indeed that Cardinal gave, in that very Conclave, a very convincing proof of the uprightness of his intentions for the service of that Crown, on an occasion where it might be said, that the Cardinals of the French faction were wanting to their duty. For the Spanish Ambassador having given to his master the title of Eldest Son of the Church, in a memorial which he presented to the Conclave, without meeting with any opposition from those gentlemen, Cardinal Chigi, who was seated next to the Cardinal de Retz, not only engaged him to protest against that innovation, but shewed him the manner of doing it; after which the Cardinal de Retz rising up, said, that the title of Eldest Son of the Church being reserved for his most Christian Majesty, he was too good a Frenchman and too faithful a servant of the King's, to suffer that that title should be bestowed on any other, that if the Cardinals who were attached to the interest of that Crown were remiss in their duty, he would not be so in his that the rigour which he was treated with would never stifle in him the sentiments he had always preserved for the honour and interest of his Prince, and that he begged of the sacred College not to accept of the memorial in that form, and to give him an act of the opposition he made to it in behalf of the King his master *.

Let that be as it will, Cardinal Sachetti's letter had its effect with Cardinal Mazarin, who immediately sent the necessary order to prevent his exclusion. After this, none but Cardinal Barberini was to be won. He was at first hard to be prevailed on, and for some time resisted the sollicitations of Cardinal Bichi, and

* This fact is related by the Cardinal de Retz in his memoirs, but without any mention made, that it was Chigi who first made the Cardinal de Retz take notice it. See this vol. p 31.

of thoſe of the ſquadron who in the end openly declared themſelves for Cardinal Chigi. But at laſt the King of Spain's anſwer being come pretty near to the purpoſe which he deſired, with an expreſs promiſe to give him ſatisfaction as to the releaſing his goods; and Cardinal Lugo having aſſured him of the protection of Cardinal Chigi for his houſe and that of the Signora Olympia; he conſented to a conference with the Cardinals de Medicis, where the principal Chiefs of all the factions being met, they all agreed to concur the next day, being the 7th of April, 1655, in the election of Cardinal Chigi, which was made by the unanimous conſent of all the Cardinals except Cardinal Roſetti, who, though of the Spaniſh faction, being unwilling to ſubmit to the naming a Cardinal whom he mortally hated, gave his vote for Cardinal Sachetti, after having offered it, with four others whom he was aſſured of, to Cardinal Barberini, who told him, that it was then too late, and that he was engaged.

This reſolution was ſo ſudden, and was kept ſo ſecret till the time that it was executed, that it amazed thoſe who did not inwardly approve of it, and who had not failed to declare for Cardinal Sacchetti, if they had had time to turn themſelves about, but ſeeing their chiefs run to the adoration of the new Pope, they ſuffered themſelves to be hurried away with the torrent, for fear of bringing themſelves into trouble by an uſeleſs and unſeaſonable reſiſtance.

This, ſir, is all that I can let you know concerning this Conclave. God grant that what Paſquin ſaid, about the Pope's guards and the length of the Conclave, may not prove true, and that all the world may not ſay after him,

Parturient montes naſcetur ridiculus mus *.

I am, SIR,

Apr.l 5, 1655 Your, &c.

* Joli ſays afterwards of this new Pope, that it was ſaid of him that he was Minimus in Maximis and Maximus in Minimis.

CONTENTS

OF THE

FOUR VOLUMES.

VOL. I. BOOK I.

The

BOOK II.

The

The

The

VOL

CONTENTS OF VOL. II.

VOL. II. BOOK III.

Troubles

The

The

His

VOL. III. BOOK IV.

The

great

VOL IV. BOOK V.

The

ADDI-

CONTENTS OF VOL. IV.

ADDITIONAL PIECES.

verner

B O O K S

SOLD BY

THOMAS EVANS.

CAMDEN's Britannia, or Chorographical Description of Great Britain and Ireland, improved by Bishop Gibson 2 vols. folio, with maps and plates; a new edition.

The Natural, Civil, and Military History of Canada, Louisiana, and all the French Dominions in North and South America, with an Account of the Indian Nations; illustrated with maps, plans, and other cuts; by Jeffreys. 1 vol folio.

Original Letters and Papers, addressed to Oliver Cromwell, relating to the Affairs of England. Published by J. Nicols, in folio, sewed 4s.

Sir Thomas Roe's Negotiations at the Ottoman Porte, with a Variety of curious Matters relating to the Turkish Empire, and instructive Particulars relating to Trade, Commerce, ancient Manuscripts, Coins, and Inscriptions, with his Literary Correspondence with the most illustrious Persons. 1 vol. folio, price bound 1l 1s.

Memoirs of the Duke de Sully, Prime Minister to Henry the Great, with the Life and Reign of that Monarch, and the Trial of Ravillac. Translated from the French, by Mrs. Lennox. 6 vols. 12mo. price bound 18s.

The

The Life of Henry St. John, Viscount Bolingbroke; by Dr. Goldsmith. Sewed 1s 6d.

Bossu's Voyage to Louisiana, with a large Account of American Plants; translated by Mr. Forster. 2 vols. octavo, 12s.

Count Algarotti's Letters to Lord Harvey, containing the State of the Trade, Marine, Revenues, and Forces of the Russian Empire, their Wars with the Turks, &c. 2 vols. 6s.

Reflections on the Painting and Sculpture of the Greeks, with an Essay on Grace in the Works of Art, and Instructions for the Connoisseur, by Abbé Winkleman. 4s. 6d.

The Adventurer, by Hawkesworth and Warton. 4 vols. 12s.

The Rambler; by Dr. Johnson. 4 vols. 12s.

The Idler; by Dr. Johnson. 2 vols. 6s.

The Plain Dealer, or Essays on Curious Subjects. 2 vols. 10s.

Clarissa, or the History of a Young Lady, by Mr. Richardson. 8 vols. 1l 4s.

Mr. Locke's Discourses on Government; octavo, 5s.

Dr Davenant's Works relating to the Trade and Revenues of England, the Colonies, and the East Indies; a new edition, by Sir Charles Whitworth. 5 vols. 1l. 10s.

The

BOOKS ſold by T. EVANS.

The Britannic Conſtitution, or Fundamental Form of Government in Britain; and many important original Powers and Privileges of both Houſes of Parliament; by Roger Acherley, Eſq 1 vol. folio, 15s.

The Univerſal Mentor, containing Eſſays on the moſt important Subjects in Life, compoſed of Obſervations, Sentiments, and Examples of Virtue, ſelected from the moſt approved Ethic Writers, Biographers, and Hiſtorians, ancient and modern; by Sir John Fielding 1 vol. 3s.

The Works of Henry Fielding, Eſq. with an Eſſay on his Life and Genius; by Mr. Murphy. 12 vols. 1l. 16s.

Lightning Source UK Ltd.
Milton Keynes UK
UKHW05f2140100418
320799UK00008BA/508/P